Affectionately, Jayne Mansfield

Published in the USA by:
BearManor Media
P O Box 71426
Albany, Georgia 31708
www.bearmanormedia.com

ISBN 978-1-59393-299-2

Printed in the United States of America.
Book design by Brian Pearce | Red Jacket Press.

Affectionately, Jayne Mansfield

RICHARD KOPER

TABLE OF CONTENTS

ACKNOWLEDGMENTS

A special word of gratitude to the following people: First of all to my partner Angelo for supporting me and giving me the freedom to lock myself up in the study and write. Many thanks to all my friends and relatives who are so supportive and interested in my projects.

Frank Ferruccio — author of two Jayne books — and Kim Rosenthal of *The Jayne Mansfield Online Fan Club*; thanks for answering my questions about Jayne and for letting me use some of the information from your archives. Most photos from Jayne's private life and stage plays are from the collection of Frank Ferruccio: thank you very much for letting me use them in my book!

Thank you Auke Bergsma *(www.aukebergsmafotokunst.nl)* for providing a wonderful picture of Jayne's visit to Holland. Paul Hogan, thank you for the information provided — especially your Jayne Mansfield article for *Outré* magazine — considering copyright and for your enthusiasm on my projects. John O'Dowd; writer of the fabulous *Kiss Tomorrow Goodbye — The Barbara Payton Story*. Thanks for your supportive emails and success with your own projects.

Many thanks to Darin Sturgill and a special note of gratitude to my friend Robert Wiseman for reading the manuscript and helping me with text editing. And last, but by no means least, I'd like to express my appreciation to Miss Gloria Pall. Thanks Gloria for sharing all those wonderful stories about Hollywood in the 1950s with me. I appreciate our email correspondence and hope we will continue our contact for the years to come.

A HAND-SIGNED PUBLICITY PHOTO, 1963.

PREFACE

"I FEEL THAT SEX APPEAL IS ONLY ONE FACET OF THE MANY
IMPORTANT FACETS TO AN INTERESTING PERSONALITY –
HOWEVER, IT IS A VERY IMPORTANT ONE IN MY ESTIMATION."

JAYNE MANSFIELD, 1958

Another book about movie star and pin-up celebrity Jayne Mansfield?
The question can be asked, what will it add to the already existing list
of books about her? About a dozen books have been written about her
sensational life and career. Some of them were written by people who
worked with or lived closely to Jayne Mansfield. Her press agent for ten
years, Raymond Strait, published two books about her. Her longtime
friend, columnist May Mann, wrote a book that was received controver-
sially, because she said she'd been in contact with the spirit of Jayne while
writing it. Nevertheless it gives an account of Jayne Mansfield through
the eyes of another woman; a woman she confided in and who stood by
her until the end.

Most books feature Jayne from the perspective of how male audiences
saw her: As the lust object, the sex goddess. While researching Miss
Mansfield's life it was interesting to read author Martha Saxton's book,
which was written from a feminine (and to some a 'feminist') point of
view. The sexual behavior of Jayne Mansfield was translated in a more
psychological way. The loss of her father at a young age was linked with
the many relationships Jayne had with men and the desire to be loved and
admired by men. And almost simultaneously that evoked a problematic
mother-daughter relationship. The latter is what the books of Saxton,
Mann and Strait have in common. They all describe Jayne's love & hate
relationship with her mother. All these books were written within ten
years after Jayne Mansfield's death in 1967.

Recently three new books were written about her. Huge Jayne fan
Frank Ferruccio wrote two to show his admiration for Miss Mansfield.

They tell the story of Jayne's life and are illustrated with many rare photographs from mister Ferruccio's collection. The third book is a study about the sex goddesses Mae West, Jean Harlow, Lana Turner and Jayne Mansfield. It's an interesting study by Jessica Hope Jordan about Jayne's sex image and opens up the discussion "on the importance of recuperating Mansfield and her image for pro-sex feminists as an important figure in the construction and sexual liberation of the hyper-feminine sexualized body in American culture."[1] In my opinion that's an interesting perspective of looking at the actress, woman and persona of Jayne Mansfield. Looking solely at her as 'the sexy movie star' or the 'Monroe clone,' doesn't do her justice. I will try to illustrate that by putting Jayne in the line-up of blonde pin-up actresses that had walked the route from starlet to featured player at 20th Century Fox studios before her.

In the first chapter of this book, I describe how Jayne was the last of a series of sexy, fun generating — blonde — stars, who were contracted by 20th Century Fox to please the filmgoers and movie star fans, and not unimportantly, make profit at the Box Office. As said before, Jayne came last in a row of actresses that were hugely popular in their moment of fame.[2] Eventually Jayne Mansfield was to become the bright star that would illuminate the stature of Fox studios again, but as time has proved, she lit the Hollywood firmament just briefly, before she faded away.

The second chapter defines Jayne Mansfield's life and untimely death. Her story is illustrated and enlivened with quotes from Jayne Mansfield herself and from the people who knew her and who were close to her. Although some details or views may be confronting in a positive or negative way, they merely add to the image that Miss Mansfield was a true person of flesh and blood, who struggled through serious incidents and life changing events during her life which shaped the person she became.

The third chapter is a short introduction on the blonde, sexy ladies who were also on the scene alongside Jayne Mansfield. They provided casting directors the choice to decide who was the best for specific productions. Some lost a part or career chance to Jayne, some only hit the spotlight because of Jayne. And some were (used as) a threat to Jayne. Mentioning

1. Jordan, Jessica Hope. *The Sex Goddess in American Film 1930-1965 — Jean Harlow, Mae West, Lana Turner, and Jayne Mansfield.* Amherst, New York: Cambria Press, 2009.

2. Some would consider actress Raquel Welch (1940) as Fox last successful manufactured movie star, but I draw the line at the late fifties by describing the end of the Hollywood star building system. Also the fact that Miss Welch's screen personality has not homogenized into a definite image, separates her from predecessors at 20th Century Fox.

these stars and starlets provides a knowledge of Jayne's competition and comparison in the fifties.

The fourth chapter is an interlude to Jayne's filmography. While the fifth chapter looks in depth at her films, the fourth chapter holds them to the cultural light of that particular era and time Jayne starred in them. Since the fifties was an era where men pulled the strings, it's interesting to speculate what a strong-willed girl like Jayne Mansfield had to endure to make a successful career. Of course that era's schizophrenic views towards women and sexuality effected women as independent as Jayne Mansfield, especially in terms of career decisions and their private life.

The last three chapters are a summary of Jayne Mansfield's cultural outings: her film parts, stage plays and television appearances. Together they enclose the largest part of this book. For it is Jayne Mansfield's acting and performing that will allow her to live on forever.

In my writing I have tried to be as complete and accurate as possible. I have verified many sources of information and think I have come up with solid material that eventually resulted in this book. I hope that you, while reading, will discover new things about Jayne Mansfield or can see her in a different light than in which she is normally portrayed. If you want to share your thoughts about this book and the information I have provided, than feel free to contact me at *fiftiesblondes@hotmail.com* or visit *www.fiftiesblondes.com.*

And lastly, I want to add a personal note. From my own point of view — that of an European author and film lover — Jayne Mansfield brought something more to the film world than many of her contemporaries, predecessors or successors. Never before had an actress of her stature ever been so approachable than Jayne Mansfield. She was probably the first major Hollywood star that visited Europe regularly. Her trip to Europe in 1957, her visits to Cannes, Venice and the Berlin film festival, her European made films and her marriage to Mickey Hargitay (a native European), secured Jayne a place in the heart of many people here. Donald Zec, famous British show business journalist in The Daily Mirror, described Jayne Mansfield in a way many other European film journalists and filmgoers saw her: "She has been as good an actress as her bubble-and-squeak roles have permitted her to be. The lady is friendly, the lady is warm-hearted, the lady is always good for a laugh. She is also one of the most pleasing bits of scenery in the whole pulchritudinous landscape of show business."[3] While Jayne's star status devaluated in

3. Zec, Donald. *This Show Business.* London: Purnell and Sons Limited, 1959.

the United States in the late fifties, she was considered star material in Europe throughout her entire career. No wonder three books about Jayne found their origin in Europe. The wonderfully illustrated Dutch book *Sexbomb — The Life and Death of Jayne Mansfield*, the sturdy British entry *Pink Goddess — The Jayne Mansfield Story* and my personal favorite: *Jayne Mansfield* an outstanding pictorial/coffee table book from France.

Affectionately,
Jayne Mansfield

KISS THEM FOR ME PUBLICITY PHOTO, 1957.

Introduction

"I DON'T REALLY THINK I AM THE MOST BEAUTIFUL WOMAN IN
THE WORLD AT ALL. IF I CAN CREATE SOME ILLUSION TO THAT
EFFECT, AND IT SEEMS I HAVE, THEN THAT IS WHAT SPELLS
SUCCESS FOR ME."

JAYNE MANSFIELD, 1964

JAYNE MANSFIELD AND 20TH CENTURY FOX:
A HISTORY OF BLONDES

Her name is Jayne Mansfield. A name that has become associated worldwide with blonde, bawdy, big busted and brazen. She was an icon of Hollywood in the fifties. An icon of a super star created by the well oiled machinery of the US film industry, cultivated as the dumbest of blondes which the fifties seemed to have a copyright for. She played her role so well that she never escaped this restricting tag. But underneath that blonde hair, seductive smile and eye-popping hourglass figure, an educated woman with an above average IQ pulled the strings. "It was an act; the whole thing was an act. She was a concert violinist and pianist and she spoke five languages. I think she was misunderstood, but it was her own doing. I mean she was the one that walked in there and said 'this is what I want' and 'I'll take it' and 'I'll do it', not realizing the consequences."[1]

She was America's Smartest Dumb Blonde in an era when women weren't supposed to expose their sexuality. Those who did were women of a certain signature, commonly named floozies. Some of them made a career in the entertainment business, posing for pin up stills or starring in cameo parts in the movies. Most of them ended on the wrong side of the tracks. Although these 'jobs' were considered unbecoming for a lady, hundreds of so called starlets flocked towards Hollywood anyway, trying

---

1. A quote from daughter Jayne Marie Mansfield.

17

PUBLICITY PHOTO, 1956.

to influence lady luck and become a superstar. Jayne Mansfield was definitely one of them. It was the era of über-blonde Marilyn Monroe when Jayne materialized her dreams.

Marilyn Monroe (1926-1962) first appeared on the scene as a promising starlet in the early fifties, when Vera Jayne Mansfield was already a young married mother. Hollywood always liked to mold their new faces based on

JEAN HARLOW.

established stars from the present and the past. Starlet Marilyn Monroe was showcased as the *new* Jean Harlow[2] in films like *Let's Make it Legal* (1951) and *Monkey Business* (1952). Jean Harlow was the embodiment of the thriving and sexually free blonde American girl who led an independent life when it came to relationships and men. She was the reigning sex queen of the 1930s. Her predecessor in an earlier era was Theda Bara,[3] the muse of

2. Born as Harlean Carpenter in 1911, Jean Harlow became one of the greatest icons of Hollywood. Mostly type casted as a sexpot and comedienne she stood under contract to MGM. She was loaned out once to 20th Century Fox for a movie called *Goldie* (1931). Jean Harlow died in 1937 form a cerebral oedema.

3. Dark haired vamp Theda Bara (1890-1955) is considered the first sex goddess Hollywood manufactured. Her credits include silent classics like *Sin* (1915), *The Vixen* (1916), *Cleopatra* (1917), *When a Woman Sins* (1918) and *The She-Devil* (1919). The titles say it all…!

pioneer film mogul and founder of the Fox Film Company, William Fox. When Theda left Fox he contracted Janet Gaynor (1906-1984). But while she certainly was no vamp, she did become the symbol of brightness and optimism in the Depression days. Fox also needed a new star to compete with Harlow and found one in blonde starlet Alice Faye (1912-1998). Faye made her film debut at Fox Films in 1934. When Darryl F. Zanuck

JANET GAYNOR WITH SHIRLEY TEMPLE (LEFT), AND ALICE FAYE (RIGHT).

headed production at the new Twentieth Century-Fox Films he had her shed the tough brassy Jean Harlow style and adopt a much softer appearance. The other blonde star, who warmed people's hearts during the harsh Depression days, was just four years old when she first stepped in front of a film camera. Lovely Shirley Temple (b. 1924) became the nation's sweetheart and every little girl wanted to be just like her. She was signed to a contract by Fox in 1934 and was let go at the age of sixteen in 1940.

When six year old Vera Jayne had visited the cinema for the first time, she knew she was to become a movie star herself. At least that's what most of her biographies try to tell us. "I came home and imitated the stars in some of the scenes. I knew then I was going to be a movie star some day. When Momma saw me acting in front of the mirror in the bedroom I told her that I was going to be a movie star."[4] Biographer Martha Saxton writes how Jayne's mother never missed a single Shirley Temple film with her

4. Mann, May. *Jayne Mansfield: A Biography.* New York: Drake, 1973.

daughter. Friends and relatives told Vera that her young daughter was just as cute and seemed destined for the movies. A prediction Jayne's mother loved to recall to Saxton: "I used to promise her if she was a good little girl we'd go to the movies and she could have chewing gum, lollipops and ice cream. And you know, I might have instilled something in her at that tender age."[5]

BETTY GRABLE AND JUNE HAVER (LEFT), MARILYN MONROE AND BETTY GRABLE (RIGHT) IN *HOW TO MARRY A MILLIONAIRE* (1953).

While America and the rest of the world faced WW II, Jayne was growing up in Dallas, attending school, going to Sunday Mass in the Methodist Church with her parents and taking piano and violin lessons and enrolled in various dance and musical programs. Married at seventeen and a mother six months later, Jayne was a graduate from Highland Park High School excelling in foreign languages. In 1953 Jayne had acted on the Dallas stage in *The Death of a Salesman* and was infatuated by the acting bug. She wanted nothing more than to leave Texas for California, Hollywood to pursue her acting career. The year 1953 was the big breakthrough for Marilyn Monroe. She surpassed Betty Grable as 20th Century Fox favorite blonde contract player.

In all its history, 20th Century Fox kept their stars in line with the threat of a new and younger face to take over in case their stars were

5. Saxton, Martha. *Jayne Mansfield and the American Fifties.* Boston: Houghton Mifflin Company, 1975.

disobedient. Betty Grable (1916-1973) was signed by Fox in 1940. She became a favorite pin up girl during WW II and was the epitome of the clean cut American girl next door. Always realistic about her qualities and her success, Betty held on firmly to what she believed were her limitations and strengths in acting. When 20th's founder Darryl F. Zanuck[6] tried to stretch her acting abilities to play a dramatic part originally intended for

MARILYN MONROE AND JUNE HAVER IN *LOVE NEST* (1951).

Shelley Winters, Betty declined. When she also refused to do *The Girl Next Door* (1953) that same year, he put her on suspension. The movie was made with June Haver in the lead.

June Haver (1926-2005) came under contract at 20th Century Fox in 1943. Fox tried to groom Haver as the successor to Grable, and they were quite successful at it. All of June's features at Fox were lensed in Technicolor. She was the only star in the 1940s who could boast such a status symbol, since shooting in the color process raised production costs by another third of the original budget. Fox had co-starred their two

6. Darryl F. Zanuck (1902-1979) founded 20th Century Films in 1933. When he bought Fox studios in 1935, 20th Century Fox was born. Zanuck was vice-president until 1958.

singing and dancing blondes in *The Dolly Sisters* (1945) and featured the so called 'Pocket Grable' in a string of comedies, dramas and musicals.

Marilyn Monroe had appeared in two of June Haver's films. In one she was a bit player, just signed at Fox and the other had her featured in a co-starring part. The first film was *Scudda Hoo, Scudda Hay* (1948) and the latter was a comedy called *Love Nest* (1951). When Monroe — instead of Betty Grable — was cast as dumb blonde Lorelei Lee in *Gentlemen Prefer Blondes* (1953), June Haver was released from her contract to enter a convent.[7] Only the Fox image creators could have made a pin up star of a girl whose deepest wish was becoming a nun!

Meanwhile, 20th Century Fox could no longer ignore the growing popularity of a starlet they just hired for her physical attributes. After the success of *Gentlemen Prefer Blondes*, they cast their two top blondes in *How to Marry a Millionaire* (1953). Expecting a feud between Grable and Monroe, the studio bosses and the press were watching closely. But instead of fighting, the two actresses got along fine. Grable confided to Marilyn that there was room enough for the both of them. She later said of Monroe: "She did an awful lot to boost things up for movies when everything was at a low state, there'll never be anyone like her for looks, for attitude, for all of it."

When Marilyn took over the throne from Betty Grable, Vera Jayne Mansfield was determined to become a star in Hollywood also. She persuaded her husband Paul Mansfield to take her and their toddler Jayne-Marie to Los Angeles. While Jayne knocked on various studio doors and screen tested at Warner Bros. with the piano scene from *The Seven Year Itch*, Fox was already having trouble with their new blonde star. Monroe demanded better scripts and declined one film project after the other. Searching for a way to intimidate its difficult star, Fox hired the talents of the newest blonde sensation of Broadway: Sheree North.

Sheree (1933-2005) had just scored an enormous success as a jitterbug dancer in the musical *Hazel Flagg* (1953) and was brought to Hollywood by Paramount for the remake of the play with comedy duo Jerry Lewis and Dean Martin. *Living it Up!* (1954) made Sheree's name in Hollywood and convinced Fox to sign her up to a contract while simultaneously feeding the press that they found the perfect bait to keep Monroe in place. It worked for a while. Marilyn agreed to do *There's No Business Like Show Business* (1954) but refused a role in another movie with Betty Grable. Sheree, waiting in the wings, stepped in.

7. After a few months she left the convent to marry actor Fred MacMurray in 1954.

MARILYN MONROE.

Sheree North was no Monroe. She proved to be too temperamental to become the carbon-copy sexpot replacement Fox had hoped for. Very outspoken, she told columnist Earl Wilson: "If I lose more weight, there won't be enough falsies in the United States to help me." Sheree escaped the 'dumb blonde trap' just in time, by convincing the Fox executives she could actually act. In the mean time starlet Jayne Mansfield had played small parts under her Warner Bros. contract and left Hollywood to become the star in a new Broadway play by George Axelrod, the writer of *The Seven Year Itch* (1955), Marilyn's latest hit film. *Will Success Spoil Rock Hunter?* proved to be such a hit that the play and Jayne became Broadway's sensation of 1955. 20th Century Fox took notice and started negotiating with Jayne's agent. They finally ended up buying the play to get Jayne over to them as soon as possible. "It was said that 20th Century Fox hired me as a threat to Marilyn Monroe, but when I brought up the subject everyone denied it. Marilyn wasn't very happy about it because she thought I was her type."[8]

Marilyn Monroe had formed her own production company and had appeared in *Bus Stop* (1956) for Fox and had just left the country for England to make a film with Sir Laurence Olivier which Warner Bros. distributed. While Marilyn was in Europe, Fox put Jayne Mansfield under contract. Now the studio had three blonde stars in their stable. Sheree North was deglamorized and was transformed into a brunette. By mid 1958 Sheree found herself at liberty when 20th Century Fox let her go. She was asked about her feelings about Miss Mansfield while filming *No Down Payment* (1957) in December 1956. Sheree replied: "This is my second picture as a natural blonde — without bust pads. So I know they're through giving me the Monroe buildup. Now they've got Jayne Mansfield on the lot. She's much better equipped than I am to compete with Marilyn."

Times changed quickly. All major studios had to cut down their budgets and let many of their contractees go. With the coming of television people stayed home rather than going to the cinema. Production costs had risen sharply and with fewer films in production, each one was vital to the success or failure of the company. Besides the economic changes, social changes also emerged. Renowned actors spoke up for themselves and were freelancing instead of being groomed by one studio in particular. At this point Jayne Mansfield started her career at 20th Century Fox.

8. Mansfield, Jayne and Hargitay, Mickey. *Jayne Mansfield's Wild, Wild World.* Los Angeles: Holloway House Publishing Company, 1963.

SHEREE NORTH WITH MARILYN MONROE'S MANNEQUIN.

"The American economy soared even higher, and the tailfins on cars swelled, along with women's busts and bouffant hairdos. The time was ripe for the Blonde as Bombshell, a new, over-the-top, *va-va-voom* icon. She arrived in the form of Jayne Mansfield."[9] Her first films were not disappointing. *The Girl Can't Help It* grossed $2.8 million, while *Kiss Them for Me* and *Will Success Spoil Rock Hunter?* made $1.8 million and $1.4 mil-

BETTY GRABLE AND SHEREE NORTH IN *HOW TO BE VERY, VERY SUCCESSFUL* (1955).

lion respectively at the box office. But these films were not built entirely around Jayne Mansfield. 20th Century Fox merely used Jayne's presence in these productions to successfully run the film's jokes and comical scenes. 20th Century Fox never gave Jayne the buildup they had given their earlier blondes and with already two outspoken blondes on their books, they had no room for another one.

Jayne's career at the studio was fully controlled. Jayne let them choose the material she was to appear in. She was allowed no artistic freedom or to make any decisions for herself. Jayne did her best to make the most of the parts she was given. What the studio couldn't control was her hunger

9. Conrad III, Barnaby. *The Blonde — A Celebration of the Golden Era from Harlow to Monroe.* San Francisco: Chronicle Books, 1999.

for publicity. Cultivating Jayne the movie star was a hopeless task. She made sure she was featured in every magazine or paper on a regular basis. If 20th Century Fox had wanted to build up Jayne as their new superstar and create an image of exclusiveness around her, Jayne herself tore it down with all the outrageous stories and photos she delivered to the press.[10] "Jayne was one of the new, modern breed of stars. She was starting to stand

WARNER BROS. PUBLICITY PHOTO, 1955. BEHIND JAYNE STANDS LANCE FULLER AND TO HER RIGHT, NATALIE WOOD.

up for her rights, something unheard of unless you were a Bette Davis. If there were signals of trouble ahead, Jayne ignored them."[11] When Jayne was advised not to marry Mickey Hargitay because Fox thought it would damage her carefully built up image, she stated to the press: "I know the

---

10. Some articles that appeared in 1957: "This is Too Much Like Monroe" *Picturegoer*, March 16, 1957, "Too Much is Too Much" *Movie TV Album*, July 1957, "Will Jayne Mansfield get Hollywood in Trouble?", *On the QT*, July 1957, "Will Success Spoil My Jaynie?" *Photoplay*, December 1957.

11. Strait, Raymond. *The Tragic Secret Life of Jayne Mansfield*. London: Robert Hale & Company, 1976.

THE GIRL CAN'T HELP IT PUBLICITY PHOTO, 1956.

studio doesn't want me to marry Mickey, but I'm too much woman. I've already told the studio my decision. They were very gracious about it. But I don't blame Fox for being bitterly disappointed. I would be too — if I had a Jayne on my hands."[12]

In 1958 Zanuck left the studio to start his own production company. He assigned Buddy Adler[13] to be his successor. But unlike Zanuck, Adler wasn't a man who tended to follow through on every detail of production. While Adler originally groomed Jayne Mansfield as a super-sized Monroe, building her up for a career as their top blonde sex bomb, he didn't know what to do with her anymore at the time he was president of the studio. While he led the studio, Jayne was constantly loaned out for European productions. The studio was getting between $250,000 and $300,000 a picture for her on loan-out while all Jayne received was her normal salary.[14] When Adler died in 1960, the studio's president Spyros Skouras[15] had trouble finding a replacement for him. During these years Skouras did everything he could to keep the studio going even if that meant he had to reduce the payroll by almost a thousand workers. Jayne was one of those once promising stars that met their obligations to fulfill their contract agreements. Her films were not box office hits any longer. Still she felt that Skouras wanted her to become and stay one of Fox's biggest names. She once said about him: "Mr. Skouras was the only man I ever really respected in my life. He was as firm as any father and a real gentleman. He was a very straightforward person. He was honest enough to bluntly state his convictions. Too honest, maybe."[16]

Eventually Fox chose to release Jayne from her contract on July 4, 1962. Exactly one month later, Marilyn Monroe was found dead. 20th Century Fox was without a blonde star for the first time in three decades. And with Monroe's passing an era of dizzy blondness came to a definite end. "It was very strange how Marilyn's death affected the industry, and the need for blonde sex symbols. It was like all parts and work for

12. Mann, May. *Jayne Mansfield: A Biography.* New York: Drake, 1973.

13. Buddy Adler (1909-1960) was a successful freelance producer when he joined 20th Century Fox in 1954. While he was head of production at Fox he negotiated with the producers of the stage play *Will Success Spoil Rock Hunter?* to get Jayne to sign a contract with his studio. Of course he succeeded. Adler died of cancer at the age 51.

14. Jayne got $1250 a week from 1956-1958. On January 28, 1959 the rate was changed to $1500 per week.

15. Spyros Skouras (1893-1971) helped merge Fox with 20th Century Films. He later served as president from 1942 to 1962. Spyros was a major stockholder of 20th Century Fox.

16. Strait, Raymond: *The Tragic Secret Life of Jayne Mansfield.* London: Robert Hale & Company, 1974.

WILL SUCCESS SPOIL ROCK HUNTER? PUBLICITY PHOTO, 1957.

blondes disappeared to honor her."[17] Just like the other blondes[18] who made a career for themselves in Marilyn's shadow, Jayne found it harder and harder to find a decent part in a quality picture. "In the fifties, Jayne and American men had conspired to keep sex a secret. By the sixties the secret was out."[19]

The swinging sixties proved to be an era of free sexuality, the struggle for equality between men and women out of which came the birth of feminism. This era where the studio-trained fifties glamour girls suddenly found themselves in, was unknown territory for their old fashioned techniques of how to be feminine and attractive, eventually leading to the end of many professional careers. A long time colleague of Jayne, Mamie Van Doren, described it as follows: "In all due respect to Jayne, I do not excuse myself from this near-desperate attempt to hold on to a passing style. I was trying to keep my head above the waters that were fast closing around us in that decade. But while I saw the end coming for us all too clearly, I don't think Jayne realized what was happening."[20]

Lost in abominable grade Z features, appearing in mediocre stage versions of *Gentlemen Prefer Blondes* and *Will Success Spoil Rock Hunter?* or entertaining truck drivers in seedy bars and clubs with a song and (strip) tease show; the remaining fifties blondes struggled to make a living for themselves in a forever changed world. Jayne Mansfield wasn't spared this downward spiral either. She was still a well known name to the public, but she had taken the blonde sex doll image so far that she was now being ridiculed for it. While Jayne Mansfield held on to the image that had given her a ride to stardom and fame, the people no longer took her seriously and saw her as a caricature of feminine sensuality of an era gone by. Jayne slipped into a depression at this stage in her career. Her eldest daughter Jayne-Marie summarized it as follows: "Unfortunately the first role that pivoted her up to semi stardom was that of a dumb blonde. And I think that that unfortunately, down the line, was the downfall. Because you're talking of an era that ended pretty quickly."

20th Century Fox Studios survived the hard times and is still in business today. It seems as if Marilyn Monroe never died, her image is still

---

17. Jordan, Jessica Hope. *The Sex Goddess in American Film 1930-1965 — Jean Harlow, Mae West, Lana Turner, and Jayne Mansfield.* Amherst, New York: Cambria Press, 2009.

18. E.g. Mamie Van Doren, Anita Ekberg and Joi Lansing.

19. Saxton, Martha. *Jayne Mansfield and the American Fifties.* Boston: Houghton Mifflin Company, 1975.

20. Van Doren, Mamie with Aveilhe, Art. *Playing the Field — My Story.* New York: G.P. Putnam's Sons, 1987.

PUBLICITY PHOTO FROM JAYNE'S LAST PHOTO SESSION AT 20TH CENTURY FOX, 1962.

LONI ANDERSON AND ARNOLD SCHWARZENEGGER IN *THE JAYNE MANSFIELD STORY.*

everywhere. And Jayne Mansfield's memory is kept alive today by her beautiful and talented daughter, actress Mariska Hargitay and by the books, internet fan clubs and publications that took flight about twenty-five years ago. In 1980, the TV film *The Jayne Mansfield Story* was made. Loni Anderson[21] and Arnold Schwarzenegger played Jayne and Mickey. And although the film wasn't always accurate on the facts, it was enter-

ANNA NICOLE SMITH (LEFT), AND PAMELA ANDERSON (RIGHT).

taining and managed to get nominated for three Emmy Awards in the categories for hairstyling, makeup and costume design.

In 1999 the English BBC featured a documentary series called *Blondes*; a triptych which featured Diana Dors, Anita Ekberg and Jayne. And recently Jayne was one of three blondes that were featured on a BBC Radio program called *Blonde on Blonde*.[22] Jayne was also featured in the award winning A&E Television Networks series *Biography* in an episode titled *Jayne Mansfield: Blonde Ambition* (2004).[23] Film maker Quentin Tarantino also made references to Jayne in two of his productions. In *Pulp Fiction* (1994) John Travolta and Uma Thurman visit a

21. Loni Anderson (1945) was the perfect actress to portray Jayne. She was a buxom, blonde pin-up and television actress in the seventies and eighties and was once married to butch actor Burt Reynolds.

22. The others were Lana Turner (episode 1) and Peggy Lee (episode 3). Jayne's episode was broadcasted on August 24, 2010.

23. The TV series won an Emmy Award in outstanding non-fiction TV series category in 2001.

restaurant where the staff are lookalikes of fifties stars like Elvis Presley, Buddy Holly, Marilyn Monroe, and Mamie Van Doren. When Thurman is confused by the appearance of two blonde waitresses, assuming there are two Marilyn's, Travolta answers: "That's Marilyn Monroe and that's Mamie Van Doren. I don't see Jayne Mansfield; she must have the night off or something." And a decade later Tarantino introduced an all Asian girl band called the *5.6.7.8's* who performed *I Walk Like Jayne Mansfield* in *Kill Bill: Vol.1* (2003).

Blonde 'actresses', *Playboy* centerfolds and pin up girls like Pamela Anderson and Anne Nicole Smith[24] — both born in the year Jayne died — had their moment of fame in the 1990s being playmates of Playboy magazine and appearing in popular TV shows and box office hits, before the lack of talent overshadowed the pin-up craze that they provoked. They revived the name Jayne Mansfield by the comparison that was made with the pin-up/movie star of the fabulous fifties. Like Anderson and Smith, Jayne was also a model for Hugh Hefner once. *Playboy* featured Jayne Mansfield as their Playmate of the Month in February 1955, there appeared several layouts of her during the following years, with the best sold issue to date being the June 1963 issue with photographs from her nude scenes in *Promises, Promises!*[25] Jayne Mansfield, the name and image, has proved to be a phenomenon of popular culture; a celebrity in her own time, a myth in ours.

24. Miss Anderson was born as Pamela Denise Anderson on July 1, two days after Jayne Mansfield's death. Anna Nicole Smith was born as Vickie Lynn Hogan on November 28 and died in 2007 at the age of 39 from an accidental drug overdose.

25. *Playboy* issues featuring Jayne Mansfield include February 1955 (Playmate of the Month), February 1956, February 1957, February 1958, December 1958, February 1960 (The best of Jayne Mansfield), July 1963, Annual 1964 (first issue of *The Best of Playboy*), December 1965, Newsstand Special 1989 (100 Beautiful Women), January 1994 and Newsstand Special 1999 (45th Anniversary Special), as well as the *Playboy* calendar in 1959.

PUBLICITY PHOTO, 1956.

BEFORE SHE WAS FAMOUS, IN A PHOTO FROM 1955.

Biography

"WHEN SHE WALKED OUT THERE SHE WAS THE PROFESSIONAL, SHE NEVER LET ANYONE KNOW SHE WAS HURTING, EVER. SHE FORGAVE EVERYBODY EVERYTHING AND SHE NEVER UNDERSTOOD WHY PEOPLE WOULDN'T FORGIVE HER. SHE WAS LIKE A LITTLE GIRL THAT NEVER GREW UP."

RAYMOND STRAIT

EARLY YEARS

Born on April 19, 1933 at Bryn Mawr Hospital, Pennsylvania, under the sign of Aries, Jayne Mansfield saw the day of light at 9:07 AM. Jayne showed great pride in her birth-sign, she once commented: "Aries people are the most energetic and the most stubborn. They have tremendous drive."[1] The infant was baptized a few months later in June in the Methodist Church of Bryn Mawr. Her parents Vera and Herbert Palmer christened her Vera Jayne. Herbert was a lawyer, Vera a school teacher. "We had an average small white frame house in an average middle class neighborhood in Phillipsburg, New Jersey. My mother was very strict, too strict! She had taught elementary school, and rules and regulations were natural to her. I know she loved me, but she expected perfection from a little child."[2] Jayne's father held a healthy practice in Phillipsburg.

1. In her life Jayne Mansfield consulted astrologers regularly. Since 1956 she sought the advice of 'astrologer to the stars' Carroll Righter (1900-1988). Righter honored Jayne at his Aries party in 1962. Lesser known celebrity astrologer, Adrian Don, said of her: "Jayne Mansfield is a child of the new age, born in the artistic and humane sign of Aries. Jayne is a distinct individualist but her nature is somewhat complex…she loves freedom and prefers to follow her own dictates rather than be bound by traditional conventions. At times this charming actress may appear vacillating and indecisive, but inwardly she is strong and unyielding as the Rock, very fixed in her desires and opinions." Mansfield, Jayne and Hargitay, Mickey. *Jayne Mansfield's Wild, Wild World.* Los Angeles: Holloway House Publishing Company, 1963.

2. Mann, May. *Jayne Mansfield: A Biography.* New York: Drake, 1973.

He was a bright man, who had been a brilliant student at University and also proved to be a fine musician.

When Jayne was three years old her father died from a heart attack while driving his car with his wife and daughter next to him. He was thirty-three. "My father's death made a great impression on me. I was always asking to go to the cemetery to visit his grave. I'd sit there and talk to him. I'd cry and cry. 'Daddy, you understand me and Momma doesn't,' I'd sob. He was the only man I ever knew who really loved me unselfishly, who never used me for personal gain," Jayne recalled to her friend May Mann. When Vera went to work, Jayne was given into temporary custody of a lady called Sally Rice, a housekeeper.

About two years after Herbert's death, Vera met Harry Peers, a travelling sales engineer from Fort Worth, Texas. They were married in St. Louis in 1939. At first Jayne was upset seeing her mother with a new man, but in the end Harry won Jayne's heart and she con- **BABY JAYNE.**
sidered him a second father. The family moved to Dallas. According to her press agent Raymond Strait she resented the Texan city. Still she had a happy childhood. "My fondest memories of Dallas are those on Amherst Street as I came to be a young woman."[3]

According to her parents Jayne was a precocious child. At six her vocabulary was that of a twelve year old, and in High School Jayne was an above average student, excelling in languages like French and Spanish. Besides being a good student, her parents enrolled her in all kinds of classes. She attended ballet classes and violin and piano lessons. Jayne's mother is described as a strict woman with a set of high morals. Jayne was supposed to live up to these standards. By getting good grades and always giving of her best at everything she did, she would get her mother's affection. "Momma was the important woman in our home. She never

3. Strait, Raymond. *The Tragic Secret Life of Jayne Mansfield*. London: Robert Hale & Company, 1976.

let me forget that she was boss. I was always in the shadow. Every time I tried to step out on my own, I was in trouble with her."[4]

With growing up Jayne found it more difficult not to rebel against her mother. Her friends at that time described her as a pretty girl, but not outstanding. Although she seemed not particularly interested in school, she kept her grades up so not to get in conflict with her mother. She did date, but not with the glamorous guys she boasted to the press about when she became famous. Her girlfriends remember her dating the dull guys and making up stories of how wonderful it all was, just to belong. That all changed when Jayne set eyes on Paul Mansfield in the year of her graduation.

On Christmas Eve of 1949, she attended a party with her girlfriends. Paul was invited to the party also. Jayne immediately had a crush for the black haired, mature looking twenty year old guy. They started dating secretly, because Vera had started keeping a close eye on her daughter's growing maturity. "It was the most conservative Christmas Eve I ever spent. He was not a great talker. He had a silent way of moving and in taking over. I liked that and I was enveloped by his subtle masculinity. I don't mean sexually. I mean the firmness with which he handled himself. I respected him."[5] Paul Mansfield liked Jayne too, but when he had to leave town for a while, Jayne started dating another man. A twenty-four year old gas station attendant, called 'Inky' by Jayne, took her to several parties during the holiday season. He also bought Jayne her first alcoholic drink. First timer Jayne drank way too much, so Inky decided to leave and get some coffee and something to eat to sober her up before he returned her home. "On the way home we stopped in the park. Inky kissed me. All the rest followed. I was certainly ready and willing. It was my first time."[6] When her parents learned about her escapades she was denied all privileges, wasn't allowed to see Inky again and denied to drink alcohol.

After the holidays Paul returned to Dallas and he and Jayne started dating again. Paul, becoming more serious about his relationship with Jayne, took her to meet his parents. Around this time Jayne found out that she was pregnant. Not daring to tell her parents, she called Paul. He directly offered to marry her. Paul Mansfield remembered the following from that period: "I began calling her and then we began dating. I felt really proud when we walked down the street with this gorgeous thing

4. Mann, May. *Jayne Mansfield: A Biography.* New York: Drake, 1973.

5. Strait, Raymond. *The Tragic Secret Life of Jayne Mansfield.* London: Robert Hale & Company, 1976.

6. Strait, Raymond. *The Tragic Secret Life of Jayne Mansfield.* London: Robert Hale & Company, 1976.

on my arm. Late January we just decided to elope. We didn't tell anybody about it. She was sixteen, I was twenty, twenty-one. I was young and in love and she was too. We got married in a fever, hotter than a couple of cats."

Paul and Jayne were married on January 28, 1950 in Fort Worth, Texas. Jayne wanted to keep her marriage a secret because she feared her parents reaction. After the wedding she discovered that she was not pregnant at

WITH PAUL MANSFIELD IN A 1950 WEDDING PHOTO.

all, but a month after the wedding she did become pregnant and in April she decided to tell her parents. Because both Paul's and Jayne's parents believed they were still unmarried, they arranged a wedding ceremony for May 10, 1950. Jayne graduated from Highland Park High School a month later and went to SMU; Southern Methodist University in Dallas. Paul attended the University in Austin, so Jayne stayed with her parents.

Jayne Marie Mansfield was born on November 8, 1950 in St. Paul's hospital. Within a few months after giving birth Jayne joined Paul and attended the University of Texas in Austin also, taking her young daughter with her to classes. Jayne developed a daily routine that would have staggered anyone with less driving ambition. Taking classes in the afternoon, coming home to do her household chores and working from 7 until 11 at evening for eighty cents an hour as a receptionist at the Gregg Scott Dance Studios. "I did Jayne Marie's laundry in the bathtub, and I cooked and cleaned too, just like any young wife. And it didn't hurt my marks either. I even got an A in chemistry!"

In January 1951, Jayne came into a small inheritance. It wasn't terribly much, but it was just enough to support some special studies. In that summer she went to Los Angeles, where she enrolled for drama courses at UCLA. She stayed in the women's dormitory and took summer courses.

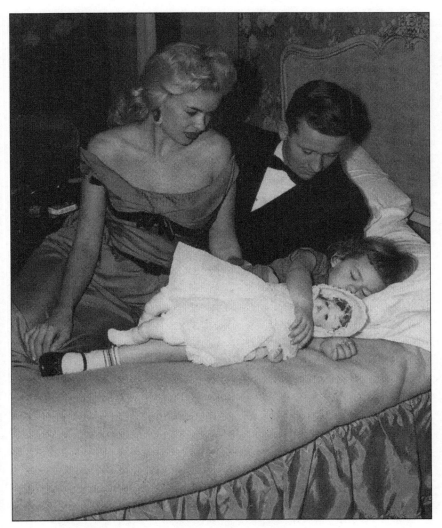

WITH PAUL MANSFIELD AND JAYNE MARIE, 1954.

WITH MARLA ENGLISH AT THE ANNUAL DEBUTANTE STARS BALL, 1954.

Meanwhile Paul had joined the US army, and because of the Korean War (that had broken out in 1950) he was called to active duty. Jayne joined him to live on Camp Gordon, Georgia. When Paul was shipped to Korea in 1952, Jayne returned to Dallas and enrolled at SMU again. She took courses in drama, abnormal psychology and biology.

Besides studying she earned some money with modeling. It was around this time she posed in the nude for the first time. This photo shoot resulted with Jayne becoming the model for a sculpturing class. "I found I could pose in the nude in front of a women's sculpturing class without any embarrassment, or even a feeling of uneasiness. Soon after that a men's sculpturing class asked me to pose for them. They even offered to up the price, but that I didn't like."[7] In 1952 Jayne also studied at the Dallas Institute of the Performing Arts, which was founded by Baruch Lumet, director Sidney Lumet's father. After a year of study he took her in to play in the first stage production of Arthur Miller's *Death of a Salesman* with the Knox Street Players.

STARTING OUT IN HOLLYWOOD

When the Korean War ended in 1953, Paul took up his promise to take his wife to Hollywood to seek a career in the movie business. The couple agreed that they would give it a half year to make Jayne's plan succeed. "I saw the Los Angeles area as good as any to establish myself too. And I was willing to take her there and look for work myself. She changed her hair to blonde; they liked blondes back then. She was getting better looking every day, you know, and I was playing my role. I told her that I would take her to California and I would standby and give her her opportunity." Before Jayne left she prepared herself for a possible screen test and worked on a scene from *Joan of Arc* with Baruch Lumet. Lumet rang his friend Milton Lewis at Paramount to notify him of Jayne's coming.

On April 30, 1954, Jayne screen tested at Paramount with her studied soliloquy from *Joan of Arc*. Eight days later Paramount tested her again in a scene from *The Seven Year Itch*, but declined to put her under contract. But Jayne wasn't a girl to be put aside, that summer she visited various studios. "So on a bright Tuesday morning, I got on a bus to go to the nearest studio to my home, Republic Studios. In the casting office it was

7. Mansfield, Jayne and Hargitay, Mickey. *Jayne Mansfield's Wild, Wild World.* Los Angeles: Holloway House Publishing Company, 1963.

JAYNE IN THE FAMOUS RED LAMÉ BATHING SUIT, 1955

all routine. Name, address, height, experience. I was one of several other young girls, some of them very pretty, in fact prettier than I was. It was a shock. It was a pretty discouraging session. From there I went to Universal Studios where I went through the same experience. At Warner Brothers, my next stop, they had certain hours for interviewing talent and I was there at the wrong time."[8] In November she managed to get a screen test at Warner Bros., again with the piano scene from *The Seven Year Itch*. Unfortunately she also failed to impress them.

Her luck changed when she landed herself a small part in a television show called *An Angel Went A.W.O.L*. As a result of this appearance, her photographer friend Frank Worth talked the producers of an independent made movie into using her. So at last Jayne made her film debut in a cheap thriller called *Female Jungle*. Unfortunately the film wasn't released until two years later, because it failed to find a distributor. But Jayne didn't give up. She signed up with a press agent called Jim Byron.[9] Frank Worth remembers Byron as a cunning business man: "[a press agent] usually just works for a star or an actress or actor, and they don't get a percentage of their business. He signed her for five percent. But what this guy did at the time was brilliant by the way. He signed twenty or thirty girls and hoped one of them was gonna make it. And that'll help him. So he signed them all for five percent of their gross. And she was one of the girls."[10] Byron put her to work immediately, he designed a Christmas gimmick were Jayne was to visit the local newspaper city rooms dressed in a brief Santa costume. The next day her picture was in all the newspapers! In January of the next year Byron and Worth arranged for Jayne to join the press junket for Jane Russell's new picture *Underwater*. The other girls who went along were Debbie Reynolds, Mala Powers, and Lori Nelson. Jane Russell was delayed a few days in New York so wasn't there when Jayne managed to steal all the attention from every other beautiful starlet around when she 'lost' the top of her bathing suit. Frank Worth was there to capture the stunt on film, he recalled: "The next day Jane Russell arrived. She came out to be photographed,

8. Mansfield, Jayne and Hargitay, Mickey. *Jayne Mansfield's Wild, Wild World*. Los Angeles: Holloway House Publishing Company, 1963.

9. Press agent Jim Byron once said how lucky he felt when he met Jayne: *"I was looking for a chick to prove I was the world's greatest living press agent."* Byron also worked with blondes Marilyn Maxwell and Yvette Mimieux. Feeney Callan, Michael. *Pink Goddess — The Jayne Mansfield Story*. London: W.H. Allen, 1986.

10. *Jayne Mansfield fan club newsletter*, May 1987.

WITH DAUGHTER JAYNE MARIE IN A 1955 WARNER BROS. PUBLICITY PHOTO.

but most of us had run out of film!"[11] Overnight Jayne became known as 'that girl in the bathing suit'. "It wasn't even my own costume. I borrowed it from Peter Gowland, the still photographer, who kept it in his studio for models. It was red lame and skin tight, it covered everything but didn't hide anything. When I took off my robe at the beach I thought I'd forgotten to put it on."[12]

Paul Mansfield started to get annoyed with his wife's career hunt: "I had began to not like what I saw and I told her that. I just couldn't stand the attention she was receiving from other men, I didn't know how we were going to take care of little Jayne Marie in a family kind of atmosphere with that going on. Of course you could say that my leaving didn't help that, but still it seemed wrong to me so I chose to tell her that. I could see myself as a Mr. Jaynie Mansfield and that really wasn't what I had sought for my life. So along about the Spring of 1955 we separated and I took a job in San Francisco and moved away." Although Paul remembers it being the Spring, Jayne and Paul actually separated on January 7, 1955. Later Jayne told Raymond Strait about her break up with Paul: "Hollywood broke up our marriage — my desire for stardom. I was a real bitch after we came to Hollywood."[13] Still aiming a career as a movie star, Jayne boosted her career with the help of Jim Byron and his buddy Bill Shiffrin, who became Jayne's agent. Because he believed Hollywood could use another blonde glamour girl besides Kim Novak and Marilyn Monroe, he took Jayne in as a client.

In January Jayne had posed semi nude for Playboy magazine, the photos were featured in the magazine in February. It was the beginning of a long term collaboration with the magazine that featured a pictorial about Jayne every coming year in February. Meanwhile Bill Shiffrin negotiated with several studios to get Jayne under contract. Finally he maneuvered her into a seven-year contract with Warner Bros. Warner Bros. were producing entertainment for the whole family in the early fifties. It was the home studio of Doris Day and Gordon MacRae who appeared in honey sweet musical comedies. But Jack Warner was cautious over contracting this publicity eager starlet. A couple of years earlier he had another blonde under contract who made a lot of negative headlines and soiled the studios name with bad publicity. The thoughts of her were still lingering in his mind. The blonde starlet who had caused Jack Warner

11. Mann, May. *Jayne Mansfield: A Biography*. New York: Drake, 1973.

12. *Photoplay*, August 1957.

13. Strait, Raymond. *The Tragic Secret Life of Jayne Mansfield*. London: Robert Hale & Company, 1976.

all the trouble was Barbara Payton.[14] Her tragic fall from stardom (and grace) was still rumored around town as a lesson in modest behavior to eager starlets like Jayne Mansfield who sought every kind of attention to make their name. Also notable is that Warner Bros., at the time, was the only major studio that didn't have its own sexy female star, nor had created one in all the years of its existence. But they always had a dozen

ON THE SET OF *ILLEGAL* (1955).

sexy stock players on hand who filled the bill when a movie called for a sexy dame in a small part.

On February 8, Jayne became a contract player at Warner's. For the first time she felt things were moving up in the right direction. That same day she also filed for divorce from Paul Mansfield, which was granted in

---

14. Sexy blonde Barbara Payton (1927-1967) got involved with the wrong men, created all kinds of bad publicity and was found to be unmanageable by the Warner's studio executives. She was released from her seven-year contract after 22 months. "Jack Warner allegedly loathed Barbara from her earliest days on the lot and was said to have viewed her as little more than a loose broad with a big mouth…Warner felt that she was an embarrassment and more trouble than she was worth; a dime-a-dozen chippie who watched everything she touched turn to dust." O'Dowd, John. *Kiss Tomorrow Goodbye: The Barbara Payton Story*. Albany: BearManor Media, 2006.

October the following year.[15] At Warner's she had a promising start in *Illegal* with Edward G. Robinson. She held a key role in a well reviewed film. Her next two parts were mere cameos, but when Warner's announced she would appear in their upcoming productions *Sincerely Yours* and *Rebel Without A Cause*, her future couldn't be brighter. "Many girls might have been discouraged or even insulted by the caliber of roles. It didn't bother me — I was happy. I figured this was all the training for the big part I'd eventually get."[16] Although Jayne screen tested with actor Dennis Hopper for the part of Judy in *Rebel Without A Cause*, she was unsuccessful. Jayne was dating the film's director Nicholas Ray at the time and he remembered that the whole test was a hoax and he considered it 'an hallucination' of Warner's casting department[17]: "I didn't even put any film in the camera for the screen test."[18] Instead of putting her to work in one of their own productions, Jayne was loaned out for an independent picture called *The Burglar* to be filmed in Philadelphia. "On the set in Philly, everyone was gathered around to read the trade papers which had been air-mailed from Hollywood. Someone exclaimed, "There's a big story here on you, Jayne." Smiling, I picked it up to read, 'Warner Bros. Drops Jayne Mansfield.'"

BROADWAY, FOX AND FAME

Desperate with the loss of her contract she called Bill Shiffrin. He told her that in New York they were testing actresses for the lead in a comedy by writer George Axelrod. At first Jayne declined because she wanted to be a movie star, not a Broadway actress. But Shiffrin insisted she would read for the producers of *Will Success Spoil Rock Hunter?* He thought she was perfect for the part of Rita Marlowe; a role modeled on Marilyn Monroe. And he was right. The producers were wildly enthusiastic about Jayne, so she landed the part that blondes like Marilyn Maxwell, Sheree North and Mamie Van Doren had turned down. *Will Success Spoil Rock Hunter?* opened at the Belasco Theatre on October 13, 1955. Jayne

15. Due to paperwork problems the divorce didn't become final until January 1958.

16. Mansfield, Jayne and Hargitay, Mickey. *Jayne Mansfield's Wild, Wild World.* Los Angeles: Holloway House Publishing Company, 1963.

17. Kashner, Sam & Macnair, Jennifer. *The Bad and the Beautiful — A Chronicle of Hollywood in the Fifties.* London: Little, Brown, 2002.

18. Originally Warner's studio executives thought it would make an excellent co-starring vehicle for their two new stars Tab Hunter and Jayne Mansfield. But Nicholas Ray refused to make the picture with anyone but Natalie Wood and James Dean. Dowdy, Andrew. *The Films of the Fifties — The American State of Mind.* New York: William Morrow & Co, 1975.

WITH CLEO MOORE AT THE 28TH ANNUAL ACADEMY AWARDS, 1956.

became an overnight success and New York celebrated her success with her: "Almost every store window in New York City had my picture in front, and those that didn't — I would go in personally and hand them one. Then I got the idea of blow-ups, five-feet-by-three. I'd autograph them to a respective shop or store and walk in with one and give it to the owner. I had many different poses, so each would have an exclusive. No one refused me. And there I was, block after block, smiling out at the public."[19]

During her stay in New York Jayne lived with her daughter Jayne Marie in a one-bedroom suit in the Gorham Hotel on West 55th Street. She hired a maid to take care of Jayne Marie and her three dogs and four cats when she was working. Being a single working mother was considered to be inappropriate at the time, and having been the centerfold of a girlie magazine didn't do her reputation any good also. But Jayne simply explained: "I read little Bible stories to Jayne Marie every night and she is a well-balanced and intelligent child. Those pictures in Playboy magazine I posed for to get milk and bread for the baby."[20] Jayne Marie remembers her mother's Broadway success: "I was four and she got the lead in *Will Success Spoil Rock Hunter?* on Broadway and that was a big deal. She was extremely excited and this is really what sky-rocketed her up." Still Jayne wanted to get back to Hollywood as soon as possible. She confided in her press agent Raymond Strait: "A Broadway star may be a great actress, but Hollywood and making films — that's where you get worldwide fame. That's what I want."[21] During this time Jayne was invited to the Latin Quarter to see the Mae West show.

On May 13, 1956, Jayne and *Rock Hunter's* producer and composer Jules Styne watched Mae West and her muscle men clad in loin cloths. One of them was the Hungarian born Mr. Universe of 1955, Mickey Hargitay. He remembers the night as follows: "And I see a girl with blonde hair, just like Mae West, and she had a milkshake. I fell in love, and so did she!" It seemed love at first sight and Jayne sought contact with him after the show. "I knew I wanted Mickey ten minutes after we were introduced at the Latin Quarter. We have been so close since. I've had to go it alone, with my family and Paul putting obstacles in my path all the way. Mickey wants to devote himself to helping my career."[22] Hearing of the romance infuriated Miss West. She demanded that Mickey stop seeing Jayne and make public that their 'romance' was for publicity reasons

19. Mann, May. *Jayne Mansfield: A Biography.* New York: Drake, 1973.

20. Saxton, Martha. *Jayne Mansfield and the American Fifties.* Boston: Houghton Mifflin Company, 1975.

21. Strait, Raymond. *The Tragic Secret Life of Jayne Mansfield.* London: Robert Hale & Company, 1976.

22. Mann, May. *Jayne Mansfield: A Biography.* New York: Drake, 1973.

JAYNE AS A PRESS GIRL, 1956.

only. But Mickey told Miss West that this was different. When asked about her opinion about Miss West, Jayne replied: "There is no truth to the story that I'm having a feud with Mae West. I admire her — as a performer. I hope I can look that good when I'm her age." When the show left New York and moved on to Washington Jayne and Mickey kept in contact through telephone or flew out to each other when they were free. Eventually Mae West fired Mickey. Hargitay confronted his wife, Mary, that he had fallen in love and wanted a divorce.[23]

When Jayne's contract for *Will Success Spoil Rock Hunter?* ended on September 15, 1956, she immediately left for Hollywood. The news of the success of the play and its leading lady had reached Hollywood and several producers/studios showed interest in Jayne. Jayne eventually chose 20th Century Fox. Buddy Adler was sent out to New York to negotiate with the producers of *Rock Hunter*. He came up with a package deal to buy the play with Jayne for a staggering sum of $120,000. But since the play was a satire on Hollywood, Fox had the story re-written by director/scriptwriter Frank Tashlin. "Then I was handed *Rock Hunter*. It was anything but what a movie studio would want, for it lampooned Hollywood. I rewrote it, replacing the movies with a TV background."[24] To prepare for her role in the film Jayne studied at the Actors Studio in New York. "I'm studying dancing, singing and dramatic acting," she told columnist Louella Parsons. "20th has promised to build me as one of their important stars." Before they starred Jayne in the film version they tested her with the public in *The Girl Can't Help It*. Adler had promised Jayne to build her up to become the biggest blonde in Hollywood. She was to become the blonde bombshell to rival Columbia's Kim Novak and their own flaxen haired Marilyn Monroe. Monroe had turned thirty and was loaned out to Warner Bros. to star in *The Prince and the Showgirl*. She had turned down all the sexy parts she was lined up for and had formed her own production company a year earlier. Her last film for Fox was *Bus Stop*, which was a dramatic part. Jayne was to become Monroe's successor in the comedies that required a dizzy, sexy blonde for its lead.

The rock 'n' roll musical/comedy *The Girl Can't Help It* turned out to be a huge success. It confirmed that the studio indeed had a talent in Jayne which could reach super star status with the right grooming. But with Jayne being a mother and given the fact that she came over to Hollywood with a soon to become Mr. Mansfield, the studio had a hard time molding her. "It was a contrast — the shapely Jayne in her sex-symbol clothes

23. The divorce was granted on September 6, 1956.

24. Mann, May. *Jayne Mansfield: A Biography*. New York: Drake, 1973.

JAYNE IN HOLLAND, 1957.

snuggling the child on her lap in affectionate, motherly poses. This was unique. It aroused even greater interest than Jayne photographed with men she dated."[25] So Fox was torn between building her up as a sexy dumb blonde, filling the void Marilyn had left open with her refusal to play these parts, or having her compete with the more sultry blonde Kim Novak, who was considered the hottest property of Columbia studios since Rita Hayworth. After the comedy part in *The Girl Can't Help It*, Jayne was put to work on *Rock Hunter*. Director Frank Tashlin recalled later: "It was one of my most colorful experiences in film making. Mickey would carry Jayne in his arms from the dressing room on to the set. There was always romantic by-play between them. They exuded happiness and it touched everyone."[26]

Then Jayne was cast in a dramatic part in *The Wayward Bus*, inspired on the novel by John Steinbeck. Her two former pictures were filmed in Technicolor, this one was shot in black and white. It received a low key release, without much publicity. It seemed Fox decided at the last minute to place all its money on shaping Jayne as the new, dizzier and improved Marilyn, instead of giving her more varied roles and a build up like Novak received at Columbia.[27] Jayne didn't seem concerned about the way her image building was heading, she had other worries. She desperately wanted to marry Mickey, but Buddy Adler and Darryl F. Zanuck were strongly opposed to that idea. They believed that this marriage would harm her career. Therefore Jayne and Mickey had to live in separate houses, pretending they were merely dating instead of having serious plans to share the rest of their lives together. Jayne had to agree to arranged studio dates with actors like Robert Wagner and Hugh O'Brian.

When she was lined up for another film, *Kiss Them For Me* Mickey was forbidden to travel with her to the shooting location, San Francisco. Although she missed Mickey, Jayne was excited about working with Cary Grant. She said about him: "He is one of the most marvelous men I've ever met. A gracious co-star who sent me little gifts every day to cheer me up. He knew how much I missed Mickey and he understood."[28] Her

25. Mann, May. *Jayne Mansfield: A Biography*. New York: Drake, 1973.

26. Mann, May. *Jayne Mansfield: A Biography*. New York: Drake, 1973.

27. Kim Novak (1933) was build up as a blonde bombshell, but opposite to the one-dimensional image 20th Century Fox created for Jayne Mansfield, Columbia starred Novak in serious parts (*Picnic*, 1955), femme fatale roles (*Pushover*, 1954), sexy and musical parts (*Jeanne Eagles* and *Pal Joey*, both 1957). In 1958 Columbia loaned her out to Paramount to star in Alfred Hitchcock's *Vertigo*.

28. Strait, Raymond. *The Tragic Secret Life of Jayne Mansfield*. London: Robert Hale & Company, 1976.

WITH PARENTS HARRY AND VERA PEERS, 1957.

agent Bill Shiffrin and friend Frank Tashlin had advised her not to do this film. Jayne also had doubts but was persuaded by the film's producer Jerry Wald that if she accepted the part than she would be offered the lead in *The Jean Harlow Story* afterwards.[29] This never materialized and Martha Saxton mentioned in her book that Wald had lied to Jayne, because Fox already decided she was unsuitable for the part of Jean Harlow.

Three months after the completion of *Kiss Them For Me* the studio arranged a forty day tour around Europe, to promote *Will Success Spoil Rock Hunter?* Jayne left on September 25, leaving Mickey behind to take care of Jayne Marie and their numerous pets. The studio insisted that she went alone, making a personal appearance tour that started in England. In England Jayne was welcomed as a superstar. Thousands of fans gathered at the London airport to greet Jayne. A large police presence was assigned to handle the crowds. Jayne was ecstatic about her reception and on returning to England at the end of her European tour, she was introduced to Queen Elizabeth at the Royal Command Performance on November 3, 1957. Jayne later described it as the most exciting moment of her life. Three days later she arrived at Los Angeles airport and at a press conference held that day announced that she would marry Mickey Hargitay the next year. 20th Century Fox executives realized that they had lost the battle with their strong-willed contract player. She was uncontrollable and made it clear that she managed her own life and career. Still, with Jayne under contract, 20th Century Fox knew that they had a very popular star in their stable. She appeared in about 2,500 newspaper photographs between September 1956 and May 1957, and had about 122,000 lines of newspaper copy written about her during this time.[30] Her publicity stunts were covered by every film magazine and newspaper in the United States and beyond.

Probably her most famous stunt up until then had occurred in April 1957. Jayne attended the Hollywood welcome party for Italian star Sophia Loren. She wore a very low cut evening dress, and while bending over to greet Miss Loren, a nipple was exposed. The lucky photographers who were there couldn't stop flashing! The look on Sophia's face makes those

---

29. In September 1956 *Photoplay* magazine announced that Jayne wanted to play Jean Harlow on the screen. The same magazine wrote in January the next year that both Marilyn Monroe and Jayne were considered for the part. Buddy Adler had purchased the film rights for *The Jean Harlow Story* in 1956. He commissioned Adela Rogers St. John to write the screenplay and wanted Marilyn in the lead. Because Marilyn objected the production was shelved. Nearly ten years later Paramount made *Harlow* with Carroll Baker in the part of the 1930's blonde star. Another production with the same title was also made in 1965, it starred Carol Lynley. It was said that Columbia pictures also considered making a Harlow biopic with either Cleo Moore or Kim Novak.

30. Pendergast, Sara & Tom. *St. James Encyclopedia of Popular Culture*. London; St. James Press, 2000.

pictures still famous today. Jayne herself said about the incident: "I really had no idea so much of me was showing. I only realized when I saw the expression on Miss Loren's face and I noticed that she was staring down my dress. Some enemies said I planned the strategy to take the play away from Miss Loren. Not at all. Though I did show Miss Loren that American girls have bosoms too."[31] The designer of the dress, Elgée Bové,

SIGNING AUTOGRAPHS IN 1957.

excused Jayne with the explanation that Jayne had lost weight following the original fitting, "so the dress sort of fell away from her at the top."

Late 1957 Jayne wanted to respond to offers to bring a nightclub act to hotels and nightclubs all over the States. Fox declined to let her do it at first, but when Jayne received an offer to work at the Tropicana hotel in Las Vegas — and insisted she wanted to do it — the studio gave in to her. She was scheduled to start working one month after her wedding to Mickey Hargitay. On January 13, 1958, Jayne became Mrs. Hargitay.

31. Mansfield, Jayne and Hargitay, Mickey. *Jayne Mansfield's Wild, Wild World.* Los Angeles: Holloway House Publishing Company, 1963.

Reverend Kenneth W. Knox led the services at the Wayfarer's Chapel in Palos Verdes, California. In preparation of the wedding, Knox invited them to his home. But the Reverend's wife objected and did not want to see Jayne, thinking she represented and portrayed the wrong kind of womanhood. But Knox himself thought different. "She was ladylike, sweet, kind and exceptionally attentive," he said of Jayne. Although Jayne had

JAYNE MARRIED MICKEY HARGITAY ON JANUARY 13, 1958.

told the studio and the Reverend that it would be a private, intimate wedding ceremony, she had printed pink cards announcing the wedding and had them dropped from a helicopter all over Los Angeles. This resulted in a huge crowd of people and pressmen to gather around the glass chapel. The marriage was covered all over the world, affirming again that Jayne Mansfield was a true Hollywood star. A star who shared her life and fame with the public in a time when stars were becoming more secretive about their private lives.

In March the Hargitays had bought a new home. The house had been built in 1929 and was owned by actor/singer Rudy Vallee, from whom they bought it for $76,000. Jayne financed the house with the inheritance of $81,340 she received after the death of her grandfather Elmer Palmer. The three-story Spanish-style house, soon to become the 'Pink Palace' had eight bedrooms and thirteen bathrooms.[32] After the wedding and their

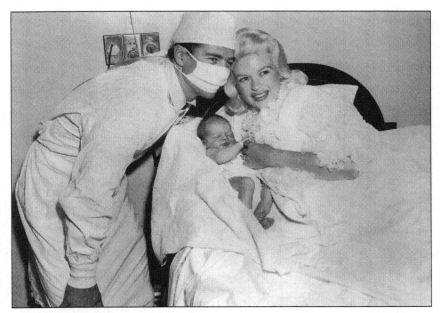

DECEMBER 21, 1958 SAW THE BIRTH OF MIKLOS HARGITAY, SEEN IN THIS FOX PUBLICITY PHOTO.

four week stint at Las Vegas in their *Tropicana Holiday* show, Fox handed her the script of *The Sheriff of Fractured Jaw*. The film was to be shot on location in England and Spain. In the summer of 1958 Jayne, Mickey and Jayne Marie travelled to Europe. While in London, Jayne announced that she was expecting a child that was to be born in December. On returning to the United States, Fox put Jayne on a non-pay suspension because of her pregnancy; a common practice female workers experienced when pregnant. On December 21, Miklos Hargitay, Jr., was born. After giving birth it was a case of losing the extra weight as soon as possible. Studio

32. Jayne and Mickey painted the house pink. It was situated at 10100 Sunset Boulevard, but was torn down in 2002. Many of the thirteen bathrooms had heart-shaped baths. The living room had pink carpets and wall decorations. Mickey also built Jayne a heart-shaped pool. The house was later owned by Ringo Starr from The Beatles and singer Engelbert Humperdinck.

BEHIND THE SCENES OF *THE SHERIFF OF FRACTURED JAW* (1958).

doctors were eager to lend a helping hand by prescribing diet pills. In the meantime, Jayne was lined up to play the other woman in Paul Newman's *Rally 'Round the Flag, Boys!* (1958). But Newman wanted Joan Collins for the part and the studio gave in to his pleas.

FALLING FROM GRACE

In May 1959 Jayne was back to her old glamorous self when she appeared on the Las Vegas stages again in the revival of the *Tropical Holiday* show. The show lasted a month, and in July Jayne was sent to England again to appear in two Soho situated B-movies. Jayne didn't want to make them, but 20th Century Fox threatened her with suspension otherwise. Jayne was becoming more unhappy with the direction her career was heading. She complained to the studio and her friends and thought of starting her own production company. This was the time that the major studios tried to compete with the growing and popular medium of television. Movie stars released themselves from their contracts and became their own agents, picking out their own scripts. Marilyn Monroe drove a hard bargain with 20th Century Fox when she founded her own production company in 1955. Jayne also stepped on the band wagon by firing her press agent Jim Byron and leaving her agent Bill Shiffrin. From now on she negotiated with the studio executives herself. "I want good dramatic roles. If the studio won't give them to me, then I'll go on the stage. If I have to, I'll do my own plays with my own company!"[33]

The year was 1960, which would prove to be the beginning of Jayne Mansfield's career decline. She was no longer considered star material by the men in charge at Fox. Times were changing. The need for dumb blondes was decreasing. Marilyn Monroe had made a hit movie, *Some Like it Hot*, that was released in 1959. But her next movie, *Let's Make Love*, was a box office flop. Mamie Van Doren was freelancing and appeared in B-movies that were aimed at the teenage market, Diana Dors had left Hollywood after an unsuccessful try at stardom, Anita Ekberg also left Hollywood and had just appeared — receiving much critical acclaim — in *La Dolce Vita* in Italy and Kim Novak had made the change of becoming a more sophisticated blonde, and appeared in two dramas that didn't emphasize cheesecake; *Middle of the Night* (1959) and *Strangers When We Meet* (1960). Jayne couldn't or didn't want to change her image of sex

33. Mann, May. *Jayne Mansfield: A Biography.* New York: Drake, 1973.

symbol. She did give it a try when she played the dual role in the sword and sandal epic *The Loves of Hercules* (original title: *Gli Amori di Ercole*). Wearing black and red colored wigs and acting in the best Shakespearean way she knew; Jayne Mansfield and Mickey Hargitay, as the Greek muscleman, made complete fools of themselves. Although her two British movies were not all that bad, Jayne only got publicity out of them because

WITH MICKEY HARGITAY IN 1958.

she wore a transparent dress in one and was said to have made a topless appearance in the other. The films themselves died a death and were released in the United States years later. The tag 'sexbomb' seemed to backfire on her. Her earlier roles were sexy and emphasized her figure, but they also gave Jayne the chance to show her comedy skills in acting. Her parts after 1958 left this essential ingredient out.

Jayne gave birth to a second son, Zoltan, on August 1, 1960. In December 1960 Jayne was the subject of attention in the television show *This is Your Life*. Jayne is celebrated as a true Hollywood star in the first stage of the show, later on the emphasis is more on her family and Jayne as a devoted wife and mother. Ten year old daughter Jayne Marie, who was dressed up like a six year old, clearly answered the show's host questions with answers they made her learn by heart. In the finale, host Ralph

Edwards mentions Jayne's two last films — *Gli Amori di Ercole* and *It Happened in Athens* — not knowing at the time that they were not to be released in the United States for two years. With the studio sending her on and off to Europe, Jayne was no longer a popular star among the Hollywood elite. Jayne decided that she would return to Las Vegas to do another show.

On December 29 she opened at the Dunes Hotel, with a show called *The House of Love*. Jayne received a salary of $35,000 a week. Besides the effect that the Las Vegas shows kept her name in the papers, they also provided her with an income that 20th Century Fox would never pay her. Although the show was a success, Jayne wasn't happy. Press agent Raymond Strait recalled: "Jayne phoned me at three one morning, crying and complaining that she wanted to come back to Los Angeles. I knew immediately that she had been drinking."[34] The girl who wanted to be a movie star more than anything else in the world, found herself without a hit picture, doing a Las Vegas stage show and married to a man who adored her, but didn't excite her anymore. "So far Mickey has been everything to me that I need. But now he is turning into just a husband. He gets up early and wants to go to bed early. He forgets that I diet, starve myself to stay slim. When I am between pictures, I have to go out and see and be seen or I'm dead."[35] Mickey Hargitay said of it later: "Pressures. A lot of people were getting in at her, saying she should do this and do that. I think she wanted to please everyone, and I felt sorry for her, for what she was trying to live up to." Mickey always seemed to be considerate of Jayne's temper, but when Jayne's drinking habits worsened, he became more and more the victim of her pestering and verbal aggression. However he stood by her side, even when she announced publicly she wanted to divorce him.

For a little while things seemed to get better. Jayne was announced to appear in several movies. *Fabiola*, a biblical spectacular that was never made[36], and *The Chapman Report*, that was filmed without Jayne and released in 1962 by Warner Bros. She was also mentioned in connection with *Something's Got To Give*, a film that started production in 1962 with

34. Strait, Raymond. *The Tragic Secret Life of Jayne Mansfield*. London: Robert Hale & Company, 1976.

35. Mann, May. *Jayne Mansfield: A Biography*. New York: Drake, 1973.

36. It was to have been a new version of the French movie *Fabiola* that was made in 1949 and starred Michèlle Morgan and Henri Vidal. Jayne mentioned the film in her newsletter *Magnificent Mansfield*, that was published January 15th, 1960. "This is a story set in biblical times and much of the filming will be in the Coliseum of Rome. It will really be an extravaganza — with a $10,000,000 budget."

WITH MICKEY HARGITAY IN LONDON, OCTOBER, 1959.

Marilyn Monroe but that was never finished because of her death. Jayne talked about a new project for 20th Century Fox that was also never made: "In *Solo* I'm to play a woman who's married to a man that's impotent. It's very dramatic and affords a nice change of pace."[37] The one film that was made in 1961, was a biopic about actor George Raft. Ray Danton played the title role in Allied Artists' *The George Raft Story.* Jayne was proud of her work in it, but unfortunately she played just one of many women in Raft's life. Nevertheless Jayne was sent off to visit several cities in the United States to publicize the movie.

While visiting the Bahamas in February 1962, Jayne and Mickey decided to take a boat trip and do some water-skiing before they would make their appearance to the press. Considered by some as a second honeymoon, Jayne, Mickey and Jack Drury, a promotion man from the hotel where they were staying, sailed out for a couple of hours of water fun. By the time of the press conference Jayne and her company were nowhere to be found. A large search was started and the following morning they were found stranded on Rode Island, a tiny coral island. Mickey later wrote about the accident: "Jayne got too daring and skidded around a wave on one ski, lost her balance and plopped into the ocean. The side of the boat hit her. I couldn't see Jayne at all, just the foam marking the spot she had hit. I dived in the water and swam to that spot. Jack motored the boat there. Lungs bursting, I held Jayne with one arm and swam toward the shadow of the boat. She grabbed subconsciously for the boat rim and pulled, catapulting Jack into the water and capsizing the boat."[38] If this was another of Miss Mansfield's publicity tricks, it stays unanswered. Both she and Mickey never admitted that it was originally all a publicity stunt that had gone terribly wrong. Jayne's stigma as a publicity seeker didn't help convince anyone to the contrary. Meanwhile, 20th Century Fox seemed not interested in putting Jayne to work. Mostly seen on television, 1961 had been a disappointing year for Jayne's career.

She had turned 28 and in the early sixties Jayne questioned herself if that was an age where portraying the sexpot was becoming unsuitable. "I believe a girl is at her physical best, as far as throwing out sparks is concerned, during the ages of eighteen to twenty-nine," adding, "but that doesn't mean a woman of forty can't generate a lot of wolf whistles." Jayne

37. Saxton, Martha. *Jayne Mansfield and the American Fifties.* Boston: Houghton Mifflin Company, 1975.

38. Mansfield, Jayne and Hargitay, Mickey. *Jayne Mansfield's Wild, Wild World.* Los Angeles: Holloway House Publishing Company, 1963.

JAYNE FALLING OUT OF HER DRESS IN ROME, 1962.

was in need of a good movie part that restored her fame. Fox decided to loan her out again, and this time Jayne was pleased. *Panic Button* was a comedy with a good script, a nice part for herself and a bunch of good actors were signed up to fill the other roles. Versatile French born actor Maurice Chevalier and rugged film and television star Michael Connors were cast along with Eleanor Parker who filled in the other female lead. Jayne was happy and looked lovely during filming. She was in love again, and according to her press agent Raymond Strait, being in love always got the best out of Jayne Mansfield. With Mickey looking after the children, Jayne had fun with Michael Connors on as well as off set. But what really rocked the Hargitay marriage, was Jayne's affair with Italian film producer Enrico Bomba.

Jayne met Bomba on June 8, 1962, at a movie party in Rome. Jayne had drunk too much and to grab attention fell out of her dress, revealing her bra. Mickey, who was not amused, slapped Jayne; making matters worse. At the end of the evening Jayne tried to leave with Bomba, but Mickey forcibly took her home. Although Bomba was a married man, Jayne dated him openly and announced that he would marry her. A divorce from Mickey seemed inevitable. Jayne was bluntly open about her affair: "Nobody ever turned me on that way. We made the wildest love on a couch in my dressing room. I knew after him I would never be satisfied with Mickey again."[39] When she received the news that 20th Century Fox would not prolong her contract, Jayne announced she was happy with that. She said that from now on she would be making the pictures she wanted. The following month she was honored as the most popular actress of 1961-1962, as voted by the Italian press. Jayne was handed the 'Oscar of the Two Worlds'. But when she stepped off stage, a woman spectator attacked Jayne crying out that she didn't deserve the prize. Some people presumed that it was another of Miss Mansfield's publicity stunts, but considering the medical treatment Jayne received because of the scratching, makes this hard to believe. Nevertheless the press wrote that this girl would do anything to keep her name in the papers.

When Marilyn Monroe passed away in August, Jayne was affected deeply. The woman she was compared to all her career seemed to have taken her own life. Jayne was facing thirty and Marilyn had become only thirty six years old. Although Jayne always said that she would never take her own life, she was confronted with a depression that had her take to

39.   Strait, Raymond. *The Tragic Secret Life of Jayne Mansfield*. London: Robert Hale & Company, 1976.

WITH ENRICO BOMBA IN LONDON, 1962.

the bottle. Italy showed its appreciation again when Jayne was awarded with the Silver Mask Award in September.[40] When Jayne and Mickey returned from Italy in July, Jayne had announced their divorce and Mickey moved out of the Pink Palace. Hurt and angry with his wife he told the press: "I've had it. I've been patient because I held the hope that Jayne and I might get back together, but obviously this is not going to happen. I'm not calling Jayne anymore and I don't want to see her again." Jayne regularly visited Bomba during the following months and invited him to come over for Christmas. When he came, Jayne, in her whimsical way, told him she didn't want to marry him after all. So, Bomba returned to his wife and children and Jayne called Mickey telling him that it was all a terrible mistake. At least that was the statement Jayne told the press when she arrived at LAX on Christmas Eve. "I love Mickey and I feel with half a break, this time it's for keeps. It's wonderful to have a home again with the kids. It's a root I sorely need and with it my career seems so much easier to handle. Blame the Italian sunshine for the one wacky period of my life."[41] Raymond Strait says that it was also possible that Bomba had turned Jayne down. "If it had happened, she may have accepted it as a reality, but her vanity as a movie queen would never have allowed her to admit failure in romance."[42] Jayne confided in her friend May Mann that Bomba, being a Catholic, couldn't get a divorce.

Jayne's marriage had become a farce by now. Although it seemed that the couple got along, there was constant fighting and Jayne putting Mickey down. Jayne's drinking worsened again too. She became furious when he negotiated with a producer about a movie part for himself. The producer wanted Jayne as the female lead, but Mickey had suggested the newest blonde sensation in Hollywood, Eva Six, for the lead.[43] Jayne made sure that the deal fell through. Jayne was never fond of competition. She wanted to be an exclusive, and especially now she needed the confirmation that she was still in demand as Hollywood's top blonde sex symbol.

40. Among the other winners were the comedy duo Franco Franchi (1922-1992) and Ciccio Ingrassia (1922-2003). Two years later they would appear with Jayne in *Amore Primitivo*.

41. Mansfield, Jayne and Hargitay, Mickey. *Jayne Mansfield's Wild, Wild World*. Los Angeles: Holloway House Publishing Company, 1963.

42. Strait, Raymond. *The Tragic Secret Life of Jayne Mansfield*. London: Robert Hale & Company, 1976.

43. Eva Six (1937) was a Hungarian born blonde who was described as the girl with 'Marilyn Monroe's face, Jayne Mansfield's body and Zsa Zsa Gabor's accent'. She had came to the US in 1960 and made a couple of films in 1963 before fading from the scene. Columnist Dorothy Kilgallen reports her consoling Mickey Hargitay, crushed by Jayne Mansfield's Mexican divorce, in May 1963. When Mickey told the press that he probably would beat Jayne to the altar, Miss Six her name was rumored as his love interest.

AT THE PINK PALACE, 1962.

When actor/director Tommy Noonan came up with a script for a comedy, Jayne was very pleased. Filming for *Promises, Promises!* Started in January 1963. When Noonan asked Jayne to do two nude scenes to spice things up a bit, Jayne hesitated. Never before had a star of her status done a nude scene. Maybe at the start of their career some shed their clothes, but certainly not when they reached stardom. But Jayne, maybe ahead of her time and daring to take a chance, decided that she would do a bedroom and bathtub scene *au naturel*. Mickey was not aware of these scenes, Noonan had talked it over with Jayne privately. When he heard about it he strongly advised Jayne not to do it. The fact that Jayne had an affair with Noonan during filming, didn't help matters between Jayne and Mickey either. The final straw for Mickey came when he heard of the *Playboy* layout that covered the nude scenes. He was furious with Noonan and literally knocked him out. Of course the picture itself and the *Playboy* photos caused much controversy at the time. On June 4, 1963, *Playboy* chief Hugh Hefner was arrested for selling obscene literature. But the jury was unable to reach a verdict. Hefner: "When that pictorial appeared it caused a firestorm. It was the most successful magazine to date for us. Chicago sent a couple of policemen over to arrest me for supposedly selling obscenity." Mickey Hargitay, feeling unhappy with all this, felt it was a slide; Jayne taking the nude-route and gaining quite some publicity, but losing her status as a Hollywood star as a result of it. Jayne defended herself by saying sex was the most natural thing for her. "Today it seems a girl must drink, take dope or be miserable to be thought sexy. When I was a girl, it was the thing to serve sex up with a laugh. I suppose I haven't changed."[44]

Jayne had turned thirty in April. That month she also appeared in her new nightclub act which had a striptease routine called 'a satire on the strip'. Jayne's manager and nightclub promoter Paul Blane remembered how over-enthusiastic Jayne would get sometimes: "The only problem with Jayne was that she'd take a couple of drinks and would take it all off! And I had to run out on stage with her fur coat to cover her up." Besides the striptease, Jayne performed a couple of show tunes. A handsome Brazilian singer named Nelson Sardelli also took part in Jayne's

44. Mansfield, Jayne and Hargitay, Mickey. *Jayne Mansfield's Wild, Wild World.* Los Angeles: Holloway House Publishing Company, 1963.

JAYNE IN A 1962 PUBLICITY POSE.

nightclub act. Jayne fell in love with him and again announced that she would divorce Mickey Hargitay. She filed for divorce in California, but then decided to go to Juarez, Mexico for a quick divorce instead. Jayne and Nelson returned from Mexico on May 1. Awaited by the press Sardelli told that he and Jayne were deeply in love, but brushed aside questions as to when they would be married. Sardelli moved into the Pink Palace and accompanied Jayne to Germany that summer, where she was to make a musical called *Heimweh nach St. Pauli*, but at the end of filming their romance was over. Jayne said: "We had such a beautiful romance. He is young and virile and sexy and wild in love, and sweet. I really believed we would be a big thing — but then I heard he was married all along."[45] When Mickey flew to Europe to visit his family in Budapest, Jayne joined him because she was scheduled to start shooting a picture there in late August. Upon returning to the United States in the fall of 1963 Mickey and Jayne had reconciled once again. Because the Mexican divorce was never filed in California, it was invalid and that meant that Mickey and Jayne were still legally wed.

At this time Jayne had discovered that she was pregnant. As soon as the press noticed Jayne's pregnancy, they openly debated who was the father of this child. Three names dominated the discussion: Hargitay, Bomba and Sardelli. Jayne stayed low and told May Mann: "I hope Mickey won't hear too much of this." Raymond Strait mentions in his book that after the birth Jayne had him send photos of the baby to Sardelli. Nevertheless the girl that was born on January 23, 1964 was christened Mariska Magdolna Hargitay[46]. Jayne felt miserable after the birth of her fourth child. She confided to Raymond Strait that her life was a mess. The negative press she received after *Promises, Promises!* And her two romances with married men raised the question again if she was an unfit mother and wife. Falling in love with Matt Cimber, the director of the summer stock play *Bus Stop* which she was rehearsing, also wasn't helpful to promote an image of a devoted wife either. Before the play premiered, Jayne and Mickey left for Europe again to make a film in Italy. In May they arrived and started shooting for *L'Amore Primitivo*. A worthless comedy with Jayne doing a striptease as the movie's highlight. May 18, 1964 had Jayne

45. Mann, May. *Jayne Mansfield: A Biography*. New York: Drake, 1973.

46. Actress Mariska Hargitay on her mother: "I was sixteen before I became interested in what sort of person my mother had been. The kids I grew up with didn't know who she was. And I was just a child when she died. I'm not interested in being a glamorous, big star like my mother was. That was the aim of the 1950s, I guess. Me, I just want to become a good actress." Crivello, Kirk. *Fallen Angels — The lives and untimely deaths of 14 Hollywood Beauties*. Secaucus, NJ: Citadel Press, 1988.

and Mickey back in the United States to resume rehearsals for *Bus Stop*. Being attracted by Cimber, Jayne started an affair with him. Soon Cimber was promoted as Jayne's business manager. Again Mickey stood by and watched, he told the newsmen: "I don't want to fight Jayne if she wants to marry her new manager. God bless her and I hope she is happy for the rest of her life." While in New York for her second play under direction

WITH NELSON SARDELLI IN 1963.

of Matt Cimber, *Gentlemen Prefer Blondes*, Jayne spoke about her turbulent life in an interview: "I am always grateful to my mother for rearing me strictly to be a lady. There are times when I fall off of it, under some bad influence. Perhaps I had too much champagne to color my world differently."[47] Jayne had an ambivalent relationship with her mother, and alcohol alike.

In the summer of 1964, a highly successful boy band from Britain visited the United States. The Beatles crossed the Atlantic to play some gigs in San Francisco and other cities. On August 26 they visited Los Angeles and John Lennon said he wanted to meet Jayne Mansfield. Jayne accepted the invitation and met the guys at the Whiskey à Go-Go on the Sunset Strip. Mamie Van Doren also visited the night club that evening and witnessed Jayne's alcohol problem: "Jayne Mansfield lifted her head drunkenly and focused on me with some difficulty."[48] About her mother she once told Raymond Strait: "My mother was a lousy parent, but I always thought of her as a glamorous lady who loved to play bridge and get drunk. She hasn't changed too much. Now she's a lousy grandparent. She still drinks and plays bridge!"[49] The hints Jayne gave on her own abuse of alcohol were not picked up by the press. Rather they focused on her stained 'mother image'. Jayne tried to explain she could be a mother and still be a sex symbol: "A woman should be all things. I'm a mother first, and a good mother. Then I'm an actress. And finally a sex symbol. Each is divorced from the other."[50] In another interview she said: "I tried so hard in the beginning to become The Sex Symbol. I tried so hard recently to switch my image to the real me, without success. But I keep hoping."[51]

While touring the country for *Gentlemen Prefer Blondes*, with Matt, Mickey and the children, Jayne was happy and seemed to have overcome the loss of Sardelli and Bomba. She was madly in love with Cimber. Jayne received excellent reviews for the play and hoped that Hollywood, again, would take notice and upon her return would restore her movie star image. But of course that didn't happen. Hollywood had changed. By the end of the fifties, most movie stars were individual contractors and by the late sixties, the traditional studio system had disappeared. Jayne Mansfield had

47. Mann, May. *Jayne Mansfield: A Biography*. New York: Drake, 1973.

48. Van Doren, Mamie with Aveilhe, Art. *Playing the Field — My Story*. New York: G.P. Putnam's Sons, 1987.

49. Strait, Raymond. *The Tragic Secret Life of Jayne Mansfield*. London: Robert Hale & Company, 1976.

50. Saxton, Martha. *Jayne Mansfield and the American Fifties*. Boston: Houghton Miffin Company, 1975.

51. Mann, May. *Jayne Mansfield: A Biography*. New York: Drake, 1973.

always depended on a studio to make her a star. She was one of the last actors to be signed by a major studio and to receive a movie star buildup. She had been a sex symbol of the fifties, publicized and promoted by the studio's press division, but by 1964 Hollywood lost its interest in her.[52]

A NEW BEGINNING?

Jayne decided she had to take a different road for success. Although European movie offers had been her paycheck security in the early sixties, from now on she wanted to concentrate on the American film business to re-establish her fame.[53] After the run of *Bus Stop*, Jayne married Matt Cimber on September 24, 1964 in Baja, Mexico. Cimber was the man, according to Jayne, who would help her become a serious actress. Matt stated that he wanted to turn Jayne into the dramatic actress he believed she was: "She has the talent and the potential. All she needs is the roles and the direction."[54] Jayne told May Mann: "The fact that we fell in love is one thing. But the fact that our interests are so mutual, and he loves me so much that he will develop my career and make me a great serious actress. Well it's something like Sophia Loren and Carlo Ponti in a way."[55] Jayne moved out of The Pink Palace and went to the East Coast to live in a townhouse on Park Avenue and East 69th Street in New York City.

After the two successful plays they did together, Matt directed Jayne in a new play called *The Champagne Complex*, but it was no success. Together they founded their own production company, Jaynatt Productions Inc. and announced in December that their first production would be the filming of Robert H. Rimmer's novel *That Girl From Boston*. The film was never made with Jayne in the lead.[56] Lacking movie parts, Jayne did a lot of guest appearances on TV talk and game shows. In the summer of 1965, she travelled to Canada with Matt to appear in his version of

52. "...even if the tried and true methods for developing stars had largely disappeared, there was a continuing demand for new stars to replace those of the previous three decades who were either retiring or moving into character roles." Solomon, Matthew. *Larger than Life — Movie Stars of the Fifties*. New Jersey: Rutgers University Press, 2010.

53. In 1964 Jayne was to film a role opposite Mickey Hargitay in *Il Boia Scarlatto* aka *Bloody Pit of Horror* (1965). But the two divorced before the filming began. Jayne was replaced by another actress.

54. Mann, May. *Jayne Mansfield: A Biography*. New York: Drake, 1973.

55. Mann, May. *Jayne Mansfield: A Biography*. New York: Drake, 1973.

56. In 1974 Matt Cimber did direct *That Girl From Boston* with Mamie Van Doren.

Nature's Way by playwright and novelist Herman Wouk. The movie deals that Matt could arrange for her were for two appalling productions. The first one, a teenage beach comedy called *The Fat Spy*, seemed like a good deal. The script promised the film to be a swinging comedy, and the other actors involved could have made it work. However the finished film was shabby and not funny at all. Jayne was pregnant with her fifth child while

WITH MATT CIMBER, ZOLTAN, MARISKA, MIKLOS AND JAYNE MARIE IN NEW YORK, 1964.

filming. The second production she took part in was filmed after the birth of her son Tony (who was born on October 17). The grade-Z piece of hokum was called *Las Vegas Hillbillys*. The Cimber/Mansfield marriage began to show cracks.

Jayne was becoming more and more unhappy that her ultimate career goal of being a Hollywood actress seemed further away than ever. Her latest play, *The Rabbit Habit*, was a failure and had to close down after only five nights. She sang some songs in several nightclubs, but that was just to keep the money coming in. What got her hopes up a bit was the filming of her new movie *Single Room Furnished* in December. Because the movie relied on her dramatic outings, Jayne saw this production as the film that would restore her name and career. In January of the new year, Jayne was scheduled to perform a nightclub revue

1965 PUBLICITY PHOTO.

entitled *French Dressing.* The show was a huge success. Matt had Jayne on a strict schedule; no nights on the town and no drinking. Although Jayne complaint to May Mann about this, she kept to the rules and was happy with all the attention she received while performing at the Latin Quarter. But after the show stopped Jayne relapsed into her old drinking routine. When filming of *Single Room Furnished* was interrupted

AFTER THE BIRTH OF TONY WITH MATT CIMBER, OCTOBER 17, 1965.

because of financial problems, Jayne's drinking worsened and she and Matt would have fights on a regular basis. Raymond Strait, who had been best man at her wedding to Cimber remembered: "After Tony was born her attitude towards Matt changed. Not right away, but by that time Jayne was doing a lot of drinking. She'd be so erratic at night she would do crazy things after the show and Matt was going through a lot with her, she wasn't easy. She would call me and make up stories that Matt was beating her up. Well I talked to people that were on the road with her and they would tell me that's not what's happening. Matt told me Jayne used to beat herself. She get drunk and beat herself, beat her arms and make them blue and say 'He did it'." Jayne was known to drink bourbon out of Coke bottles, disguising her lust for alcohol. Normally she never drank when she had to work, but by now Jayne had messed up one or two performances because she was so intoxicated.

AT THE ACAPULCO FILM FESTIVAL IN MEXICO, WITH ACTOR SERGIO VILLAGRAN, 1966.

Matt Cimber recalled years later: "She would never face the fact that she had a drinking problem. And if she could have done that I would have stuck it out. But because she totally denied it, I knew that it would be a very long time before she'd ever be ready to really try, if ever, to try to do something about it."

On July 14, 1966 Matt and Jayne separated. Cimber tried to remain her manager, but when the couple fought over the custody of Tony, Jayne accused Matt of beating her regularly and the collaboration ended quickly. Jayne filed for divorce on the grounds of extreme cruelty and grievous mental suffering. She was assisted by a lawyer called Sam Brody. Matt Cimber later said about his relationship with Jayne: "I really admired her, I had an incredible good time with her. I think the only mistake in our relationship was that we got married." Hearing the news of the split-up while filming in Rome, Mickey Hargitay returned home to be with Jayne and 'protect' her from Matt. It was planned that he would accompany Jayne on her trip to Venezuela and Columbia, but at the last minute Jayne brushed him off, taking her new lover with her. Dutch painter/author Jan Cremer[57] had met Jayne for publicity reasons a week before her departure to South America. Cremer had written the novel *I, Jan Cremer*, which was dedicated to Jayne and translated in English in 1966. Soon afterwards they were entangled in a sexual affair. It seemed Jayne was out to fulfill her need to be loved and admired. Over the past years she had dated men who started out as 'the love of her life', but could not fulfill this promise. Now she dated whomever she fancied at that particular moment. Half a year earlier she had told her friend May Mann: "I'm sorry to say, when I get in with the swingers during long nightclub engagements away from home, I have been a swinger too. That's the long hours, the loneliness, the booze. That isn't the real me."[58]

During her visit to Caracas, Venezuela, Jayne ran into problems at the airport. Her passport was revoked because of a local tax matter. When she paid the fine of $220 she was allowed to leave the country on August 17.

On her return to the United States, Jayne was without her lover Jan Cremer. Instead she brought home a twenty-year old Venezuelan boy called Douglas Olivares. Originally she said he was her recording

57. Jan Cremer (April 20, 1940) met Jayne Mansfield before a performance of *Gentlemen Prefer Blondes*. "Jayne Mansfield stayed at the Garden City Hotel on Long Island...we met her in a restaurant; after the show we returned to this 'Westbury Chef'. Jan and Jayne ate and drank till three in the morning." Dauphin, Gerald. *Jan Cremer in New York & Jayne Mansfield.* Antwerp, Belgium: Celbeton, 1966.

58. Mann, May. *Jayne Mansfield: A Biography.* New York: Drake, 1973.

JAYNE AND MATT WITH BABY TONY AND THE OTHER CHILDREN, APRIL 19, 1966.

secretary, but to May Mann Jayne told the truth: "He's precious and so in love. I'm his first love. He won't be twenty-one for two and a half months yet. So we have to be careful, very careful."[59] When Jayne arrived at the Pink Palace, she got the news that Matt hadn't brought his son back after a visit. Jayne and Matt had arranged that he could have unlimited visits to Tony as long as he never took the child from the house. She contacted her lawyer Sam Brody about it. He was told by Matt that Jayne and all other adults were drunk when he brought Tony back, so he decided to return home with him instead. The case was settled after four weeks; Cimber had to return Tony to Jayne, he was given the right to visit his son for one hour twice a week. The papers were picking up about her affair with Olivares and the stories about the custody fights with Matt, Jayne received negative headlines. When teenage daughter Jayne Marie developed a crush on her mother's South American beau, and was making passes at him, Jayne decided that she'd had enough. A tearful Olivares returned to Venezuela and very soon Sam Brody replaced him in the Pink Palace. At first Jayne showed no intention of marrying Brody, but several months later she talked of converting to Judaism and made suggestions to wed once more.

According to Raymond Strait and May Mann, Brody forced himself upon Jayne; drugging her and oppressing her with his aggressive, jealous nature. He blackmailed her with nude pictures that were in his possession. "Sometimes I hate him," she told May. Sam Brody was known as a respected lawyer, a married man and father of two children at the time he met Jayne Mansfield. Raymond Strait remembers that Brody went out of his mind with the idea of having an affair with the blonde sex bomb; he tried to control every aspect of Jayne's life. Strait: "She was drinking a lot and so was Sam. Sam was an insanely jealous man. He was trying to be the manager, the everything and no one was keeping Jayne in check and keeping her professional." Sam used to beat Jayne up, and Jayne would ring the police to get him out of her house. The next day she took him in again. Around this time Raymond Strait tried to withdraw himself more and more from the mess Jayne was making of her life. He no longer functioned as her official press secretary, when one of the strangest publicity gimmicks in Jayne Mansfield's career occurred. She accepted a medallion that came along with the title 'High Priestess of San Francisco's Church of Satan' from Satan worshipper Anton LaVey on October 26. She had met him at the San Francisco Film Festival the day before. Why Jayne,

59. Mann, May. *Jayne Mansfield: A Biography.* New York: Drake, 1973.

CABARET, 1967.

who was known as a person who valued religion, accepted this 'honor' is not quite clear.[60] She told her friend May Mann that it was all for laughs that she accepted the invitation to LaVey's Church. Sam Brody, brought up in the orthodox Jewish religion, didn't want anything to do with LaVey and caught the fury of the high priest of Satan, because he was disrespectful in handling the church artifacts. Therefore LaVey put a spell on him and warned Jayne to stay away from Sam, because he was to die before the year was out.

On November 26, 1966 Jayne was at Jungleland in Thousand Oaks, California. It was a visit for publicity reasons, but because of the location she took her children with her. Brody joined them and together they had a wonderful day in the park with the children playing with the 'tame' animals. Then all of a sudden everything turned into a tragedy when a young lion snatched Zoltan and started to ravage his face and body. He was hurried to a hospital where his spleen was removed two days later. Jayne stayed in the hospital the whole period. The world sympathized with Jayne and her son. But when Sam joined Jayne, negative headlines soon appeared. Jayne and Sam, under influence of LSD and alcohol, were constantly fighting. It came to a point where both were ordered to leave the hospital and Jayne was given the restriction to visit her son alone or together with Mickey Hargitay. Mickey reasoned that the Brody/Mansfield relationship would meet a violent end eventually: "It seemed that something very severe had to happen." On December 25 Zoltan was released from the hospital to join his family for Christmas.

In the first months of 1967 Jayne visited the US soldiers in Vietnam. She toured the army camps from January 3 until February 27. "I was voted as one of the three most desired people, by the troops, that they wanted in Vietnam, and I was planning to come before that. But since my son had this terrible accident, being bitten and clawed by a Lion, and he almost lost his life, I had to delay my tour. But just before his accident I visited Walter Reed Hospital in Washington. I saw the ward where the boys just got back and they were severely injured, still living and I just felt I wanted to give of myself as much as I could." She gained good press coverage while visiting the soldiers, but after a couple of fights with Sam in which Jayne almost broke her back, the military asked them to leave and return to the United States.

60. *"When we were in San Francisco, Sam got jealous of Anton and myself. They had a big argument, and Anton told Sam that he would meet a tragic and violent death within a year, that he would pay to Lucifer to accomplish it. Now isn't that stupid? To get upset about something like that."* Strait, Raymond. *The Tragic Secret Life of Jayne Mansfield*. London: Robert Hale & Company, 1976.

JAYNE IN 1967.

Sam Brody seemed to be the wrong guy at the wrong time. He had borrowed thousands of dollars from Jimmy Hoffa to spend on Jayne. And when he couldn't pay him back, Jayne offered to help him out by going on the road again, doing a burlesque kind of song and dance routine. But in the United States no major nightclub would sign her up, so she ended up playing in small town clubs all over the country. On March 24, 1967 Jayne and Sam Brody traveled to Europe to tour Ireland and the North-East of England. Just like her first visit to Great Britain, ten years before, there were hordes of people and press to give her a warm welcome. The British press cited: "Not even the Queen of England has ever had such a royal welcome by the press." Her tour of several working men's clubs in Great Britain and Ireland may have seemed a low-down in her career, but in those days playing at these places was a common thing for well known performers. In Ireland her show was canceled because Catholic clergymen asked their parishioners to boycott Jayne's show. Jayne donated her $2,800 fee to the Widows and Orphans fund. In North-East England, however, her shows were a big success and even when impresario Don Arden sacked Jayne — because she turned up late for several engagements, appeared in her street clothes because she hadn't brought her stage dress and couldn't wear a skirt on one occasion because of bruised legs — she was immediately signed by other club owners. Jayne earned 20,000 pounds for her dates at 'La Dolce Vita' in New Castle, 'La Bamba' in Darlington, 'The Latino' in South Shields and 'The Variety Club' in Batley.[61] By the end of Jayne Mansfield's career, she was more popular in Britain than in the US.

When asked by the British press if she considered herself as a happy person, she answered: "No, no. I have wonderful happy moments, I consider myself tremendously fortunate for having five children. But I think a person who is tremendously complicated and involved, I don't think that person would ever really be a contended happy person." At the end of her English tour Jayne's relationship with Sam Brody deteriorated. Brody once said of their turbulent affair: "I beat her up. She didn't mind. She loves it. I am so sick of beating her. But she drives me into rages, and then I don't know what I'm doing. I don't even know myself anymore. Jayne is the most masochistic person I've ever known."[62]

61. Batley Variety Club — often called 'The Vegas of the North' — was a step up from the normal working men's clubs, for it was a Theatre Club. It had carpet on the floor and the public sat in a little "pod" on plush velvet benches, with an open end facing the stage. There were hundreds of these seats arranged in tiered rows from the huge stage right to the back of the room. The Variety Club attracted the world's top performing acts. Acts like Shirley Bassey and Tom Jones were commonplace to entertain the coal miners and mill workers.

62. Strait, Raymond. *The Tragic Secret Life of Jayne Mansfield*. London: Robert Hale & Company, 1976.

WITH SAM BRODY IN 1967.

FADE TO BLACK

By now Jayne was turning up drunk and late for her shows and her performances became increasingly erratic. She started wearing fewer items of clothing, and those items she did wear often suffered revealing wardrobe malfunctions. Many times she came on stage with the visible bruises caused by Brody. It was another black period in her life, but all got even worse when her eldest daughter charged Brody for violation in June, 1967. Jayne Marie stated that Brody had beaten her up on the instructions from her mother. The once so tight mother-daughter relationship was damaged even more when Jayne countersued that her daughter had received the beating because of her games with diet pills, sleeping pills and marijuana. Jayne's rage over her daughter's betrayal brought her near to hysteria in court. "I don't appreciate that she tried to imitate me, dropping the 'Marie' from her name. She wants to wear make-up, long eyelashes, wants to be me, wants to — the whole thing, what I do as a movie star."[63] The judge advised that Jayne Marie was to stay with Paul Mansfield's uncle and aunt; Mr. and Mrs. William Pigue. The case was recessed until July. During the trial Jayne revealed that Paul Mansfield wasn't the real father of Jayne Marie, but a certain Ian Parrish was. She claimed she was raped by him and therefore married Mansfield.[64] Jayne's life was a mess at this point. She still drank a lot and also took LSD on several occasions. Daughter Jayne Marie recapitulated these last troubled years in a BBC documentary about her mother: "A lot of it was a depression with where her career was going. I mean who wants to work in a nightclub in Biloxi? That was not her choice. There really wasn't any help from men, it was her that did it."[65] After Zoltan's accident at Jungleland, Jayne and Mickey stayed in contact. Jayne regularly spoke to him on the phone. After all the turbulence in her life it seemed she took comfort in the calmness of Mickey's personality. Her good friend May Mann also lent a shoulder to cry on. Jayne was very unhappy because of all the traumas that had occurred over the last few months. She wanted out of the relationship with Brody. "Sam can be so kind, and so horrible. I don't know what comes over him. He beats me. I'm so tired of hurting all over!"[66]

63. Feeney Callan, Michael. *Pink Goddess — The Jayne Mansfield Story*. London: W.H. Allen, 1986.

64. Ian Parrish may well have been the boy whom she dated in 1949 and called 'Inky'.

65. BBC series Arena: *Blondes*, 1999.

66. Mann, May. *Jayne Mansfield: A Biography*. New York: Drake, 1973.

On June 23 Sam and Jayne left for Biloxi, Mississippi. Jayne was scheduled to appear at Gus Stevens' Supper Club. Miklos, Zoltan and Mariska joined their mother. Between the performances at the club, Jayne had a morning booking for WDSU-TV's 'The Midday Show' in New Orleans on June 29. She had decided to leave Biloxi in the evening to spend the night at the Roosevelt Hotel in New Orleans. The children fell asleep in the back of the car. Jayne, Sam and the 19-year-old driver of the car, Ronnie Harrison were in the front seats. It was a humid, misty night. They were driving on Highway 90 between Slidell and New Orleans at 2:25, where a mosquito spraying pesticide truck had just sprayed the countryside. A tractor trailer riding in front of them had just ran into the fog and had slowed down. The Mansfield car slammed into the rear end of the trailer and subsequently went up under the truck. Both men and Jayne were thrown out of the car. Jayne died of severe head injuries.[67] Zoltan suffered a concussion and lacerations, Miklos suffered a fractured arm and Mariska received face lacerations. Two of the four Chihuahuas Jayne had taken with her were also killed. Years later Zoltan Hargitay recalled the tragic accident: "We were tired, my brother, my sister and me, we were all tired. And we got in the car and fell asleep. I don't remember anything else but just waking up in the back seat. And it was kind of an eerie weird feeling. I knew we were in an accident, but it almost seemed we were in a dream. It had happened so quick."[68]

When notified of the accident, Mickey Hargitay rushed over to his children. He was allowed to see Jayne: "I saw her, a last time. It wasn't really her anymore. You know, the soul was gone. The spirit was gone, it was just a machine...it wasn't her."

On July 3, 1967, Jayne Mansfield was buried at the Fairview Cemetery in Pen Argyl, Pennsylvania. It was the wish of her family and Mickey that she was buried there. May Mann, Raymond Strait and Matt Cimber disapproved and wanted Jayne to be buried in Hollywood. But the New Orleans court had given Hargitay the possession of the body because they found that Jayne's Mexican divorce was not valid. Although Mickey Hargitay wanted a quiet funeral, Jayne was buried in the way she had lived. Hundreds of people came over to the cemetery to be with Jayne for the last time. It was the public, the fans that stayed loyal to Jayne until the end. No Hollywood celebrities showed up. On July 6, May Mann provided a

67. Contrary to many sources, Jayne Mansfield was not decapitated in the accident.

68. BBC series Arena: *Blondes*, 1999.

memorial service at All Saints Episcopal Church in Beverly Hills. Mickey Hargitay and Matt Cimber attended, but the children didn't attend. Vera and Harry Peers moved into the Pink Palace to secure themselves of taking part in the dividing of Jayne's belongings. But Matt Cimber got a court order to get them out of the house.

On July 20, the LA court ruled that Mr. and Mrs. Pigue were to

JAYNE MANSFIELD'S FUNERAL, JULY 3, 1967.

be named the guardians of Jayne Marie Mansfield. Miklos, Zoltan and Mariska would stay with their father. Matt Cimber got custody over his son Tony. Jayne left no will. On August 23 Hargitay and Cimber reached a compromise over the appointment of administrators for Jayne's estate and reached an agreement concerning the division of her possessions. A day later, a California court ruled that Cimber is Jayne's surviving spouse for inheritance purposes. He receives one-sixth of the estate; the other five-sixth went to the children. Mickey received $180,000 from life insurance. All legal actions were covered in the press. "Jayne would have loved all the publicity. It would have delighted her to know that two former husbands were fighting for her dead body — and her estate. However she wouldn't have liked her mother being barred from her home after her death — regardless of what had happened in life. Basically, she loved her mother. She just didn't know how to cope with her, as Jayne Marie had trouble reaching her."[69] That seemed to be the tragedy of the child who missed out on the love of her mother; with becoming a mother herself she tried hard to change the pattern, but didn't succeed completely. "I was always sorry that my mother and I could not have had a close relationship. I promised myself that when I had children they would be my confidantes, and we would be always close and affectionate. I'd give them all of the love I never had when I was growing up. Momma probably had it for me — but she didn't show it."[70]

At age 34 the life of a woman who lived it to the fullest ended. A woman ahead of her time, maybe, but certainly a woman who tried to make her own decisions and who lived her own life. Romances with the wrong men, accused of bad taste in expressing her talents and an everlasting force from inside to reach the highest level in show business; Jayne's story reads like a fairy tale, but one with a gloomy side and an unhappy end. During her life Jayne Mansfield almost had it all, but through her own actions never completely accomplished reaching superstar status. However she never once stopped fighting for fame and recognition throughout her career. Looking down from heaven, reclining on her pink cloud, I think she will be delighted to see that after all, she is not forgotten.

"I think that she was a woman who was way before her time. Because I don't know how somebody can have five children and yet still be a sex symbol. She was just amazing."[71]

69. Strait, Raymond. *The Tragic Secret Life of Jayne Mansfield*. London: Robert Hale & Company, 1976.

70. Mann, May. *Jayne Mansfield: A Biography*. New York: Drake, 1973.

71. A quote from actress Mariska Hargitay on her mother.

KATHY MARLOWE.

Comparison and Competition

"I DON'T LIKE BEING COMPARED TO MARILYN ALL THE TIME.
AFTER ALL, I HAVE MY ASSETS AND SHE HAS HERS . . . AND *I*
CAN ACT."

JAYNE MANSFIELD, 1957

Publicity is a way to keep your name in the headlines; Jayne Mansfield knew that better than anyone else. Before Jayne reached Hollywood other curvaceous blondes made a name for themselves and when Jayne starred in her leading parts, many girls tried to reach the fame Mansfield achieved by also being involved in crazy publicity stunts and showing off their hourglass physique. The Hollywood starlets in the Mansfield mould, who made somewhat of a name for themselves, were: Joi Lansing, Sandra Giles and Kathy Marlowe.

Voluptuous Kathy Marlowe was under contract to Warner Bros. at the same time as Jayne. She was one of the five blondes with Tommy Noonan, master of ceremonies, at the Ballyhoo Ball in October 1956. The others were Sandra Giles, Juli Reding, Mamie Van Doren and Jayne Mansfield. Kathy Marlowe had a minor part in *Illegal* (1955) and had her one moment of fame when she was starred as *The Girl With an Itch* (1958). When Jayne was contracted by 20th Century Fox, Marlowe had cameo parts in two pictures that were shot at the Fox lot. One of them was *The Lieutenant Wore Skirts* (1956) with Tom Ewell and Sheree North. The film was directed by Frank Tashlin who repeated a breast fetish gag, with Jayne holding a milk bottle aside each breast, from *The Girl Can't Help It*. In *The Lieutenant Wore Skirts* he had Kathy Marlowe holding two water melons before her bosom.

Blonde starlet Sandra Giles was described as 'a mixture of the best of Jayne Mansfield with the best of Mamie Van Doren.'[1] She came closest to Jayne when it came to crazy publicity stunts. She revealed a nude painting of herself, and sued the artist because she claimed she had posed for him in a bathing suit. At the premiere of *Teacher's Pet* (1958) she arrived in a mink covered Cadillac, but these stunts didn't help her career the

SANDRA GILES (LEFT), AND JOI LANSING (RIGHT).

way it helped Jayne's. Giles played her biggest part in the 1959 grade-C movie *Daddy-O*, which is considered a cult classic by fans of 1950s teenage movies.

Joi Lansing was mostly seen on TV in the fifties and sixties, but made some memorable cameo appearances in films like: *A Hole in the Head* (1959), *But Not For Me* (1959) and *Who Was That Lady?* (1960). In 1967 she starred in the sequel to Jayne's *Las Vegas Hillbillys*, called *Hillbillys in a Haunted House*. In 1970 Lansing was seen on the New York stage with Jayne's second husband Mickey Hargitay, in a show that was a spoof on burlesque. In 1972 Joi Lansing died from breast cancer at age 43.

Although these women had the physique and the sex appeal Jayne had, they missed that certain charisma that lifted Mansfield up to outshine them. "She does come across as very sympathetic, a nucleus of psychological stability in a physically grotesque world. This sympathetic quality

1. Picturegoer, April 6, 1957.

is something that marks her out from others of her size. One cannot imagine, for example, Anita Ekberg managing it."[2]

Not only in Hollywood were copycats and concurrence to be found. In Europe and especially Great Britain there were blondes everywhere in the film business. In England Diana Dors ruled the screen, but found competition from blondes like Belinda Lee and Carole Lesley.

DIANA DORS.

2. Cameron, Ian & Elisabeth. *Dames.* New York: Frederick A. Praeger, Inc., Publishers, 1969.

Diana Dors made her film debut in 1946 and with the rise of Marilyn Monroe she was soon dubbed 'England's answer to Marilyn Monroe'. Just like Jayne Mansfield, Diana Dors knew how to hit the headlines. At the Venice Film Festival of 1955, for example, she wore a mink bikini while riding a Gondola. When she came to Hollywood in 1956, she was offered a contract at 20th Century Fox and they wanted her to star in *The Girl Can't Help It*. "The Monroe comparisons continued, of course, and there was an offer, which Dennis [Hamilton; Dors' husband] turned down, from Twentieth Century Fox for me to star with her former co-star, Tom Ewell, in a comedy follow-up to *The Seven Year Itch*. 'Everyone will compare you with her all the more if you do it', he maintained."[3] Maybe he was right. When Jayne did the movie, many critics compared her to Monroe. The tragedy of Miss Dors' American career was that after declining a part that would have had her compared to Marilyn, she did a film called *I Married A Woman* (1956) for RKO, that got her being compared to Marilyn Monroe and Jayne Mansfield as well. A 'Screen Story' magazine review read: "…Miss Dors, that fabulous combination of Mansfield and Monroe." In the early sixties Diana Dors had her own show in Las Vegas. She married comedian Dickie Dawson in 1959. Dawson had a cameo part in one of Jayne's films. He appeared at the beginning of *Promises! Promises!* (1963) as the comedian who does phony bird calls. Divorced and almost broke at the end of the sixties, Diana was doing cabaret shows all over Great Britain. It was around 1967 that she met Jayne, who was making a tour in England herself. Diana Dors once said about Jayne: "I could not believe that this sweet cooing dumb blonde from Texas was really as dumb as she pretended to be, and in all the time I knew her she never let the mask fall once, until at the end I finally believed she did speak and think like a Kewpie Doll."[4]

The British had always been fond of Jayne and that fondness helped to emerge the birth of pin-up girls and starlets who followed in Mansfield's footsteps. Shane Cordell was called the English Jayne Mansfield for a while, and when Jayne filmed *The Sheriff of Fractured Jaw* in England, blonde Sheena Marshe was hired to be her double. Jayne wasn't amused by Miss Marshe's likeness to her, so she demanded another double to be hired. The girl who came closest to being British Jayne Mansfield, was bosom queen Sabrina. She had the same hourglass figure as Jayne; a

3. Dors, Diana. *Dors by Diana — An Intimate Self-Portrait.* London: Macdonald Futura Publishers Ltd, 1983.

4. Bret, David. *Diana Dors — Hurricane in Mink.* London: JR Books, 2010.

tiny waistline and huge bosom she liked to show off as often as possible. However, her career never reached the same heights as Jayne's. When Jayne passed away before filming of a new project commenced, Sabrina was asked to take Jayne's role in *The Ice House* (1969).

Another British blonde actress, who was often ranked within the same region as Dors, Monroe and Mansfield, was Shirley Eaton. Eaton

SABRINA.

survived the climate change towards blondes in the sixties and starred in a couple of well received Hollywood films. Looking back at her blonde contemporaries, she commented on Jayne: "All she had to offer was an immense bosom and a huge bum. In fact, she was a joke figure, a caricature woman, someone who carried no threat for most men because she was so risible. Whether Jayne Mansfield was acute enough to know that she was

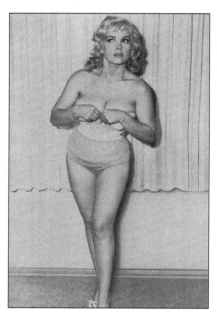

SHIRLEY EATON (ABOVE), AND JULI REDDING (RIGHT).

being used in this way, I don't know. Her main films all presented her as a dumb sex object and I think she was demeaned by that."[5]

During the fifties and thereafter, *Will Success Spoil Rock Hunter?* remained a popular play and it required the talents of different actresses when it started touring the country. Merry Anders followed in Jayne's footsteps when the play came to the West Coast in 1956. Roxanne Arlen starred in the play in 1957, Juli Reding was Rita Marlowe in 1963 and Mamie Van Doren finally played the part she had turned down all those years before, in 1971 in Chicago and later in 1974 in Florida. In Britain, blonde June Cunningham portrayed the voluptuous movie star in 1958.

At some point in the negotiations between Fox and playwright Axelrod, Swedish blonde Anita Ekberg was considered for the part of Rita Marlowe in the film version by 20th Century Fox. When Jayne had

5. Eaton, Shirley. *Golden Girl.* London: B.T. Batsford Ltd., 1999.

to meet with her obligations to the play, and Fox was eager to make the film version, Anita was named as the lead. When Jayne heard of this, she was on the phone with the studio immediately to prevent them from hiring Ekberg. Nevertheless Anita Ekberg holds no crutch to Jayne: "I was a friend of hers. I adored her. I think she was a fantastic person. She was simple, she played up with her sex and her figure. That was very smart

ANITA EKBERG.

of her because as an actress maybe she wasn't that great, but she also wasn't stupid at all, because many of her roles she played like the blonde goose."

Anita Ekberg, Hollywood's blonde sensation of 1955, made a nice career for herself in Hollywood B-movies and Italian sword and sandal epics. She reached her all time high when working with Frank Tashlin (*Artists and Models*, 1955 and *Hollywood or Bust*, 1956) and Italian director Federico Fellini on *La Dolce Vita* (1959) and *Boccaccio 70* (1962).

Another actress who was considered for the part of Rita Marlowe, was showgirl, TV and movie starlet Gloria Pall. She was featured in an article in the February 1955 issue of Playboy with five pages, Jayne was that magazine's centerfold. In an interview with the author, Miss Pall recalled her connections with her fellow blondes. She said she got along fine with everybody, but Jayne Mansfield was the exception. "I don't want to give the impression that I am envious or just sour grapes. What happened between us is the truth as I remember it."

Gloria met Jayne in 1955 for the first time: "While I was in Vegas I visited the Sahara where I was a showgirl in early 1953. I strolled over to the pool by the diving board and there was a sexy blonde posing in a red

GLORIA PALL, JUDY TYLER AND ELVIS PRESLEY IN *JAILHOUSE ROCK* (1957).

bikini bathing suit…if you could call it that. I was wearing a two piece leopard bathing suit. I stood there for a couple of minutes watching her pose and then her press agent James Byron, who I knew from Hollywood said, 'Hi Gloria, this is Jayne Mansfield. We just came from Florida where Jane Russell is shooting *Underwater*. Jane got lots of publicity. I'm going to make her a star…she's very daring!' The photographer looked at me and suggested we take a couple of photos together. Jayne turned the color of her bikini and said, 'This is my shoot and nobody but me poses for these photos. So move along.' After a few days I came back to Hollywood and got a call from famous songwriter Julie Stein who was involved with George Axelrod in helping him cast a Broadway show. I was to meet him for a reading at actress Eleanor Parker's ex-husband Bert Friedlob's mansion in Beverly Hills. After the reading, he invited me to the Luau in

Beverly Hills. That was owned by Lana Turner's ex Steve Crane. When we got there and were seated outside, we met Vince Edwards. Guess who is sitting with him but Jayne Mansfield again. Julie said to Vince: 'Gloria just read for me for a Broadway play and we're flying her back in a couple of days.' Well say no more . . . Jayne was on the next plane and got the part. I was finally going to get a big break and she got it from me."[6] Jayne's

SHEENA MARSHE.

ferocious self management eventually made her name, but as is to be expected, also took the chances of those with less shrewdness.

When Jayne appeared on the Hollywood scene, Marilyn Monroe reigned as the number one blonde love goddess. Although Jayne was, and still is, often compared to Marilyn Monroe, her real contemporary 'con-colleagues' were the blonde stars who were born around the same time as Jayne and who started their careers in the early fifties being hailed as 'the girl to compete with Marilyn'. Many studios — including Monroe's 20th Century Fox — were always on the lookout for another blonde girl who could stir a sensation; the so called 'New Monroe'. Columbia Studios found themselves a new Marilyn quite literally.

Marilyn Pauline Novak (born 2-13-1933) only had a couple of RKO musical cameos to her credit, when she was introduced to Columbia's boss Harry Cohn. He disliked her, but because he never got over his misjudgment of not giving Marilyn Monroe a contract back in 1948, he agreed to give the 'fat Pollack', as he called Kim behind her back, the big build up. Within a year Kim Novak became the biggest female box-office draw after Monroe. She was teamed up with Frank Sinatra in *The Man With the Golden Arm* (1955) and *Pal Joey* (1957), and co-starred with James Stewart in *Bell, Book and Candle* (1958) and Hitchcock's *Vertigo* (1958). Roles Jayne could only have dreamed of.

6. Part of an email from Gloria Pall to the author.

When Jayne arrived at Fox in 1956, she was the third blonde in town to compete with Marilyn. Columbia had Novak, RKO contracted British Diana Dors (born 10-23-1931) and Jayne was hired by Fox to surpass Monroe who just had turned thirty and was declining all sexy 'dumb blonde' movie parts they had lined up for her. But despite the big buildup Jayne Mansfield received, her career was over within a year

KIM NOVAK.

and a half. Unlike Jayne's, the career of Kim Novak blossomed way into the sixties. When Marilyn delayed filming of *Something's Got to Give* in 1962, 20th Century Fox threatened to replace her with Kim Novak. When Monroe was fired by Fox, Novak was offered the part. When she declined, the project was shelved. Although Jayne was mentioned as early as 1957 for this movie, her own studio preferred to contract Novak instead of her to replace Marilyn. "In contrast, however, to the careers of Mansfield and, in certain extent, of Monroe, Novak was given more opportunities to develop a nuanced and multi-dimensional star image that went far beyond her blonde hair and sex appeal."[7] Columbia created an actress out of a pin up movie star. Jayne was never given that chance at Fox.

Another girl who experienced this one-dimensional image building was Mamie Van Doren (born 2-6-1933). Universal Studio had its own answer to MM in Van Doren. Just like Jayne she was mostly cast as a glamour gal, but Van Doren's parts did have more spice to them because she was cast as the tough heroine in B-movie teenage dramas and minor crime thrillers. Her parts in *Untamed Youth* (1957), *Born Reckless* (1958) and *Vice Raid* (1959) gave her the name of Hollywood's 'Bad Blonde'. It was Van Doren who was Jayne's biggest threat in the publicity and Pin-Up department.

Mamie Van Doren had originally been offered the leading part in *Will Success Spoil Rock Hunter?* by playwright George Axelrod. She declined because she wanted to get rid of the 'other Monroe' tag. Looking back, she said it may have been the biggest mistake in her show business career. Jayne and Mamie met a couple of times in their life, but they never became close friends. And although they were never hostile to each other in their early careers, by the mid sixties they were fishing in the same pond to get some decent work. This created a sort of competition between the two actresses.

With Jayne sinking deeper into her alcohol problems Mamie seemed to be the wiser one: "Jayne appeared to live in a world midway between the fifties and sixties, holding on to the dumb-blonde persona of the fifties sex symbol while trying on sexually liberated attitude of the love generation."[8] Their co-starring in *Las Vegas Hillbillys* may have seemed

---

7. Solomon, Matthew. *Larger Than Life — Movie Stars of the Fifties*. New Jersey: Rutgers University Press, 2010.

8. Van Doren, Mamie with Aveilhe, Art. *Playing the Field — My Story*. New York: G.P. Putnam's Sons, 1987.

like a wonderful publicity stunt, but the result is a disappointment. The two blondes don't really interact. In the one scene where they cross each other's paths, a stand in was used. At the end of the sixties both Jayne and Mamie were doing a lot of personal appearance shows across the USA. Because Mamie's play *Gentlemen Prefer Blondes* was held over for a few extra weeks, she wasn't able to appear at Gus Stevens' Supper Club

MAMIE VAN DOREN.

in Biloxi, for which she was booked in July 1967. "Fortunately, Bill Loeb was able to schedule Jayne Mansfield to take my place, and reschedule me for later in the summer."[9] We all know now that this performance proved to be Jayne Mansfield's last.

In conclusion, *Will Success Spoil Rock Hunter?* co-star Orson Bean has the following to say about Jayne's feelings towards her blonde contemporaries in 1955: "She never bad mouthed any of the others. She just wanted to be one of them and ultimately head of the pack. I hadn't heard her express jealousy or anything like that at all."[10]

9. Van Doren, Mamie with Aveilhe, Art. *Playing the Field — My Story*. New York: G.P. Putnam's Sons, 1987.

10. *Jayne Mansfield fan club newsletter*, spring 1991.

WARNER BROS. PUBLICITY PHOTO, 1955.

Filmography

"I WAS DETERMINED TO FIND A JOB IN MOTION PICTURES.
YES, MY EGO WAS INFLATED BECAUSE I BELIEVED I WOULD
EVENTUALLY BECOME A STAR. BUT WITHOUT THAT EGO I
WOULD HAVE GOTTEN NOWHERE."

JAYNE MANSFIELD, 1963

INTRODUCTION

Jayne Mansfield started her career in a time when the idea of sexual freedom began to gain acceptance. The strict censorship provisions of the Hollywood Code rapidly yielded, permitting studios greater freedom, particularly with regard to sexual liberties. Since the early 1950s movies promoted marriage as the safe haven for a woman. In married life a woman's task was to take care of her husband, her children and her household. Actresses could portray free, fun loving girls as long as they would end up with a man at the end of the film. Films like Doris Day's *Calamity Jane* (1953), *How to Marry a Millionaire* (1953), with Marilyn Monroe, Betty Grable and Lauren Bacall, *Seven Brides for Seven Brothers* (1954) and Jane Russell's *Gentlemen Marry Brunettes* (1955) centered upon this marriage theme. Of course the women in these titles would only find true love if they hadn't crossed the border of chastity. Girls who did were named bad girls and as punishment for their immoral lifestyle they always lost their love interest in the end. These B-movie productions had titles which left nothing to the imagination: *Wicked Woman* (1953), *The Other Woman* (1954), *Three Bad Sisters* (1956) and *She Devil* (1957). The bad girls of these films had an unacceptable preoccupation with sex and were unfit for matrimony or any type of relationship in which fidelity was expected.

The era's schizophrenic view on female sexuality caused the film studios and producers to hesitate to explore the newfound territory. But self

BEHIND THE SCENES OF *THE BURGLAR* (1955).

made star Jayne Mansfield confronted them in being a girl who combined the two, sexpot and mother, in one person. "By a fairly brilliant move of constantly associating the maternal with her hyper-feminine sexualized body, Mansfield attempted and to some degree succeeded in naturalizing and normalizing her sexpot image."[1]

Could a woman shift her boundaries by expanding them with a little more sexual freedom and still become a respected married woman? Could a woman build a career on her curvaceous attributes and be a mother at the same time? Jayne Mansfield did. She was a married woman and a mother when she arrived in Hollywood, and a sexy one too! But if she molded her screen and public image at free will or as a sacrifice to become a star is questionable. She once said: "I had a body, yes, but I also had brains and an inborn stubbornness. I was determined to work things out and make it, my way."[2]

Jayne recalled in a 1960 interview that she was pointed out the short-cut to success when reading for a casting director: "I did a soliloquy from Joan of Arc for Milton Lewis who was the head of casting at Paramount Studios in order to audition. And he just seemed to think that I was wasting my, as he said, obvious talents." So she stepped on the road to stardom by portraying floozies.

Her early film characters were girls who were either harsh, shrewd or downright dumb and their on-film lifestyle was that of a prostitute or a kept woman. "They [Warner Bros.] promised me the star treatment and gave me little but walk-on parts as a dumb blonde or a gangster's sweetie," Jayne commented on her early parts. In *Hell on Frisco Bay* Jayne's cameo appearance consisted of her portraying a stupid, flirting dame while the character of Angel O'Hara in *Illegal* was restrained by the man who supported her. And with the portrayal of the sluttish Candy Price in the aptly named *Female Jungle*, Jayne impersonates a girl who earns her living by sleeping with men. These parts were so-called starlet parts. Starlets were interchangeable bit players who desired to become a movie's leading lady in the near future. "To establish yourself as an actress, you have to become well known. A girl just starting out, I would tell her to concentrate on acting, but she doesn't have to go around wearing blankets."

1. Jordan, Jessica Hope. *The Sex Goddess in American Film 1930-1965 — Jean Harlow, Mae West, Lana Turner, and Jayne Mansfield.* Amherst, New York: Cambria Press, 2009.

2. Luijters, Guus & Timmer, Gerard. *Sexbomb. The Life and Death of Jayne Mansfield.* New York: Citadel Press, 1985.

A SCENE FROM *KISS THEM FOR ME* (1957), WITH A PICTURE OF JAYNE AND MICKEY
ON THE WALL IN THE BACKGROUND.

By becoming a film star, an actress needed to have her own persona. Blondes with an hourglass figure were destined for a buildup as the sexy, helpless, brainless 'easy to get' girl. "The Fifties blonde was the girl to match the new utopia that postwar America was aspiring to. She was glossy, artificial and bigger than anything that had gone before, in every area of her anatomy except her brain."[3] Marilyn Monroe was the epitome

JAYNE AND JOAN COLLINS BEHIND THE SCENES OF *THE WAYWARD BUS* (1957).

of these type of girls. Films like *How to Marry a Millionaire* and *The Seven Year Itch* emphasized on this stigma which was commonly known as 'the dumb blonde'. "As far as being a dumb blonde is concerned, this certainly gave me my first chance into stage stardom first and movie stardom second," Jayne exclaimed in an interview where she also pointed out she wanted to be recognized as a serious actress. But she was right, the part of the dumb blonde headed the way to stardom.

After her success on the Broadway stage in *Will Success Spoil Rock Hunter?* Jayne was put under contract at 20th Century Fox. They cast her in *The Girl Can't Help It* as a girl who just wants a domestic life instead of

3. Yates, Paula. *Blondes — A History From Their Earliest Roots.* London: Michael Joseph Ltd, 1983.

becoming a famous singer. Jerri Jordan is a kept woman also. Her 'manager' lays out her future for her, ignoring her wish to become a mother and housewife. But without the help of another man, talent agent Tom Ewell, Jerri isn't able to break free from her unwanted destiny. In real life Jayne Mansfield herself knew just what she wanted. She just played along with the men in charge so she would become a famous movie star. It was her misjudgment to believe that she could change her dumb blonde image and become a serious actress.

Jayne did play two 'real' characters which today are considered as the parts through which she proved she could act. *The Burglar* shows a girl who is bitter about life, craving the attention of the man who considers her his sister. *The Wayward Bus* gave Jayne the opportunity to look great but still portray a harmed girl with feelings and hidden away hopes. Both films were filmed in black & white and weren't promoted in a big way. *The Burglar* was shelved for over a year and only got a nationwide release after Jayne's success on Broadway, *The Wayward Bus* was stuffed between the well publicized premieres of *Will Success Spoil Rock Hunter?* and *Kiss Them For Me*. These last two movies showed us Jayne Mansfield the dizzy, outrageous blonde sexbomb again.

The director of *The Girl Can't Help It* and *Will Success Spoil Rock Hunter?*, Frank Tashlin, is considered as the director that sculpted the movie star image that Jayne wanted to achieve. "[He] turned Mansfield into a living cartoon of postwar femininity, a kind of sexual hydrogen bomb capable of laying waste to entire male population," film critic Dave Kehr once wrote about the collaboration of Tashlin and Mansfield in *The New York Times*. Of course *Rock Hunter* is the key film in Jayne's career. It's the part that made her famous and Rita Marlowe is the character that has become synonymous with the actress Jayne Mansfield. The part she portrayed in that film seemed to have become the part she portrayed in real life. A part she portrayed so well, that it seems she couldn't free herself from it anymore.

This was the time that film studios were still led by the men that had built the star system over the last two decades. They controlled their contracted stars completely, making up an aura around their prize trophies, an image by which their creations should live. They carefully picked the parts and selected the movies that restrained the stars to play the same kind of role in different variations. Jayne Mansfield was destined to become the biggest blonde since Monroe. For that reason, 20th Century Fox didn't want her to marry muscleman Mickey Hargitay. They even tried to separate the pair by sending Jayne off to San Francisco to film *Kiss Them For Me*. It was made clear to Mickey not to follow. The publicity department aimed at an image of Jayne as the eligible bachelor girl, who is dating men, but is not seriously considering marriage. The truth was different of course. But although she seemed to adjust to the studio's demands, in the end strong-willed Miss Mansfield chose her own path. In *Kiss Them For Me* there's a scene where Jayne is telephoning in her slip, on the wall behind her are some pictures and photos. One photo shows Jayne with

ADVERTISING MATERIAL FOR *THE GIRL CAN'T HELP IT* (1956).

Mickey Hargitay. Who put the photo on the wall is unknown. Maybe it was Jayne, the rebel, herself. She was the original motor behind most of the outrageous publicity gimmicks.

A self-made woman and actress, Miss Mansfield was one of the first sex symbols that had a child when she started her career.[4] Those days sex symbols were supposed to be dream women, standing on a pedestal, being an out of this earth creature. At the same time they were supposed to be approachable and eligible for the man who made her feel like a girl, who treated her as a child; protected her and sheltered her from evil. But when a woman has children that means she has to take care of them, leaving less time to spend with her lover. A lover who has to postpone his 'quality

4. Sheree North also had one child when Fox contracted her, but she shrugged off the sex symbol tag quite quickly after her film debut.

ON THE SET OF *TOO HOT TO HANDLE* (1959).

time' with her until she puts the babies to bed. Being a mother takes in other feelings with a man, than seeing a woman as a playmate solely. Jayne Mansfield aimed at portraying both at the same time: "Mansfield's blurring of these strict patriarchal boundaries creates for…men a sense of discomfort for fear they are being disposed of their power. Mansfield crosses over from one patriarchal view to the next, from sexual object (whore) to sexual subject (Madonna)…."[5] Jayne once said about it: "I have always considered my career self and my personal self as two different and separate people. There's a Jayne Mansfield at home, a wife and devoted mother, and there's Jayne the sex symbol, which is my career. I have always kept them completely apart and separate." But the executives at 20th Century Fox thought differently. How were they going to make a profit on a star who was unable to make movies because of pregnancy?

Married and a mother of two children in 1959, Jayne wanted to break free from the dumb blonde tag that had become a straitjacket instead of the threaded bodice that gave way to pin-up stardom. In a 1957 interview while visiting France, she had said: "I want to do all kinds of parts. I want to do as many serious roles as I do comedy roles. But I as a person am much different from the comedy roles I portray on the screen and also much different from the serious ones that I have portrayed and will portray. So I like a little bit of both." Besides Miss Mansfield own motives, Fox started loaning her out for independent productions because they just didn't know how to use her anymore. Many of her contemporaries had escaped the limiting US production standards and found new artistic freedom in Europe. Jayne was loaned out for two English productions and was booked for an epic film to be filmed in Cinecittà, Italy.

Being loaned out for English co-productions mostly meant a devaluation for American actors, and filming on Europe's mainland also meant that an actor could find himself in a mediocre historical costume film. But with the French and Italian 'Nouvelle Vague' (New Wave) dictating the spirit of the times, Europe also seemed the place to be to revive one's acting career.[6] While visiting Europe in 1957, Jayne told the host of a Dutch TV show: "I think that European pictures are more progressive, more artistic and I think that they aim at a higher cultural level."

5. Jordan, Jessica Hope. *The Sex Goddess in American Film 1930-1965 — Jean Harlow, Mae West, Lana Turner, and Jayne Mansfield.* Amherst, New York: Cambria Press, 2009.

6. *"The nouvelle vague films from France and others by such directors as Federico Fellini, Michelangelo Antonini and Ingmar Bergman further accelerated the decline of censorship in the United States."* Dempsey, Michael. *Movies of the Fifties.* London: Orbis Publishing Limited, 1982.

PUBLICITY PHOTO FROM *TOO HOT TO HANDLE* (1959).

Nevertheless she always let the US press know that she would rather film in the United States.

European film making held other standards towards nudity. Italian, French and Scandinavian films showed much more flesh than the American Production Code allowed. Jayne's ventures in Europe also led to her first steps on showing onscreen nudity. Her first attempts to change her image were merely 'cross-over' productions, Jayne wasn't allowed to shake off her pin-up trademark completely. Filmed in Great Britain, *The Sheriff of Fractured Jaw* pictures Jayne as a saloon girl with brains. A smart lady who presides over the small community of Fractured Jaw, in absence of a male sheriff. Although looking conservative, clothed in long dresses and wearing colored stockings, Jayne's sex symbol status is pointed out by having her wear an outrageous costume in a musical number called "If the San Francisco Hills Could Only Talk".

Jayne's next picture pushed the limits of the Production Code even further. *Too Hot To Handle* gave Jayne some good scenes to showcase her dramatic range in acting, but it was all downplayed by her character being a striptease dancer who wears a transparent dress. Also on the Soho scene was the character of her next film; Billy Lacrosse, owner of a nightclub. *The Challenge* marked Jayne's first topless scene, but this time the character gets more depth because she's also the tough leader of a gang of crooks. Besides the dramatic overtones of this production, the wardrobe department still fitted Jayne in dresses two sizes too small. Her appearance looked grotesque rather than sexy. The same can be said about Jayne's next attempt at serious acting. The costumes she wears in *Gli Amori di Ercole* emphasized her breasts by padding them out and restraining her waist. Her appearance is so distracting that Jayne's acting, in a dual role, seems ridiculous. The nudity here consisted of a bathing scene that looks tame by today's standards. *Gli Amori di Ercole* is regarded as one of her lesser films.

Jayne's European output wasn't released in the US at all or with a delay of at least a year. Americans hadn't seen Jayne in the cinemas for over a year and a half and when 20th Century Fox also decided to postpone the release of *It Happened in Athens*, Jayne Mansfield seemed to have become a name of the past. The first time the US movie going public had the chance to see her again was in *The George Raft Story*. But it was a minor B film, filmed in black & white; a long cry from her early days at 20th Century Fox.

Since 1959 the company was in the red, with major losses in feature film production. Jayne's loan-out movies meant income for the studio and when the studio lost another $60 million, Darryl F. Zanuck came back to replace Spyros Skouras as president of the company in 1962.[7] While filming on another loan out picture in Europe, *Panic Button,* Jayne got notified that Fox had dissolved her contract. *Panic Button* wasn't released until 1964. Jayne's movie star days seemed over. She quickened her downfall by playing two nude scenes — accompanied by a *Playboy* layout — in *Promises, Promises!* Hedda Hopper[8] severely criticized Jayne for it: "I doubt

JAYNE AND ULLRICH HAUPT IN *HEIMWEH NACH ST. PAULI* (1963).

that Jayne will ever live down the nude pictures in that girlie magazine … the photographs are from the movie she made abroad. I am not surprised that the picture won't be shown in the U.S.A. I should hope not!"[9] The picture was relegated to the art house circuit.

Without a nationwide released film for four years, Jayne travelled to Europe again, this time voluntarily. She was cast in *Heimweh nach St. Pauli,* which was to be filmed in Hamburg, Germany. After completion

7. *"A loss over $60 million during 1961-62 included expenditures of over $30 million on the disastrous Cleopatra (1963) and a $2 million write-off on Marilyn Monroe's last, unfinished picture Something's Got To Give."* Finler, Joel. *Movies of the Fifties.* London: Orbis Publishing Limited, 1982.

8. Hedda Hopper (1885-1966) was a well known and feared gossip columnist. She started out as an actress herself, but reached more fame with her own radio program *The Hedda Hopper Show* and with writing her columns for Photoplay magazine and The Chicago Tribune.

9. According to various reports at the time, *Promises, Promises!* was believed to have been filmed outside the United States.

she went to the former Yugoslavia to film *Der Einer frisst den Anderen*. In the latter Jayne did really well as the mad, slutty Darlene. Finally a part for which she had to show her acting abilities again. The two German financed films were a success in German language countries only. A trip to Italy resulted in the absurd pseudo documentary picture *L'Amore Primitivo* for which Jayne bared her breast again. If her earlier

WITH TOMMY NOONAN, MARIE MCDONALD AND MICKEY HARGITAY IN *PROMISES! PROMISES!* **(1963).**

PUBLICITY PORTRAIT, 1963.

Italian film effort was considered bad, her second one was even worse. Jayne's film career was over.

While Jayne was filming in Europe and appearing in stage shows in the US, Hollywood manufactured new stars like Raquel Welch, Ann-Margret and Elke Sommer. Only a couple of Jayne Mansfield's blonde contemporaries survived the climate change. Meanwhile Jayne Mansfield and long time rival Mamie Van Doren had to take on every film offer no matter how awful the script. With Van Doren, Jayne was cast in the very low budget *Las Vegas Hillbillys*. It seems that she participated in these last films because of the paycheck only. One of Jayne's last outings as an actress was in a failed comedy with comedian Phyllis Diller, *The Fat Spy*. Here the interpretation of the sex symbol met the 'real life' expecting mother on the screen. Perceptibly five months pregnant, Jayne managed to portray a sex starved dumb blonde, charming her co-star; a bald, unattractive man who could have been her father.

A 1965 pocket book introduced a chapter on Jayne titled *The Sagging World of Jayne Mansfield* as follows: "For the movie queen — especially the Glamour Girl — there seldom is any turning back. She wiggles her assets, steps out on the road to 'success' and never gets off. Not willingly. And sometimes the road is a long downhill run to oblivion, with a dead end."[10] Forgotten by Hollywood producers and feeling unwanted Jayne returned to Las Vegas. In working with her director husband Matt Cimber, Jayne hoped to make her comeback. "Finding film roles for her would have been difficult. Because what was happening in the fifties certainly was beginning to change very obviously in the sixties. So I felt that if we could develop a nightclub act that would give her, probably, financial security forever."[11]

Her nightclub act was featured all over the United States, in some of the most mediocre theaters and supper clubs. When she took the act abroad she was forced to play in English pubs and working men's clubs. When asked, at the time, by a British reporter if she wanted to change her image, Jayne replied: "I would like to build on it, which I'm doing right now. I'm doing more dramatic things, I'm doing the same satire and wonderful things, like I mentioned *Fanny Hill* that I want to do in the West End, and more dramatic pictures but also the campy satirical fun pictures."

10. Hirsch, Phil. *Hollywood Uncensored — The Stars-Their Secrets and their Scandals*. New York: Pyramid Books, 1965.

11. A quote from ex-husband Matt Cimber.

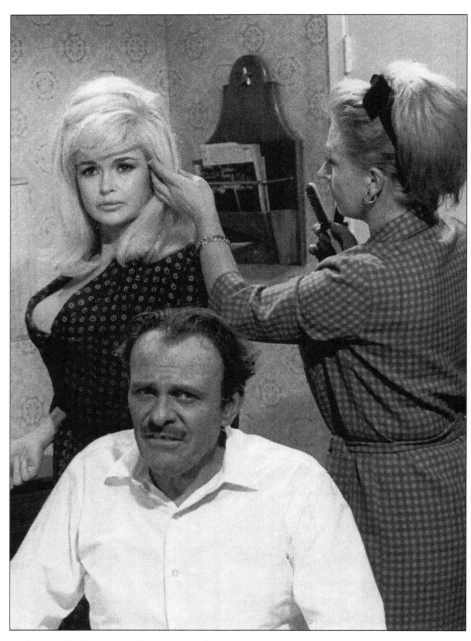

WITH TERRY-THOMAS BEHIND THE SCENES OF *A GUIDE FOR THE MARRIED MAN* **(1967).**

In late 1965 the Cimbers had started working on *Single Room Furnished*. Jayne played the character changes of a woman down on her luck quite effectively. Because financing the project was problematical, it took Cimber three years to finish the film. In the meantime he and Jayne were divorced, and by the time of the film's release Jayne had died. But lady luck gave Jayne one last opportunity to shine. One month before her death *A Guide For the Married Man* was released. The A-level movie was a success and although small, Jayne's part received positive reviews. Produced by the studio that helped her reach stardom ten years earlier, 20th Century Fox, the film rehabilitated Jayne as America's most outrageous golden blonde pin up star.

Maybe Jayne Mansfield was a wasted talent. Wasted by the Hollywood studio system that always type casted her as the glamorous movie star, sexy stripper, or blonde gang mol. Viewing her movies and watching her performances in them, shows us a woman who really wanted to act. Underneath the blonde bosomy façade lay traces of an unpolished talent and when directed by talented directors, this rough diamond did shine brightly. Taking in consideration the material Jayne Mansfield was handed it would have been a hard job for any actress to show what acting skills she really possessed.

The director that guided Jayne through her first big starring parts and who tried to guide her to a bright acting future, Frank Tashlin, thought she threw it away by over-exposing herself in the press. "Jayne had everything — beauty, talent and drive — but she blew her career at Fox with too much publicity. No one could get through to her that she was hurting herself with this constant barrage of daily publicity in the papers and press."[12]

Ex-husband Mickey Hargitay witnessed it all and commented later: "I think the problems really began with her career because she was pushing it too much; she didn't want to stop. And I kept saying, 'honey don't bother, don't …you know, sit down, relax, choose your script.'"

Biographer Martha Saxton summarized Jayne's decline as follows: "But Jayne really exterminated the dumb blonde by taking its image to its funny, insane and unpalatable conclusion. She willfully destroyed the fantasy she'd exploited."[13]

Summarizing her life and acting career Jayne herself once said: "I tried. But not everybody thought so." She couldn't have said it better…

12. Mann, May. *Jayne Mansfield: A Biography.* New York: Drake, 1973.

13. Saxton, Martha. *Jayne Mansfield and the American Fifties.* Boston: Houghton Miffin Company, 1975.

FEMALE JUNGLE (1954).

FEMALE JUNGLE

1954 — American Releasing Corporation
73 minutes, Black and white

PRODUCER: Burt Kaiser. DIRECTOR: Bruno Ve Sota. SCREENPLAY:
Burt Kaiser & Bruno Ve Sota. Based on the story by Burt Kaiser. MUSIC:
Nicholas Carras. EDITOR: Carl Pingitore. MAKE-UP: Louis J. Haszillo.
PHOTOGRAPHY: Elwood Bredell. SOUND: Roy Meadows.

CAST: Lawrence Tierney *(Sgt. Jack Stevens)*; John Carradine *(Claude
Almstead)*; Jayne Mansfield *(Candy Price)*; Burt Kaiser *(Alec Voe)*; Kathleen
Crowley *(Peggy Voe)*; James Kodl *(Joe)*; Rex Thorsen *(Sgt. Duane)*; Jack
Hill *(Captain Kroger)*; Bruce Carlisle *(Chuck)*; Connie Cezon *(Connie)*;
Robert Davis *(George)*; Gordon Urquhart *(Larry Jackson)*; Bill Layne
(Heckler); Alan Jay Factor *(Doctor Urquhart)*; Bruno Ve Sota *(Frank)*; Jean
Lewis *(Monica Madison)*.

The story involves the murder of Monica Madison, a Hollywood actress.
The three suspects include Hollywood columnist Claude Almstead, an
alcoholic policeman Sgt. Stevens and a cartoonist called Alec Voe. Voe is
married to Peggy, but has an affair with nymphomaniac model Candy Price,
who also dated Sgt. Stevens. Alec turns out to be the psychopath killer of
Miss Madison and before he is caught by the police, he also murders Candy.
Jayne has a sexy scene at the beginning of the movie when she is
visited by Police Sergeant Stevens. She refreshes his memory by kissing
him when she understands that he has forgotten their date at the Can
Can Club earlier that evening. During this visit she receives a phone call
from a stranger who she responds to in an arousing way. She asks him
how he looks and then ends the conversation by making an appointment
with him. Later on she shares a scene necking with Alec Voe. She tries
to make him leave his wife and elope with her. "Your good for nothing,
but I'm crazy for you," Candy tells him. When he says that they are over
and that he still loves his wife, Candy realizes her faith:"With or without
violins, I call this a brush off." Still hoping to get her man, we see her in
her last scene. She stops Voe from brutalizing Peggy. Voe is frantic and
in his confused state of mind he confesses to killing Monica. Candy tries
to reason with him but Voe strangles her while saying: "I love you Candy.
Whatever I did, I did it for you."
Female Jungle is a cheaply made grade Z movie. Although filming
for *Female Jungle* finished in November 1954, the movie couldn't find a

distributor until 1956. Producer Burt Kaiser tried to sell the movie to Paramount and Allied Artists, but they declined to release it. The company that finally released *Female Jungle*, American Releasing Corporation, later became part of B-movie corporation American International Pictures. They bought the picture right before Jayne's Broadway success in *Will Success Spoil Rock Hunter?* "The films backer and co-star, Burt Kaiser, was

FEMALE JUNGLE (1954).

eager to unload it so ARC got it at a bargain price. And the only reason she [Jayne Mansfield] had been hired for Kaiser's film was that her agent had asked for $50 less than the other actress who auditioned for the part."[1] The movie was finally released June 15, 1956. It was shown as the second half of a double bill package for the drive-in crowd.[2] The working titles for this production were originally *Girl Murdered* and *The Hangover*.

Jayne received a total of $150 for her debut film role. "I was to play a sexy girl of the streets, sensual and bad. It was a quick picture, made in ten days. I didn't even get two hundred dollars. But I loved every minute of being in makeup; even when I had to lay on the hot sidewalk playing

1. McGee, Mark Thomas. *Faster and Furiouser — The revised and fattened fable of American International Pictures.* Jefferson: McFarland & Company, Inc., Publishers, 1996.

2. The other movie was *The Oklahoma Woman.*

my own dead body for an hour at a time; the budget didn't allow stand-ins or a dummy corpse."

Actress Jean Lewis (b. 1930) later changed her name to Eve Brent[3] and Rex Thorsen (1921-2001) would become better known as Duane Grey. Blonde Jean Lewis was a bit player in the fifties, *Female Jungle* marked her film debut. She had her only moment of fame when she was cast as

FEMALE JUNGLE LOBBY CARD, WITH BURT KAISER.

Tarzan's mate Jane in *Tarzan's Fight for Life* (1958). Well in her eighties she still makes the occasional cameo appearance in a Hollywood production. Troubled actor Lawrence Tierney (1919-2002) had a once promising career when he starred in some solid dramas and action packed movies at RKO studios in the 1940's. Due to heavy drinking which led to aggressive encounters on and off the film set, he found his career over in the early fifties. He kept on playing parts in movies until he died.

John Carradine (1906-1988) with his distinctive deep baritone voice, played in B-movie horror films in the forties. He made over 300 movies between the 1930's and the 1990's. About 20th Century Fox executive Darryl F. Zanuck — to whom Jayne Mansfield would be under contract

---

3. Under this name she would play the part of a cheap blonde in *A Guide for the Married Man* (1967), in which Jayne played a small part also.

within two years — Carradine once said: "Nobody liked working for Zanuck, the little goddamn Napoleon, always walking around with his polo mallet. Nobody had any respect for him except as an executive." Burt Kaiser (1926-2004), who played the psychopathic murderer, was also the producer of the picture. He was a friend of Jayne's 'agent' at that moment, Frank Worth. Worth was a cameraman and photographer at the time and he introduced Jayne to Kaiser.

BELGIAN POSTER FOR *FEMALE JUNGLE*.

After Jayne viewed the movie at a local movie theatre, she proclaimed: "I loved me up there on the screen. At last being an actress! Being a star! 'I love you, Jayne Mansfield', I told my image. 'I'll work hard for you. Nothing or no one will ever make me let you down.'"[4]

In Jayne's self written pseudo-biography *Jayne Mansfield's Wild, Wild World* she recalls getting the movie part of Candy Price in a different way than the other biographies written about her. "The one day I stopped in for a hamburger. Actor Larry Tierney was sitting at a nearby table and I overheard him saying that a new picture was starting at Warner Brothers called *The Female Jungle*. I asked if I could borrow the script for a few minutes. In the cast of characters, which I turned to first, there was this notation: "Girl — busty, attractive, sexy, outgoing, alluring." Hey, that was me! I told Tierney I was an actress and I thought I was right for one of the parts. He suggested I get through to the producer and talk to him."[5] Since all of the witnesses to this story are no longer with us, there's no way of verifying this!

REVIEWS

Variety: "Since there's little help from the murky plotting, most box office changes chances will have to come from the succession of chesty femmes (including Jayne Mansfield, before her current success) who strut their brief moments across the screen, and the elongated scenes of amorous fondling which leave only the ultimate to the imagination."

Hollywood Citizen-News: "Miss Mansfield is amply endowed with the same sex appeal which is the other Miss M's stock in trade.[6] The quality she exudes is rather heavier and is minus the touch of comedy which exalts La Monroe. Comparisons are odious. In her own right, Miss Mansfield is very appealing, her uninhibited love scenes are sizzling."

Picturegoer (GB): "This is pre-Broadway and *The Girl Can't Help It* Mansfield. Even here the girl shows all the symptoms of a potential actress. As a jaded good-time girl who just wants the bad-time guy (Burt Kaiser) she registers as something more than a vigorous blonde with spectacular statistics."

4. Mann, May. *Jayne Mansfield: A Biography*. New York: Drake, 1973.

5. Mansfield, Jayne and Hargitay, Mickey. *Jayne Mansfield's Wild, Wild World*. Los Angeles: Holloway House Publishing Company, 1963.

6. Actress Marilyn Monroe is meant by 'The other Miss M'.

ILLEGAL

1955 — Warner Bros.

88 minutes, Black and white

PRODUCER: Frank P. Rosenberg. DIRECTOR: Lewis Allen. SCREEN-PLAY: W. R. Burnett & James R. Webb. Based on the play *The Mouthpiece* by Frank J. Collins. MUSIC: Max Steiner. EDITOR: Thomas Reilly. MAKE-UP: Gordon Bau. COSTUMES: Moss Mabry. PHOTOGRAPHY: J. Pervell Marley. SOUND: Stanley Jones.

CAST: Edward G. Robinson *(Victor Scott)*; Nina Foch *(Ellen Miles)*; Hugh Marlowe *(Ray Borden)*; Robert Ellenstein *(Joe Knight)*; DeForest Kelley *(Edward Clary)*; Jay Adler *(Joseph Carter)*; James McCallion *(Allen Parker)*; Edward Platt *(Ralph Ford)*; Albert Dekker *(Frank Garland)*; Jan Merlin *(Andy Grath)*; Ellen Corby *(Miss Hinkel)*; **Jayne Mansfield** *(Angel O'Hara)*; Clark Howat *(George Graves)*; Henry Kulky *(Taylor)*; Addison Richards *(Steve Harper)*; Howard St. John *(E. A. Smith)*; Lawrence Dobkin *(Al Carol)*; George Ross *(Policeman)*; John McKee *(Detective)*; Barry Hudson *(Detective)*; Kathy Marlowe *(Gloria Benson)*; Ten Stanhope *(Bailiff)*; Charles Evans *(Judge)*; Jonathan Hale *(Doctor)*; Marjorie Stapp *(Night Orderly)*; Fred Coby *(Third Guard)*; Max Wagner *(Bartender)*; John Cliff *(Barfly)*; Henry Rowland *(Jailer)*; Julie Bennett *(Miss Worth)*; Pauline Drake *(Woman)*; Roxanne Arlen *(Miss Hathaway)*; Archie Twitchell *(Mr. Manning)*; Stewart Nedd *(Phillips)*; Herb Vigran *(First Policeman)*; Chris Alcaide *(Second Policeman)*.

Victor Scott, a district attorney unknowingly sends an innocent man to the electric chair. Just minutes before the man is to be executed, Scott receives new evidence that proves the man is innocent. He tries to stop the execution but fails. This works on his conscience and he resigns from his office. Without a purpose in his life he becomes an alcoholic and eventually a lawyer for criminal clients. He cleans up his act eventually and opens a private practice and when Ellen Miles, Scott's protégée while DA, finds herself in trouble with the law through her former boss's mob connections, Scott gets Angel O'Hara, a blonde pianist and nightclub singer, to testify against her ex-boyfriend Frank Garland. Garland is the head racketeer who framed Ellen. During Angel's testimony, Scott dramatically dies in the courtroom.

Because of many plot similarities, *Illegal* is often compared to *The Asphalt Jungle* (1950). In the latter Marilyn Monroe starred as a gangster's moll. One of Jayne's scenes — where she lies curled up on a couch — is especially reminiscent of one of Monroe's scenes in *The Asphalt Jungle*. Jayne has a total of four scenes in this movie, dressed in stunning and very tight outfits. She got the opportunity to sing on the screen for the first time. The song she's singing while playing the piano is "Too Marvellous for Words".

WITH EDWARD G. ROBINSON, ELLEN CORBY AND NINA FOCH IN *ILLEGAL* (1955).

The picture's final scene ends with a close up of Jayne's chest against the background of the courtroom.

Illegal was the first production Warner's put her in. Filming began on February 14, 1955. *Illegal* was released to the public in October 1955. One of the film's taglines was: "He was a guy who marked 100 men for death — until a blonde called 'Angel' O'Hara marked him for life!"

Jayne shared most of her scenes with long-time WB contract player Edward G. Robinson (1893-1973). In *Illegal* he portrayed a DA who works for the mob, a world familiar to him because he became famous playing thugs and gangsters in productions like *Little Caesar* (1931) and *The Little Giant* (1933). Actor Albert Dekker (1905-1968) played Jayne's

ILLEGAL (1955).

WITH EDWARD G. ROBINSON AND ALBERT DEKKER IN *ILLEGAL* (1955).

suitor. Earlier in his career he played the boss of Marilyn Monroe, who was his secretary in *As Young As You Feel* (1951).

About her time as a contract player at Warner Bros. Studios, Jayne later commented: "So while I thought I was being signed for my talent, I was really signed because I was photogenic, and I would have been hurt and unhappy had I known the truth. Yet the studio was right and because they pointed me in the direction of publicity I was able to work my way up that particular ladder."

REVIEWS

New York Times: "…*Illegal* is trying to blueprint *The Asphalt Jungle's* Marilyn Monroe. Well in 'Illegal' Jayne Mansfield plays precisely the role in the apartment of Albert Dekker, the poobah of crime. Miss Mansfield, we might add, is the beauty who is imitating Miss Monroe in a feeble imitation of *Once in a Lifetime*[7] on the Broadway stage."

Hollywood Reporter: "Jayne Mansfield is his blonde girlfriend who has the same delicious attributes as Marilyn Monroe. She'll go far if the studios can find for her the tray on which to serve them."

Variety: "Jayne Mansfield battles gamely with what looks like an impersonation of an imitation of Marilyn Monroe."

Picturegoer (GB): "…the blonde they've been buzzing about, Jayne Mansfield, playing the gangster's girlfriend and acting so like Monroe you might almost imagine you were back watching *The Asphalt Jungle* …."

7. When *Illegal* was released, Jayne was already the star in Broadway success *Will Success Spoil Rock Hunter?*, which storyline was quite like the popular play *Once In A Lifetime*.

PUBLICITY PHOTO FOR *PETE KELLY'S BLUES* **(1955).**

PETE KELLY'S BLUES
1955 — Warner Bros.
95 minutes, Color

PRODUCER: Jack Webb. DIRECTOR: Jack Webb. SCREENPLAY: Richard L. Breen. MUSIC: Sammy Cahn & Arthur Hamilton. EDITOR: Robert M. Leeds. MAKE-UP: Gordon Rau. COSTUMES: Howard Shoup. PHOTOGRAPHY: Hal Rosson. SOUND: Leslie G. Hewitt & Dolph Thomas.

CAST: Jack Webb *(Pete Kelly)*; Janet Leigh *(Ivy Conrad)*; Edmond O'Brien *(Fran McCarg)*; Peggy Lee *(Rose Hopkins)*; Andy Devine *(George Tenell)*; Lee Marvin *(Al Gannaway)*; Ella Fitzgerald *(Maggie Jackson)*; Marty Milner (Joey Firestone*)*; **Jayne Mansfield** *(Cigarette Girl)*; Than Wyenn *(Rudy)*; Herb Ellis *(Bedido)*; John Dennis *(Guy Bettenhouser)*; Mort Marshall *(Cootie Jacobs)*; Nesdon Booth *(Squat Henchman)*; William Lazerus *(Dako)*; Teddy Buckner *(Cornetist)*; Matty Matlock *(Clarinetist)*; Moe Schneider *(Trombonist)*; Eddie Miller *(Saxophonist)*; George Van Eps *(Guitarist)*; Nick Fatool *(Drummer)*; Ray Sherman *(Pianist)*; Jud De Naut *(Bass Player)*; Snub Pollard *(Waiter in Rudy's)*.

Kansas City in the 1920's. Pete Kelly's jazz band is being forced to pay for mob protection. When he refuses to pay them at first, a member of his band is killed by mobster McCarg's clan. Eventually the band start working for the gangsters in their own club where Rose Hopkins, the gangster's girlfriend, is the leading singer. Jayne has the small part of a red headed cigarette girl and has one line of dialogue in a twenty second scene. When Jack Webb asks her what she is selling, Jayne answers: "Anything you want."

Although *Pete Kelly's Blues* was Jayne's second film for Warner Bros., which started filming on March 28, 1955, it was released before *Illegal* by Warner Bros. on July 31, 1955.

Producer-director Jack Webb (1920-1982) had used Jayne for a walk-on in his TV series *Dragnet*[8] before she was cast in Pete Kelly's Blues. Jack Webb was raised by his mother. One of the tenants in his mother's lodging house was an ex-jazzman who began Webb's lifelong interest in jazz. In 1951, Webb introduced a short-lived radio series, *Pete Kelly's Blues*, in an attempt to bring the music he loved to a broader

---

8. *Dragnet* ran from 1951-1959. The episode Jayne Mansfield appeared in stays untitled, because she is not credited for any of the episodes in 1955. Jack Webb played Sgt. Joe Friday who investigated crimes in Los Angeles in this very popular police drama series.

WITH JACK WEBB AND PEGGY LEE IN *PETE KELLY'S BLUES* (1955).

audience. That show became the basis for the 1955 movie. In 1959 a television version of the radio show was made. Singer, songwriter and actress Peggy Lee (1920-2002) was nominated for an Oscar for her portrayal of Edmond O'Brien's alcoholic girlfriend. She lost to actress Jo Van Fleet for her performance as James Dean's prostitute mother in *East of Eden*. Peggy Lee sings: "Sing a Rainbow"; "He Needs Me"; "Somebody Loves Me"; "Sugar"; "I Never Knew"; "Bye-bye Blackbird"; "What Can I Say After I Say I'm Sorry?" and "Oh, Didn't He Ramble".

REVIEWS

New York Times: "*Pete Kelly's Blues* is an incredible waste of tantalizing music and decor designed for the sole purpose of letting Jack Webb strut his stuff almost exactly as before. As star-director-producer of his second Warner feature, which opened yesterday at the Victoria, Mr. Webb simply swaps his *Dragnet* badge for a cornet and triumphantly battles some prohibition-era Kansas City mobsters."

Motion Picture: "A jazzed-up version of *Dragnet*."

Variety: "Webb's understatement of his character is good and Peggy Lee scores a personal hit with her portrayal of a fading singing star taken to the bottle. O'Brien registers exceptionally well as the would be big shot and Miss Leigh prototypes the era with her joy-seeking flapper."

HELL ON FRISCO BAY

1955 — Warner Bros.

58 minutes, Color

PRODUCER: George C. Bertholon. DIRECTOR: Frank Tuttle. SCREEN-PLAY: Sydney Boehm & Martin Rackin. Based on the Collier's Magazine serial "The Darkest Hour" by William P. McGivern. MUSIC: Max Steiner. EDITOR: Folmar Blangsted. MAKE-UP: Gordon Rau. COSTUMES: Moss Mabry. PHOTOGRAPHY: John Seitz. SOUND: Charles B. Lang.

CAST: Alan Ladd *(Steve Rollins)*; Edward G. Robinson *(Victor Amato)*; Joanne Dru *(Marcia Rollins)*; William Demarest *(Dan Bianco)*; Paul Stewart *(Joe Lye)*; Perry Lopez *(Mario Amato)*; Fay Wray *(Kay Stanley)*; Renata Vanni *(Anna Amato)*; Nestor Paiva *(Lou Fiaschetti)*; Stanley Adams *(Hammy)*; Willis Bouchey *(Police Lt. Paul Neville)*; Peter Hanson *(Detective Connors)*; Anthony Caruso *(Sebastian Pasmonick)*; George J. Lewis *(Father Larocca)*; Tina Carver *(Bessie Coster)*; Rodney Taylor *(Brodie Evans)*; Peter Votrian *(George Pasmonick)*; **Jayne Mansfield** *(Blonde)*; Mae Marsh *(Landlady)*.

When policeman Steve Rollins is released from prison where he sat for a murder he didn't commit, he hunts the real killer down in the Italian fishing community in San Francisco. The godfather of this community is played by Edward G. Robinson, with whom Jayne also starred in *Illegal* that same year. Joanne Dru played Rollins' estranged wife and nightclub singer Marcia.

Hell on Frisco Bay marks Jayne's first dumb blonde part. She has her shining moment when she visits a nightclub with hubby Anthony Caruso. When she sits at the table alone, a man approaches her and asks if he can bring her home. "Do you have a car?" Jayne asks. "No man, a whip!" the man replies. Filming started on April 4 and ended on May 10. The film was released in the theatres in December 1955. In Great Britain it was released as *The Darkest Hour*.

It was the second time Jayne Mansfield starred in a movie with Edward G. Robinson, but this time they don't share a scene. Leading man Alan Ladd (1913-1964) had played tough-guy roles throughout the 1940's mostly with tragic svelte blonde Veronica Lake as his co-star. By the end of the 1950's, liquor and a string of so-so films had taken their toll. In 1964 he was found dead, apparently due to an accidental combination of alcohol and sedatives. Bit player Rodney Taylor (b. 1930) who played a tough-guy underling of the ruthless San Francisco waterfront gang boss Victor Amato, would later be known as famous leading man Rod Taylor, of such sixties classic films as Alfred Hitchcock's *The Birds* (1963) and *Do Not Disturb* (1964) with Doris Day.

REVIEWS

New York Times: "There's nothing here to make you dizzy — just the usual murders, mayhems and intrigues."

Variety: "As noted, Robinson stands out. Miss Dru is good as the long-suffering wife and her singer character has two oldies, "The Very Thought of You" and "It Had To Be You", to vocalize."

WITH ANTHONY CARUSO IN *HELL ON FRISCO BAY* (1955).

WITH MICKEY SHAUGNESSY IN *THE BURGLAR* (1955).

THE BURGLAR
1955 — Columbia
90 minutes, Black and white

PRODUCER: Louis W. Kellman. DIRECTOR: Paul Wendkos. SCREEN-
PLAY: David Goodis. Based on the novel *The Burglar* by David Goodis.
MUSIC: Sol Kapan. EDITOR: Herta Horn. MAKE-UP: Josephine
Clannella. PHOTOGRAPHY: Don Malkames. SOUND: Ed Johnstone
& Norman Kasaw.

CAST: Dan Duryea *(Nat Harbin);* **Jayne Mansfield** *(Gladden);* Martha
Vickers *(Della);* Peter Capell *(Baylock);* Mickey Shaughnessy *(Dohmer);*
Wendell Phillips *(Police Captain);* Phoebe MacKay *(Sister Sara);* Stewart
Bradley *(Charlie);* Frank Hall *(News Reporter);* Bob Wilson *(Newsreel
Narrator);* Steve Allison *(State Trooper);* Richard Emery *(Harbin as a child);*
Andrea McLaughlin *(Gladden as a child);* John Facenda *(Newscaster);*
Frank Orrison, Sam Elber, New Carey, John Boyd, Michael Rich, George
Kane, Sam Cresson, Ruth Burnat *(people).*

Nat Harbin and Gladden grew up together as children. Nat is an
orphan who was raised by Gladden's father. He taught Nat the trade of
burglary. In return Nat had vowed to always care for Gladden. Gladden
helps Nat steal a diamond necklace. When one of Nat's henchmen,
Dohmer, makes a pass for Gladden, Nat sends her to Atlantic City.
Meanwhile Charlie, a corrupt policeman, hears of the necklace robbery
and plans with his accomplice Della to steal this jewellery from Nat's gang.
He seduces Gladden in Atlantic City trying to find out the whereabouts
of the necklace. When Nat overhears Della and Charlie discussing their
plan to kidnap Gladden, he drives to Atlantic City to warn her. Chased
by Charlie, Gladden and Nat are cornered on the Steel Pier. In return for
Gladden's freedom, Nat gives Charlie the necklace, but Charlie kills Nat
anyway. When the police arrive it's Charlie's girlfriend and accomplice
Della who gives him away to the police.

Jayne's agent Bill Shiffrin took director Paul Wendkos to Warner's to
show him the test Jayne did of *The Seven Year Itch.* Wendkos found Jayne
too cheap looking for the part of Gladden. But because Bill Shiffrin also
represented Dan Duryea, whom Wendkos wanted for this production, he
managed to secure Jayne the part. While filming an accident occurred on
set. A tea kettle exploded in Jayne's face. She was treated for burn marks
before filming resumed. Jayne received $5000 for this production.

Jayne did a good job with the part of Gladden. The glamour which surrounded her in many of her other pictures was not to be seen in this movie. Her make-up and costumes are rather simple and plain, but it suits her well and elevates the part of Gladden to a real person. This was one of the rare times Jayne was enabled to act, rather than to shine just as a glamour girl. Jayne was very proud of this role. "The Burglar differs

WITH MICKEY SHAUGNESSY, PETER CAPELL AND DAN DURYEA IN *THE BURGLAR* (1955).

completely from everything else that I have done so far. It's a very serious part — no make-up. It has nothing to do with my body; they play down my bust, it would detract from my acting. It presents me as an actress. I play the daughter of a thief who shacks up with a good guy. It has a happy ending. I marry the hero."[9] While filming *The Burglar* Jayne was dropped by Warner Bros. "I was really broken-hearted. I resolved, though, it wouldn't hurt my performance in The Burglar."

The Burglar benefits from the excellent performances of its leading actors. Dan Duryea (1907-1968), mostly cast as the villain, delivers good

9. The happy ending Jayne talked about is not in the print that was released to the public. The author doesn't know whether the script Jayne referred to was altered during filming.

work as thief Harbin. Although a crook, Harbin shows his human side with his love for his 'half-sister' Gladden. Beautiful forties leading lady Martha Vickers (1925-1971) made her return to the big screen after a six year break, when she was offered a part in *The Burglar*. She played the treacherous Della in a femme fatale manner. Director Paul Wendkos (1925-2009) made his directorial debut with this production. He made a

WITH DAN DURYEA IN *THE BURGLAR* (1955).

name for himself by directing several popular 50s television series, but is best remembered for his *Gidget*[10] trilogy. When Harry Cohn, the head of Columbia studios agreed to release *The Burglar*, he also signed a contract with Wendkos.

Besides the quality of work from the actors and the excellent direction, the scene setting and atmosphere are also effective to tell this gloomy story. "The brooding camerawork of Don Malkames and some highly imaginative special effects — particularly in the flashback scenes in which Richard Emery and Andrea McLaughlin portray Duryea and Mansfield as children — make this something unusual and extremely effective."[11]

10. The first in the series was *Gidget* (1959) with Sandra Dee, followed by *Gidget Goes Hawaiian* (1961) and *Gidget Goes to Rome* (1963).

11. Cocchi, John. *Second Features — The Best of the 'B' Films*. New York: Citadel Press, 1991.

WITH DAN DURYEA IN *THE BURGLAR* (1955).

The Burglar was filmed in Philadelphia and Atlantic City, on a budget of $90,000, for an independent production company in the summer of 1955 and was shelved for a couple of months. Columbia studios finally released the picture in June 1957 to take advantage of the sudden stardom Jayne had found through her role in the Broadway play *Will Success Spoil Rock Hunter?* It was restricted to a feature for adults only, because of the mature nature of some of the scenes.

THE BURGLAR (1955).

The Burglar is considered as a — minor — film noir.[12] Film noir includes stylish Hollywood crime dramas, particularly those that emphasize cynical attitudes and sexual motivations. Hollywood's classic film noir period is generally regarded as stretching from the early 1940s to the late 1950s. The sexual motivation in *The Burglar* is represented by the apparently incestuous affair of Nat and Gladden. They grew up as brother and sister, raised by the man they both called father. Although the movie makes clear

12. *"Like other works by David Goodis, The Burglar is more concerned with the feelings of its characters than with its melodramatic pulp story.".... "Like many late noir films, The Burglar suffers from a self-consciousness which makes its artistry less impressive than that of earlier works with a more subtle ambience."* Silver, Alain and Ward, Elizabeth. *Film Noir — an encyclopedic reference guide.* London: Bloomsbury Publishing Limited, 1988.

that Nat is the adopted son of Gladden's dad, their relationship seems forbidden and wrong and at times almost violent in interaction.

After the robbery the gang waits for the heat to cool down. Tension amongst themselves heat up resulting in Dohmer making advances towards Gladden. The impatient Baylock blames her for the delay in fencing the loot, so Nat sends Gladden out on her own to Atlantic City until the fence can be made. At this point, it's obvious that Gladden has unreciprocated amorous feelings towards Nat. Feeling the burden and conflict of his oath to his mentor to always protect and look after Gladden, Nat falls into the web of a mysterious woman called Della and considers giving up his criminal life. But it's Gladden who stays in his

BELGIAN POSTER FOR *THE BURGLAR.*

mind and when Della's feelings for him turn out to be deceitful he hurries back to Gladden. He explains the situation to her, but she refuses to leave Atlantic City. He asks her what's the matter. "You don't know? You really don't know? Look at me, I'm a woman. I'm flesh and blood and I've got feelings. But you never knew. You never wanted to know. I'm starving for you," she confesses to Nat in tears. The scene is quite effective and is one of a couple of scenes where Jayne is allowed to show her acting abilities. Jayne underplays her role wonderfully and adequately conveys a sense of helplessness and confusion, rather than the Monroe-like sex kitten she was becoming by the time the film was released.

In 1971 a remake of *The Burglar* was made in France. Based on the novel by David Goodis[13] it starred Jean-Paul Belmondo, Dyan Cannon and Omar Sharif in director Henri Verneuil's *La Casse*. In many critics' opinion is the original film the winning picture, although *La Casse* did set the record for the highest grossing opening week in France at that time.

REVIEWS

Picturegoer (GB): "In this gloomy, off-beat thriller, made in 1955, most of the characters are slightly dotty — Jayne's most of all ...I'm glad she quit this arty trap in time."

Motion Picture Herald: "Miss Mansfield is providing a non-singing portrayal, and there's sufficient talent shining forth to indicate adequate grasp of what is apparently the main feminine role here."

Box-office Magazine: "Jayne Mansfield is a good marquee name and the chief selling angle of this modest budget crime film. The picture was produced just before Miss Mansfield scored her Broadway hit in 1955 and she looks and acts in a less flamboyant manner than the current 'glamour girl' status necessitates. However, it's a quietly effective portrayal, even if some fans may scarcely recognize her."

The Monthly Film Bulletin: "This thriller is expounded with a display of technical virtuosity which eventually becomes merely tricky. Dan Duryea and Jayne Mansfield both give very competent performances."

13. David Goodis (1917-1967) wrote *The Burglar* in 1953. In his novels he was most adept at creating the darkest and most innerly troubled characters. The things that drive these characters, their hurts and their pains, were difficult to convey on film. He also wrote the original story for films like: *Dark Passage* (1947) and *Nightfall* (1957).

PUBLICITY PHOTO FOR *THE GIRL CAN'T HELP IT* **(1956).**

THE GIRL CAN'T HELP IT

1956 — 20th Century Fox
99 minutes, Color

PRODUCER: Frank Tashlin. DIRECTOR: Frank Tashlin. SCREENPLAY: Frank Tashlin/Herbert Baker. MUSICAL DIRECTOR: Lionel Newman. EDITOR: James B. Clark. MAKE-UP: Ben Nye. PHOTOGRAPHY: Leon Shamroy. SOUND: E. Clayton Ward & Harry M. Leonard.

CAST: Tom Ewell *(Tom Miller)*; Jayne Mansfield *(Georgiana 'Jerri' Jordan)*; Edmond O'Brien *(Fats Murdock)*; Henry Jones *(Mousie)*; Julie London *(Herself)*; John Emery *(Wheeler)*; Juanita Moore *(Hilda)*; Barry Gordon *(Barry, the paperboy)*; Phil Silver *(the milkman)*; Sandy White *(cigarette girl)*; Henry Kulky *(iceman)*; Barbara Gould *(secretary)*; Sue Carlton *(teenager)*; Garry Stewart *(teenager)*; George Givot *(Lucas)*; Milton Frome *(Nick)*; Alex Frazer *(Rogers)*; Ray Anthony, Little Richard, Fats Domino, Gene Vincent and his Blue Caps, The Platters, The Treniers, The Chuckles, Eddie Fontaine, Abbey Lincoln, Nino Tempo, Johnny Olenn and Eddie Cochran *(themselves)*.

Alcoholic talent agent Tom Miller is hired by ex-gangster Fats Murdock to make his girlfriend Jerri Jordan into a singing star. The girl however, has no interest in showbiz fame. She just wants to be a housewife and have kids. At rehearsals, Miller learns Jerri is a real bad singer. When Miller and Jerri fall in love, they refuse to pursue their romance because of Murdock and his underworld connections. Afraid of the consequences of not working with her, Miller uses Jerri's scream in a record called *Rock Around the Rock Pile*,[14] written by Murdock when he was in prison. Murdock plugs the song by smashing his rival's jukeboxes and replacing them for his own all over town. The song becomes an instant hit. The rival and his gang decide to kill Murdock at a Rock 'n Roll festival, but with the help of Miller he gets away and rushes on stage. There he keeps the audience entranced with his own singing. His rival decides not to kill him, but to make him pay back by making him into a star instead. Jayne proves in the final scenes of the movie that she actually is an excellent singer.

---

14. *Rock Around the Rock Pile* was played by bandleader Ray Anthony. At the time he was the husband of Jayne's rival, blonde sexpot Mamie Van Doren. *"Anthony's appearance in the film was ironic as his career was on the decline, which he blamed on rock music."* McGee, Mark Thomas. *The Rock and Roll Movie Encyclopedia of the 1950s.* Jefferson: McFarland & Company, Inc., Publishers, 1990.

The surprised Miller and Jerri find their way to romance open when Fats Murdock gives up Jerri, when he realizes it's Miller she really loves. Jayne said of her part in *The Girl Can't Help It*: "I play a girl that has the most gorgeous body in the world, but who is totally unaware of her sex-appeal. The only thing she wants to be is a wife and mother. But sex interferes all the time. You could say that this character is really like me.

WITH EDMOND O'BRIEN AND TOM EWELL IN *THE GIRL CAN'T HELP IT* (1956).

That is why it is such a perfect part for me; I understand this character."[15] After the success of her Broadway show, 20th Century Fox bought the rights of *Will Success Spoil Rock Hunter?* to re-write it into a satirical movie about the advertising trade and television world. Before they would star Jayne in this movie, they wanted to try out their new star with the public. So Jayne was given the part in *The Girl Can't Help It* first. (The part was originally intended for Sheree North).[16] The movie was

15. Faris, Jocelyn. *Jayne Mansfield. A Bio-Bibliography.* Westport: Greenwood Press, 1994.

16. Sheree North (1933-2005) also had her big Hollywood break after playing a part in a successful Broadway play, *Hazel Flagg* (1953), for which she won the 1953 Theatre World Award. The part of a sexy jitterbug dancer landed her a part in the film version produced by Paramount, *Living it Up!* (1954) with Jerry Lewis. 20th Century Fox took her in as a threat to Marilyn Monroe, their star who declined to play scheduled film parts. Sheree played in some of the movies Marilyn refused to do, but she never reached the status of Monroe's fame. In 1958 she left Hollywood, only to return in the late sixties, playing character parts.

originally under development at 20th Century Fox with producer-writer Nunnally Johnson. But Frank Tashlin was assigned soon afterwards. He started filming on September 14, 1956; a day before Jayne arrived in Hollywood. Tashlin first shot various rock and roll numbers and was trying to cast either Paul Douglas, Broderick Crawford or Orson Welles for the Fats Murdock role. Finally Edmond O'Brien was signed at the

WITH TOM EWELL IN *THE GIRL CAN'T HELP IT* (1956).

end of the first week of shooting. Filming ended on November 5.

Not sure of how the public would react to Jayne, 20th Century Fox made the movie a rock and roll musical, ensuring that it would make profit. *The Girl Can't Help It* was the most lavish of all rock and roll movies that were produced during the fifties. It is filmed in Cinemascope, with stereophonic sound and in Technicolor. Not only aiming at the teenage market, but also wanting to appeal to a mature audience, the producer attracted the talents of famous singers like Little Richard, who sang the title song "She's Got It" and "Ready Teddy", Fats Domino, who performed "Blue Monday", Eddie Cochran with "Twenty Flight Rock", The Platters, who sang "You'll Never Know", Gene Vincent did "Be Bop a Lula", Eddie Fontaine sang "Cool It Baby" and sultry Julie London (as the ex client/girlfriend of Tom Ewell) with "Cry Me a River". Jayne's singing ("Every Time You Kiss Me") was dubbed. "The story is put together out of 347

THE GIRL CAN'T HELP IT (1956).

gags — Tashlin counted them himself — with seven or eight musical numbers that are remarkably well directed and elevate rock and roll even as they satirize it."[17]

Frank Tashlin[18] was the director that provided Jayne with her best and memorable film appearances. "The blonde comedienne's overstuffed proportions were a perfect foil for Tashlin's cartoonist sensibility. Neither

WITH TOM EWELL IN *THE GIRL CAN'T HELP IT* (1956).

adult, nor child, Mansfield's bubbly enthusiasm and total lack of self pretense complemented the spirit of rock and roll to a tee."[19] By some critics Tashlin was attacked because he used cartoon ingredients in *The Girl Can't Help It* (as well as in his other films). In retrospect he denied that accusation: "I did a picture with Tom Ewell and Jayne Mansfield, and as far as they [the reviewers] were concerned, that was a Tom & Jerry cartoon,

17. Truffaut, François. *The Films in My Life.* New York: Simon & Schuster, 1978.

18. Frank Tashlin (1913-1972) wrote and illustrated children's books and , worked as an animator at Walt Disney Studios and directed animated films before he made a successful crossover to live-action films. Among his directorial credits are *Artists and Models* (1955), *The Lieutenant Wore Skirt, Hollywood or Bust* (both 1956) and *Cinderfella* (1960).

19. Ehrenstein, David and Reed, Bill. *Rock on Film.* New York: Delilah Communications Ltd., 1982.

U.S. POSTER FOR *THE GIRL CAN'T HELP IT* (1956).

and the fact that his name was Tom and hers was Jerri — which I never thought of — they said, 'she's the cat and he's the mouse.'"[20]

Nevertheless Tashlin's visual and cartoonist style is evident throughout the whole picture. In the opening scene Jayne walks across the street and makes a pedestrian's glasses shatter, ice blocks melt down with her presence and milk bottles explode with boiling milk. A paper boy exclaims:

THE GIRL CAN'T HELP IT (1956).

"If that's a girl, than I don't know what my sister is!" Jayne struts her stuff seemingly not aware what kind of reactions she evokes. While picking up his milk bottles before entering Miller's apartment, she holds them against her chest when she encounters him. Later that same scene she confides to Miller that she just wants to be a mother instead of the celebrity he is supposed to make of her. "Don't you think I'm equipped for motherhood?" Jerri asks Miller while bending over to put the breakfast on the table. Jayne's got plenty of witty lines in this movie. On a trip to the beach Jerri tells Miller that they are going to visit a special place of Murdocks. Miller assumes it's his place of birth. "Oh no, Mr. Murdock wasn't born there, but most of his best friends were killed there." Noticing

20. Garcia, Roger. *Frank Tashlin.* British Film Institute, 1994.

the shocked look on Miller's face Jerri tells him, "Oh don't worry, Mr Murdock put new carpets in all over."

Hollywood's number one 'blonde handler' Tom Ewell (1909-1994), was a famous and beloved character actor and comedian during the fifties. He had played with blondes like Lana Turner in *A Life of Her Own* (1950), Marilyn Monroe in *The Seven Year Itch* (1955) and Sheree North in *The Lieutenant Wore Skirts* (1956), before he was teamed up with Jayne Mansfield.

The movie had all the typical "Jayne Mansfield" ingredients, used in the right doses and portrayed in good taste. Jayne plays a nice girl and has her famous giggles and squeals, but unlike in other productions they are used properly and in small amounts. She is costumed wonderfully, showing off her figure without becoming vulgar. Fashion designer Charles Le Maire[21] was responsible for Jayne's spectacular outfits. (Jayne's wardrobe had costs $35,000). And she got good dialogue; stressing on her dizziness as well as on her vulnerability. "I knew Jayne was perfect for a picture I had ready," Tashlin said when he was asked to re-write the play *Will Success Spoil Rock Hunter?* for the screen. "I had only seen pictures of her, but I knew she would be perfect. When I met Jayne it was love at first sight. She was adaptable, marvelous and eager. She was an instant hit here in the press, with newspaper and magazine interviews scheduled around the clock. Our picture was a big success."[22]

Many reviewers claimed that Jayne acted with Monroe in mind. Her mannerism and sultry speaking voice reminded them of the way Marilyn moved and spoke. Nevertheless the public loved the picture and most of the film critics did too. *The Girl Can't Help It* (working title: *Do-Re-Mi*) was released in December 1956. The film grossed $2.8 million at the box office.

REVIEWS

New York Times: "Miss Mansfield's range at this time appears restricted to a weak imitation of Marilyn Monroe."

21. Charles Le Maire (1897-1985) and William Jack Travilla (1920-1990) were *the* costume designers at 20th Century Fox studios during the 1950's. Among the actresses Le Maire designed the costumes for are Marilyn Monroe (*Let's Make It Legal*), Sheree North (*The Best Things in Life Are Free* and *The Way to the Gold*) and of course Jayne Mansfield (*The Wayward Bus, Will Success Spoil Rock Hunter?* and *Kiss Them For Me*). Travilla was famous for Monroe's dresses in *Gentlemen Prefer Blondes, The Seven Year Itch* and *Bus Stop* among others.

22. Mann, May. *Jayne Mansfield: A Biography.* New York: Drake, 1973.

Film Review 1957-1958 (GB): "Gay, witty and satirical comedy which has something amusing to say about Rock 'n' Roll, shapely blonde dolls (new star Jayne Mansfield, a lovely, real funny performance) and other things. First rate entertainment."

Cue: "Jayne Mansfield is the epitome of the dumb blonde who looks kept, but is innocent as a new born babe: a gal whose greatest passion is cooking, housekeeping and dreaming of a homely husband and a houseful of little pattering feet."

Photoplay (GB): "As the blonde, Jayne Mansfield is stunning. The film's comedy is centered upon her physical attributes, which gives Tom Ewell plenty of good lines."

Time: "*The Girl Can't Help It* marks the debut as a movie star of Jayne Mansfield, who has already achieved a tape measure's worth of fame through publicity stills. The plot is frankly built around the twenty-three year old platinum blonde's physical proportions."

Variety: "It is an hilarious comedy with a beat, and the younger set will take to it like a double malt and cheeseburger. Miss Mansfield doesn't disappoint as the sexpot. Nature was so much more bountiful with her than with Marilyn Monroe that it seems that Miss Mansfield should have left MM with her voice."

Picturegoer (GB): "Maybe the girl can't help it, when she looks, walks and talks like Monroe. She tries too hard at being the successor to Monroe. Wiggle by wiggle you've seen it all before. Where? In *The Seven Year Itch*."

Los Angeles Mirror News: "Instead of a horde of frantic teenagers expressing themselves we have Miss Mansfield expressing herself in this rock and roll opus. Somehow, she makes the big beat sound better."

Cahiers du Cinema (France): "Tashlin exaggerates Jayne Mansfield's statuesque figure with false breasts and all the rest of it, but instead of ridiculing her, he makes her a likeable and moving personality, like Marilyn Monroe in *Bus Stop*."

WILL SUCCESS SPOIL ROCK HUNTER? (1957).

WILL SUCCESS SPOIL ROCK HUNTER?

1957 — 20th Century Fox
95 minutes, Color

PRODUCER: Frank Tashlin. DIRECTOR: Frank Tashlin. SCREENPLAY: Frank Tashlin. MUSICAL DIRECTOR: Lionel Newman. EDITOR: Hugh S. Fowler. MAKE-UP: Ben Nye. PHOTOGRAPHY: Joe MacDonald. SOUND: E. Clayton Ward & Frank Moran.

CAST: Jayne Mansfield *(Rita Marlowe)*; Tony Randall *(Rockwell Hunter)*; Betsy Drake *(Jenny)*; Joan Blondell *(Violet)*; John Williams *(Le Salle Jr.)*; Henry Jones *(Rufus)*; Lili Gentle *(April Hunter)*; Mickey Hargitay *(Bobo Brannigansky)*; Groucho Marx *(George Schmidlapp)*; Georgia Carr *(Calypso Singer)*; Ann McRea *(Gladys)*; Lida Piazza *(Junior's Secretary)*; Bob Adler *(Mailman)*; Phil Chambers *(Mailman)*; Dick Whittinghill *(TV Interviewer)*; Larry Kerr *(Mr. Ezzarus)*; Sherrill Terry *(Annie)*; Mack Williams *(Hotel Doorman)*; Patrick Powell *(Receptionist)*; Carmen Nisbit *(Breakfast Food Demonstrator)*; Richard Deems *(Razor Demonstrator)*; Don Corey *(voice of Ed Sullivan)*; Benny Rubin *(Theatre Manager)*; Minta Durfee *(scrubwoman)*; Edith Russell *(scrubwoman)*; Alberto Morin *(Frenchman)*; Louis Mercier *(Frenchman)*; Barbara Eden *(Miss Carstairs)*.

ADVERTISING MATERIAL FOR *WILL SUCCESS SPOIL ROCK HUNTER?* (1957).

Rockwell Hunter works for an advertising company in New York. He needs a winning ad campaign for the 'Stay-Put' lipstick account. In Hollywood, voluptuous movie star Rita Marlowe has an argument with her Television Jungle series star, boyfriend Bobo, and leaves for New York. Rockwell wants Miss Marlowe, who is known for her famous lips, for his campaign. Rita agrees if Rockwell will pretend to be her lover, in

WITH JOAN BLONDELL IN *WILL SUCCESS SPOIL ROCK HUNTER?* (1957).

order to make her boyfriend jealous. The campaign is a success. When Jayne meets the man — George Schmidlapp — she has always loved, she chooses married life above stardom. Rockwell marries his girlfriend Jenny and leaves the advertisement business to work as a chicken farmer!

The comparison between Jayne and Marilyn Monroe was made again, when Jayne/Rita Marlowe leaves Hollywood for New York to start her own production company and when Rita confides in Hunter that the film studio bosses are doubtful about casting her in a movie about two Russian brothers. Both are obvious references to Marilyn Monroe.[23] While leaving

23. Marilyn Monroe left Hollywood for New York in 1955. In New York she attended Lee Strasberg's acting classes. Upon her return to Hollywood she formed her own production company with photographer and friend Milton Greene. She also wanted to play the part of Grushenka in *The Brothers Karamazov* (1958), but the executives of 20th Century Fox disapproved, so the producers chose Maria Schell instead.

Hollywood at the airport with her secretary Violet, Rita answers the TV interviewer's question over why she's going to New York: "I'm just going to New York with my secretary to rest and seclusion." In doubt about the use of the word seclusion she consults Violet: "Seclusion sounds so dirty." Arriving in New York, she descends the steps from the plane wearing a luxurious fur coat which she throws back to reveal a one-piece swimsuit.

WILL SUCCESS SPOIL ROCK HUNTER? (1957).

"I have no romances," she tells the reporters, "All my lovers and I are just friends."

Besides the Monroe imitation of Jayne, actress Betsy Drake did a Jayne Mansfield imitation. Being the girlfriend of Rockwell Hunter and although knowing of the 'business' side of the agreement between Miss Marlowe and her fiancée; the flat-chested girl becomes insecure and intimidated by the voluptuous appearance of the blonde bombshell Rockwell is seen all over town with. She therefore buys a bullet bra and starts cooing "I feel just divoon!" and whispering in a sexy voice, hoping that Rockwell will notice her again and that he will understand the silliness of becoming Miss Marlowe's 'loverdoll'.

Actor Tony Randall was splendidly cast as the nervous and plain Rock Hunter. Originally Frank Tashlin wanted to use Tom Ewell again. Since he was committed to a new play, Randall was signed just two weeks

PUBLICITY PHOTO FOR *WILL SUCCESS SPOIL ROCK HUNTER?* (1957).

before shooting commenced. Boyish Tony Randall (1920-2004) started his acting career at the start of the 1950's on Television; the medium that *Will Success Spoil Rock Hunter?* satirizes. 1957 was the year his motion picture career took off. In the sixties he starred with Marilyn Monroe in *Let's Make Love* (1960) and played opposite Doris Day and Rock Hudson in several comedies. Randall was nominated for the Golden Globes of

WILL SUCCESS SPOIL ROCK HUNTER? LOBBY CARD, WITH TONY RANDALL.

1958 in the category 'Best Motion Picture Actor in a Musical/Comedy'. He lost the award to Frank Sinatra.

About working with Jayne, Randall said: "She was funny. She wasn't a great actress or anything like that, but she was very amusing. She said funny things all day long. She was genuinely funny and much brighter than most people think."[24] He preferred working with Jayne above working with Marilyn Monroe. "At least Mansfield tried to be a professional. She'd show up and rehearse and work and shoot it. At that, she was good. And she had some humor about her. Monroe! I never could understand what it was all about. She was absolutely talentless. To work with her was agony. In the first place, she was never there. You'd wait; five o'clock at night, she'd show up on the set."

24. Agan, Patrick. *The Decline and Fall of the Love Goddesses.* Los Angeles: Pinnacle Books, Inc., 1979.

Thirties and forties wisecracking blonde showgirl Joan Blondell (1909-1979) was superb as Rita Marlowe's imperturbable secretary, always ready to assist and attentive to the needs of her famous employer.[25] Hollywood's obsession with well endowed girls, was parodied by director Frank Tashlin in many of his films.[26] "Most movies of the fifties were filled with rampant Bosomania, what feminist critic Marjorie Rosen

WITH TONY RANDALL IN *WILL SUCCESS SPOIL ROCK HUNTER?* (1957).

eventually labeled Mammary Madness. But Rock Hunter rates as the only film of the fifties to be about Bosomania and its absurdity."[27] Many of the jokes in this movie are about Jayne's bosom. When Rita is finally in the arms of her true love Schmidlapp she asks him why he never tried to kiss her before. "I never could get close enough", he replies. And when asked about Rita's production company, Rockwell answers: "That's right

25. *"Joan finished the year in* Will Success Spoil Rock Hunter? *(1957), director Frank Tashlin's bright spoof of Madison Avenue and television. Though the movie was a showcase for Fox's latest Marilyn Monroe wannabe, Jayne Mansfield (repeating her stage role), Joan made the most of her role as Mansfield's secretary, and was delightful in her scenes with huckster Henry Jones."* Bubbeo, Daniel. *The Women of Warner Brothers — The Lives and Careers of 15 Leading Ladies.* Jefferson: McFarland & Company, Inc., Publishers, 2002.

26. In earlier films, Frank Tashlin used the charms of another blonde and big busted movie star, Anita Ekberg (in Paramount's *Artists and Models,* 1955 and *Hollywood or Bust,* 1956).

27. Brode, Douglas. *Lost Films of the Fifties.* Secaucus, N.J.: Citadel Press, 1988.

Sweetie, I'm president of Rita Marlowe Productions, Incorporated, but Miss Marlowe is the titular head."

When asked about this breast fetish Frank Tashlin answered in an interview: "Imagine a statue with breasts like Mansfield's. Imagine *that* in marble. We don't like big feet or big ears but we make an idol of a woman because she's deformed in the breasts. There's nothing more hysterical to me than big-breasted women — like walking leaning towers." In their earlier film *The Girl Can't Help It*, Tashlin let Jayne portray a super sexy girl who was unaware of her physique, but in *Will Success Spoil Rock Hunter?* Jayne played completely the opposite as the star who used her built to gain publicity and fame for her own success.

The character Rita Marlowe is the most crucial role of Jayne's career. The part brought her fame on Broadway, and upon her return to Hollywood she wasn't the pin-up starlet when she left for the East coast, but achieved the status of an important celebrity who had the opportunity of becoming a mega star. Besides this new career perspective, the part and name of Rita Marlowe of course stands for all that Jayne Mansfield desired to be when she was dreaming of becoming a well known and beloved movie star and all that she became and stood for in real life as the outrageous, publicity keen glamour star the world had come to know.

Most critics were enthused with Jayne and the movie, but some thought it to be vulgar and in bad taste. The Los Angeles Times, for example, commented that Jayne was playing the dumb blonde role over and over. Maybe Jayne should have taken a warning in this remark. In her autobiography Jayne showed a hint of insight on the effect of her being typecast as a sexpot: "My new bosses at 20th-Fox had to realize they had signed a star personality. It *had* to be. My publicity continued to make the papers every day. People knew me now. I was invited to big parties and premieres. I was recognized wherever I went. But this wasn't enough. I needed to prove that I could act too. As yet I was coasting on my face and figure and my publicity. I proved something to Broadway, but could I to Hollywood? So the picture was made and I never worked so hard. It was released and was a big success. The critics liked my dizzy, extroverted, funny Rita Marlowe. I was a hit. I had arrived on all levels."[28]

Will Success Spoil Rock Hunter? started filming on March 19, 1957. Tashlin called it a wrap on May 2. Since Paramount studios producer

28. Mansfield, Jayne and Hargitay, Mickey. *Jayne Mansfield's Wild, Wild World.* Los Angeles: Holloway House Publishing Company, 1963.

Hal Wallis didn't allow Tashlin to use comedian Jerry Lewis for the part of George Schmidlapp, he cast Groucho Marx at the end of shooting. Jayne came back to the studio to shoot her scene with him on June 10.

20th Century Fox advertised a lot of their productions in this movie. Posters and advertisements for *Peyton Place* and Jayne's own *Kiss Them For Me*, *The Girl Can't Help It* and *The Wayward Bus*, appear in several scenes.

WILL SUCCESS SPOIL ROCK HUNTER? (1957).

The movie was released June 29th, 1957. In Great Britain and the rest of Europe the film was released as *Oh! For A Man!* 20th Century Fox planned a publicity tour through 16 European countries for Jayne. On September 25th, she arrived in England. In October she visited Belgium, The Netherlands, Germany, Bulgaria, France, Italy and Sweden among other European countries. On November 6, 1957 Jayne arrived in Los Angeles. In the United States only the film brought in $1.4 million for 20th Century Fox.

In 2000, the film was selected for preservation in the United States National Film Registry by the Library of Congress as being "culturally, historically, or aesthetically significant".

REVIEWS

Los Angeles Times: "Jayne Mansfield repeats the role which created a sensation when she played it on the stage. Is the joke stale now that it repeats itself? That depends on your reaction to the girl. There are some men who find her a satisfying symbol of nature in all its bounty. There are others who feel that nature has overstepped comfortable limits — a fact that Miss Mansfield emphasizes by choosing her wardrobe slightly too small."

Film Review 1958-1959 (GB): "Wittily screened version of the George Axelrod Broadway stage comedy. Slim story but plenty of slick touches all poking fun at TV. Jayne Mansfield as the movie star who agrees to Tony Randall's suggestion she shall endorse a lipstick on condition he does a little public loving with her! Great fun".

New York Times: "Miss Mansfield, with her frankly grotesque figure and her lead pipe travesty of Marilyn Monroe, is one of the lesser exaggerations. She is lurid but comparatively tame alongside the rubber-faced mugging of Tony Randall as the advertising man".

Variety: Miss Mansfield (deliberately, or not) looks and moves and sounds like Marilyn Monroe, does a sock job as the featherbrained sex-motivated movie star. She's stunningly dressed (with all the expected exposures) and is handed some very strong laugh lines which she delivers competently."

Time: "Actress Jayne Mansfield, a comic genius whenever she plays Jayne Mansfield, slithers into the skin-tight role of Jayne Mansfield."

The New Yorker: "You may be sure that Mr. Tashlin utilizes Miss Mansfield's massive contours to the fullest."

Picturegoer (GB): "The fun flounders towards the end. But happily, few of the obvious jokes are aimed at Mansfield. This forward lass, with a built-in squeal and wiggle, is a delight."

THE WAYWARD BUS (1957).

THE WAYWARD BUS
1957 — 20th Century Fox
89 minutes, Black and white

PRODUCER: Charles Brackett. DIRECTOR: Victor Vicas. SCREENPLAY: Ivan Moffat. Based on the novel by John Steinbeck. MUSICAL DIRECTOR: Lionel Newman. EDITOR: Louis Loeffler. MAKE-UP: Ben Nye. PHOTOGRAPHY: Charles G. Clark. SOUND: Alfred Bruzlin & Frank Moran.

CAST: Joan Collins *(Alice Chicoy)*; **Jayne Mansfield** *(Camille Oakes)*; Dan Dailey *(Ernest Horton)*; Rick Jason *(Johnny Chicoy)*; Betty Lou Keim *(Norma, the counter girl)*; Dolores Michaels *(Mildred Pritchard)*; Larry Keating *(Elliott Pritchard)*; Robert Bray *(Morse)*; Kathryn Givney *(Mrs. Bernice Pritchard)*; Dee Pollock *(Ed 'Pimples' Carson)*; Will Wright *(Van Brunt)*; Roy Bourgeois *(Andrews)*; Tom Greenway *(Mr. Breed)*; Mary Carroll *(Mrs. Breed)*; Harry Carter *(Bus Driver)*; Joe Devlin *(Bus Dispatcher)*; Milton Frome *(Stanton)*; Harry Tyler *(Ticket Seller)*; James Stone *(Jowett)*; Anna Luther *(extra in bus depot)*; Mina Cunard *(extra in bus depot)*; Minta Durfee *(extra in bus depot)*; Ruth Warren *(extra in bus depot)*.

Johnny Chicoy and his alcoholic wife Alice own a gas station and a café. Johnny also drives a bus between Rebel and San Juan in Southern California. While on route, the bus is stranded due to bad weather. Among the passengers are Camille, who claims to be a dentist assistant, but actually is an ex-stripper and model for magazines like 'Naked Truth', Ernest Horton a travelling salesman, and Elliott and Bernice Pritchard, a couple with marriage problems, travelling with their rebellious teenage daughter Mildred. Joining the bus passengers are bus stop employees Ed 'Pimples' Carson, the young handyman and mechanic, and Norma, the star-struck waitress who dreams of being discovered in Hollywood. During the emergency stop Mildred and bus driver Johnny, unhappy with his married life, get close and the travelling salesman wins the heart of Camille. Finally the passengers are rescued by a helicopter and Camille and Ernest plan to get married. The dramatic part in this movie is registered by the reactions of the travellers, the action is provided with a landslide, a washed out bridge and the helicopter rescue finale.

At first sales man Ernest Horton encounters tough cookie Camille in the cafeteria at the bus station. He flirts with her and she lets him know right there and then that she's not interested. Later on in the bus, Horton sits behind Camille and starts to make conversation again. "If I were smart I'd be settled down and married instead of peddling stuff around like this." Camille laughs. "Hey how about that, marrying …you and me," Horton continues. "It's original. No question about it," Camille answers. "It's as simple as ABC" Horton says. To which Camille replies: "S.E.X. you mean.

THE WAYWARD BUS (1957).

Look, you're a sales man. So am I. We both know what the score is; it's even. So why don't we call it that and quit. OK?"

The movie was filmed after *Will Success Spoil Rock Hunter?*, but released earlier; in June 1957. Jayne's portrayal of Camille was one of the best in her career. Jayne never looked lovelier and more vulnerable. The critics were divided in their opinion about *The Wayward Bus*, but most of them were enthusiastic about Jayne's performance. Film journalist Ruth Waterbury[29] wrote in an article for *The Los Angeles Examiner*: "Among the bus passengers the most touching is Jayne Mansfield. As an actress she should be considered something more than a phenomenon of nature. If

29. Ruth Waterbury (1896-1982) was the former editor of Photoplay and Silver Screen magazines. She covered Hollywood film industry news for over 50 years dating back to the late 1920s. She wrote for The New York Daily News, The Los Angeles Herald, Coronet Magazine and countless movie fan magazines throughout her career and served as assistant to legendary Hollywood gossip columnist Louella Parsons.

ever she gets a role that doesn't use her body first, but let's her ability and personality shine through, there'll be some box-office records smashed."

Despite these favourable reviews Jayne was again compared to Marilyn Monroe. The part of Camille reminded many reviewers of Monroe's Cherie from her movie *Bus Stop* (1956). Both girls are B-girls, one posing for pin-ups in tawdry men magazines and a dancer at stag parties, the

WITH BETTY LOU KEIM IN *THE WAYWARD BUS* (1957).

other a mediocre chanteuse and dancer in a small honky tonk establishment. The other thing they had in common is that both girls were unlucky in love until they met their hero with whom love blossomed on a bus trip. Jayne's Camille though, is a girl who is hardened by life not expecting anything from people without them wanting something in return; while Monroe's Cherie is a dependent, insecure girl who clings to the person nice to her.

It seemed at this point of Jayne's career that this constant comparison to Monroe would damage her build up to stardom. Jayne's press secretary Raymond Strait mentioned the following insight on Jayne's thoughts about the constant Mansfield-Monroe comparison: "The inevitable comparisons to Marilyn Monroe intensified. One afternoon during an interview [in 1957], Jayne was probed on the subject until she did what

WITH DAN DAILEY IN *THE WAYWARD BUS* (1957).

she rarely did with columnists — She blew her stack. "Look," she told the inquiring magazine writer, "I don't wiggle. I walk. I'm a good actress — an original. I don't know why you people like to compare me to Marilyn or that other girl, what's her name, Kim Novak."[30]

Jayne was supported by several versatile contemporaries. British born Joan Collins[31] (b. 1933) first came to Hollywood in 1955. 20th Century Fox signed her up to compete with MGM's Elizabeth Taylor. In England Collins was known as a 'bad girl'. Joan once said of Jayne in an interview: "If [she] would stop trying to be so glamorous all the time, she would probably be a good actress." Blonde Dolores Michaels (1933-2001) made her debut as an actress in *The Wayward Bus*. She started her professional career in 1953 as a bit player in RKO musicals and was seen on TV before Fox signed her up.

Director Henry Hathaway[32] was replaced by Russian born director Victor Vicas (1918-1985) during filming. *The Wayward Bus* was Vicas's first English spoken production. He mostly directed German and French films throughout his career. On his weblog[33] actor Rick Jason (1923-2000) recollects working with Vicas as very unpleasant. "Vicas showed no respect nor patience for anyone on the set, and put up with the actors as a necessary evil. Every morning as Dan [Dailey] and I stepped onto the sound stage we'd say to each other, "Which one of us is going to murder the bastard today?" One day it would be me who'd pull Vicas through the ringer, the next day Dan would make life hell for him. The crew knew what we were doing and they loved every minute of it. He treated them like shit and we were the only ones who could get back at him. Vicas hadn't the slightest idea how to handle actors."

Jason, signed by Fox the same year as Jayne, remembers her as a clever and amiable person: "I came to see Jayne Mansfield in a completely

30. Strait, Raymond. *The Tragic Secret Life of Jayne Mansfield*. London: Robert Hale & Company, 1976.

31. Joan recalled a bizarre incident while filming with Jayne. One day she entered her trailer and found Jayne totally naked: *"She smiled sexily and licked her lips. 'Dick's trimming things into a heart-shape down there, aren't you, Dick? Mickey can't get enough of it. We both want lots more kids.' Since I knew she already had several I wondered how much longer she was going to keep her eighteen-inch waist, but then, glancing at her again, I realised that it wasn't that small. A tight Merry Widow had obviously done wonders for her."* Collins, Joan. *Past Imperfect — An Autobiography.* New York: Simon & Schuster, 1978.

32. Henry Hathaway (1898-1985) also directed Marilyn Monroe in her breakthrough movie *Niagara* (1953). "Producer Charles Brackett soon discovered that while Hathaway could be relied upon to handle the San Juan location scenes with great vitality and imagination, he "mismanaged" untalented people like Joan Collins and Jayne Mansfield. Hathaway was replaced by Victor Vicas." Reid, John. *These Movies Won No Hollywood Awards.* Lulu.com, 2005.

33. *www.scrapbooksofmymind.com.*

different light than that which she projected. Jayne was shrewd. She knew her limitations as an actress, and she knew exactly how to sell herself. She was a master at obtaining publicity and kept gigantic books of all her press clippings. She had a great sense of humor, particularly about herself. Most important, of course, up on that screen Jayne had a presence."

WITH LARRY KEATING AND DAN DAILEY IN *THE WAYWARD BUS* (1957).

The director of her two recent box office hits, Frank Tashlin, told Jayne not to make this picture: "I advised her not to do this film. In God's name, what can you do when you have to sit in a bus for more than one hour?"[34] Although the movie did not contain as much sex as John Steinbeck's novel on which it was originated, it received an 'adult' rating from the film censors, probably also because it was advertised with the following tagline: "Violent love: Alice who clung like a tigress to the man every woman wanted. Second-hand love: Camille the girl who danced at stag parties. Bold love: Mildred who ran after a married man."

In one scene Jayne telephones the person who hired her to dance at a stag party, telling him that she will be delayed. The music that is playing

34. Luijters, Guus & Timmer, Gerard. *Sexbomb. The Life and Death of Jayne Mansfield.* New York: Citadel Press, 1985.

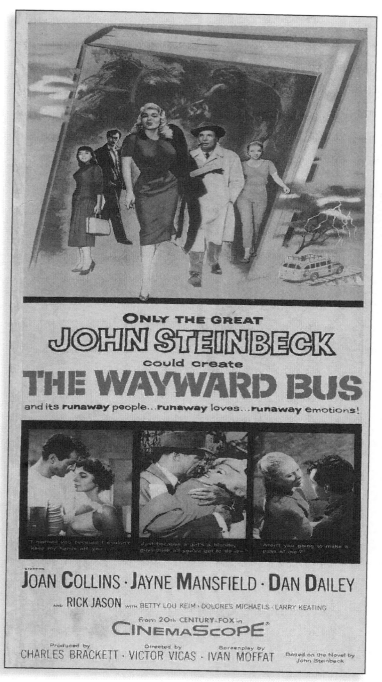

U.S. POSTER FOR *THE WAYWARD BUS* **(1957).**

in the background is a tune called *Something's Got To Give*, ironically it was also used in Marilyn Monroe's unfinished last film project of the same title.[35] The film was shot on location in the remote hamlet of Las Virgenes, beyond Agoura in the San Fernando Valley. The barn that was used in a love scene was originally built for the 1932 Will Rogers & Janet Gaynor film *State Fair*. According to a Fox press release Jayne had to stay

JAYNE AND DAN DAILEY.

away from filming for three days after she came in contact with poison oak and she broke out in a rash.[36]

Jayne won the Golden Globe in 1957 in the category of *Most Promising Newcomer — Actress*, for her performance in *The Wayward Bus*. The film

35. In a 1960 fan club letter Jayne announced that she probably would be starring in this movie and that Frank Tashlin would write the screenplay. The shooting location would have been Hawaii. "*Something's Got To Give* was originally intended as a B-movie and it was designed specifically for Jayne Mansfield and Joan Collins in 1959. This version was shelved after Mansfield and Collins' unsuccessful pairing in Fox's 1957 film *The Wayward Bus*." Marshall, David. *The DD Group: An Online Investigation Into the Death of Marilyn Monroe*. Bloomington, IN: iUniverse, Inc, 2005.

36. The truth was that Jayne needed time off to do a photo shoot for Look magazine and they could not wait for her to finish the film.

was also nominated for the Golden Bear at the 7th Berlin International Film Festival, but lost to Sidney Lumet's *12 Angry Men* (1957). The film also did well at the box office, it grossed $1,750,000.

REVIEWS

Showman Trade Review: "Jayne Mansfield plays attractively as the entertainer who calls herself a salesman and who falls in love with a real salesman, Dan Dailey. Their romance is one of the film's highlights."

New York Times: "As for the acting of all and sundry — Rick Jason as the driver of the bus, Joan Collins as his moody helpmate, Jayne Mansfield as the stag party girl, Dan Dailey as the travelling salesman, and maybe a half-dozen more — it looks as if it is being delivered by a stock company that might be travelling on a bus."

Film Review 1958-1959 (GB): "Excellent treatment of basically confected story about a wild journey by a bus down Mexico way, and the manner in which it cosily solves the personal problems of the driver and passengers."

Variety: "There is, inevitably, the glib salesman and the girl to figure the romance. Dan Dailey and Jayne Mansfield do these parts in close to mechanical fashion. They have an occasional humorous line to help lighten matters but the material for the most part lacks sparkle. The onlooker is not likely to be concerned whether or not Miss Mansfield, as a bubble dancer, and the drummer get together romantically."

Picturegoer (GB): "A spectacular landslide and a perilous trip across a bridge, straining above a swollen river, are almost as startling as the really expert performances of Joan Collins and Jayne Mansfield."

Motion Picture Herald: "Miss Mansfield is seen as a vacuous bubble dancer, on her way to appear at a stag party but yearning for the life respectable...."

WITH CARY GRANT IN *KISS THEM FOR ME* (1957).

KISS THEM FOR ME
20th Century Fox — 1957
103 minutes, Color

PRODUCER: Jerry Wald. DIRECTOR: Stanley Donen. SCREENPLAY: Julius Epstein. Based on the novel *Shore Leave* by Frederic Wakeman. MUSIC: Lionel Newman. EDITOR: Robert Simpson. MAKE-UP: Ben Nye. PHOTOGRAPHY: Milton Krasner. SOUND: Frank Moran & Charles Peck.

CAST: Cary Grant *(Andy Crewson)*; **Jayne Mansfield** *(Alice Krachner)*; Suzy Parker *(Gwenneth Livingston)*; Leif Ericson *(Eddie Turnbill)*; Ray Walston *(Lt. "Mac" McCann)*; Larry Blyden *(Mississip)*; Nathaniel Frey *(C.P.O. Ruddle)*; Werner Klemperer *(Cmdr. Wallace)*; Jack Mullaney *(Ens. Lewis)*; Ben Wright *(RAF Pilot)*; Michael Ross *(Gunner)*; Harry Carey Jr. *(Roundtree)*; Frank Nelson *(Neilson)*; Ann McCrea *(Lucille)*; Caprice Yordan *(Debbie)*; John Doucette *(Shore Patrol Lieutenant)*; Kip King *(Marine)*; Barbara Gould *(WAC Corporal)*; Mike Mahoney *(Marine)*; Jan Reeves *(Blonde)*; Sue Collier *(Girl at Party)*; Jack Mather *(Man)*; Peter Leeds *(Reporter)*; Jonathan Hale *(Nightclub Manager)*; Hal Baylor *(Big Marine)*; Jane Burgess *(Girl)*; William Phipps *(Lt. Hendricks)*; Ray Montgomery *(Lt. J.G.)*; Larry Lo Verde *(C.P.O. Submarine)*; Kathleen Freeman *(Nurse Wilinski)*; Nancy Kulp *(WAVE at Switchboard)*; Richard Deacon *(Hotchkiss)*; Maudie Prickett *(Chief Nurse)*; Linc Foster *(Co-Pilot)*; Rachel Stevens *(WAVE)*; Michael Fox *(War Correspondent)*; Robert Sherman *(War Correspondent)*; Harry Carter *(War Correspondent)*; Richard Shannon *(War Correspondent)*; James Stone *(Bellhop)*; B. Suiter *(Bellhop)*.

During World War II, three sailors (Andy Crewson, "Mac" McCann and Mississip) are in San Francisco on leave. They hire a luxurious suite and throw a party. Among the guests are blonde floozy Alice Krachner and icy Gwenneth Livingstone. Although Alice is the one who goes after Crewson it is Gwenneth he falls in love with. When Gwenneth falls in love with him too, she breaks off the engagement with her fiancée Turnbill, a wealthy businessman. In revenge, Turnbill uses his influence to have the three sailor friends restricted to a navy hospital. When "Mac" learns that he has been elected a senator in his home state, he uses his new found power to get them released. Losing Crewson to Gwenneth, Alice starts flirting with the already married McCann. The men continue to party with Alice and Gwenneth, until they have to board ship to the Pacific Ocean again.

Director Frank Tashlin advised Jayne not to take this part and play second fiddle to Suzy Parker:[37] "The two films we made together were big box-office hits. Jayne was ready for a next hit movie: 'One with Cary Grant as my co-star!' She was ecstatic. I begged her: 'Don't do it. Don't

WITH RAY WALSTON AND CARY GRANT IN *KISS THEM FOR ME* (1957).

do it, Jayne! You'll only play second fiddle to Suzy Parker'. I pointed out to her that it is she who gets Cary Grant in the movie."[38] But Jayne absolutely wanted to play opposite Cary Grant.

Cary Grant (1904-1986) started his career in the 1930's playing opposite Mae West, Marlene Dietrich and Jean Harlow. In the 1940's and 1950's he was directed by Alfred Hitchcock, with co-stars Ingrid Bergman, Grace Kelly and Eva Marie Saint. He was married five times, but that didn't stop the persistent rumours that he was actually bi-sexual. Grant

37. Suzy Parker (1932-2003) was a former fashion model who was put under contract to 20th Century Fox, because they sensed a new Grace Kelly in her. She never reached the fame and acclaim Fox hoped for. Suzy Parker made a couple of movies after *Kiss Them For Me* (*Ten North Frederick*, 1958 and *The Best of Everything*, 1959) before she turned to television in the sixties.

38. Luijters, Guus & Timmer, Gerard. *Sexbomb. The Life and Death of Jayne Mansfield.* New York: Citadel Press, 1985.

was the most famous actor Jayne Mansfield got a chance to work with in her career and although the film was one of the least successful of Grant's career, Jayne and Grant made a wonderful pair.

Actor Ray Walston recalled an incident on the set involving Jayne and Grant: "In one scene he is in bed with malaria having chills. The covers are over him. Jayne Mansfield pats him on the stomach…she patted him

WITH RAY WALSTON IN *KISS THEM FOR ME* (1957).

right below the navel. On one take, just to be extremely mischievous, he scooted up in the bed so she patted him on his genitals."[39]

The movie was promoted with catch lines like: "See Cary Grant as the handsome, debonair navy flyer, and Jayne Mansfield as the girl the whole navy wanted to kiss." It seemed Fox decided to build up Jayne as a sex doll. In that light it's best to look at the part of Alice Krachner in *Kiss Them For Me*. Was Rita Marlowe the identification of Jayne herself, Alice was just too much Jayne. Although Jayne looked beautiful and happy in the film, Alice stays a girl you like to look at, but when you get to know her better, you soon grow tired of. She swings her hips, squeals and squeaks when she's around Cary Grant or in the midst of attention from the navy boys. In one party scene she's dancing with Grant's character Andy Crewson

39. Nelson, Nancy. *Evenings with Cary Grant*. New York: Citadel Press, 2003.

PUBLICITY PHOTO FOR *KISS THEM FOR ME* (1957).

who, while dancing with her keeps his eye on Miss Parker all the time. Alice whispers in his ear, "Say something sweet to me." Crewson replies, "I can say this to you, you have beautiful hair." "And it's natural; except for the color!" Alice answers.

In comparison to Rita, a calculating star who wants to benefit from her outrageous publicity stunts, Alice is just the dumb blonde who gives

WITH NATHANIEL FREY IN *KISS THEM FOR ME* (1957).

her all to anyone who's nice to her. She loses the attention of the hand-some Grant, but just as easily gives Grant's less attractive married friend Ray Walston the same treatment. When he reminds her again he has a wife, Alice answers: "Married. So what! Everybody's married." Still she tells Walston later that it does bother her. He tells her that while he's been kissing her, he was thinking of his wife. Then Jayne tells him she is so friendly with all navy men because an acquaintance who is serving in the army, wrote to her about his ordeals in the pacific: "So he said, Alice; every feller you see, army or navy…you'll kiss them for me!"

This scene is the best scene Jayne got in the whole film. You can see here that underneath all the glamour Jayne Mansfield was a competent actress when given the right material and direction. It must have been hard for Jayne to make this character believable and sympathetic. Taking in consideration the fact that director Stanley Donen didn't treat her as his muse, like Frank Tashlin had done before, it was a hard task for Jayne to follow direction. "The cartoonish excesses of Frank Tashlin were her metier; in the hands of a restrained director like Donen, Jayne merely seems vulgar and inappropriate."[40] Jayne's mother, Miss Vera Palmer, vis-

LOBBY CARD FOR *KISS THEM FOR ME* (1957).

ited Jayne at the studio one time and remembered getting up with Jayne at 5:00 a.m. and watching her rehearse a scene with Grant over and over. Jayne was exhausted after this rehearsal. On the way back she told her mother crying: "Mama, I just have to do it."[41]

The original stage play opened on Broadway on March 20, 1945. The play featured blonde Judy Holliday in her Broadway debut in the part played by Jayne in the movie. When playwright Luther Davis heard that Jayne was cast in the Holliday role, he remarked: "She [Holliday] played a little girl who thought sex was clean. Then who does Stanley Donen cast in the movie but Jayne Mansfield, who could make a spoon dirty. What sort of supine director would allow Jayne Mansfield to be cast in

40. Hogan, David J. *Jayne, Jayne — The Vera Palmer Mansfield Story.* Outré magazine #1, 1994.

41. Saxton, Martha. *Jayne Mansfield and the American Fifties.* Boston: Houghton Miffin Company, 1975.

his picture?"[42] Actually director Stanley Donen[43] didn't have any say in the casting of Jayne: "When I found out it was to be Jayne Mansfield in the part Judy was so adorable in, I was horrified."[44]

The play had been sent to several studios before it ended up with Fox in 1956. Warner Bros. and Columbia showed no interest in the project. RKO had already turned it down as early as 1950. Although Darryl F. Zanuck

disliked the story, producer Jerry Wald believed that the original novel would make a great movie. On March 20, 1957, he hired Stanley Donen to direct the movie. Jayne had arrived in San Francisco in the spring of 1957 and she finished shooting her scenes for the film on June 19, 1957. Most of the outdoor shooting took place in and around the city of San Francisco, the hotel scenes were filmed at the Fairmount Hotel. The rest of the film was shot in the studio in Los Angeles.

42. Silverman, Stephen M. *Dancing on the Ceiling — Stanley Donen and his movies.* New York: Alfred A. Knopf, Inc., 1996.

43. Choreographer, producer and director Stanley Donen (1924) directed such classic musicals like *Singin' in the Rain* (1952), *Seven Brides for Seven Brothers* (1954), *Funny Face* and *The Pajama Game* (both 1957) and *Damn Yankees!* (1958). *Kiss Them For Me* was the first non-musical he directed.

44. Silverman, Stephen M. *Dancing on the Ceiling — Stanley Donen and his movies.* New York: Alfred A. Knopf, Inc., 1996.

Kiss Them For Me received poor reviews from the critics and is considered one of Grant's lesser films. It marked the last big budget production for Jayne at 20th Century Fox to be made in Hollywood. Fox just didn't know how to use Jayne to full effect. Originally contracted as a dizzy sexbomb to attract the male public, she proved to them that she could really act as well as giving her a part in *The Wayward Bus* emphasized.

BELGIAN POSTER FOR *KISS THEM FOR ME.*

Jayne didn't disappoint them, but for some reason Fox put the picture out quickly before *Will Success Spoil Rock Hunter?*, which resulted in the fact that Jayne's dramatic outings in *The Wayward Bus* were overshadowed by the publicity and acclaim for the Rita Marlowe — read: ultra blonde, sexy and a dizzy publicity seeker — part.

Kiss Them For Me was released to the public on December 10, 1957. It grossed $1.8 million at the box-office.

Cue: "Miss Mansfield postures, poses, thrusts herself about (forward and aft) squeals, coos, moos and gets pretty tiresome emphasizing her single level of body mugging."

Motion Picture Review: "The leading ladies don't have much to do, although Mansfield as a defence worker who wanders in and out every so often shows promise of being a light comedienne."

Los Angeles Times: "The undeniably spectacular Miss Mansfield continues her broad burlesque of Miss Monroe, but I must say it is beginning to bother me. That cooing gurgle, for instance."

New York Times: "The other half, played by Jayne Mansfield, he has artificially flung to the other boys. They can have her. She is grotesque, artificial, noisy, and distasteful — and dull."

The New Yorker: "As just one added handicap, the cast includes Jayne Mansfield, whose suggestive simpering and wiggling could exhaust the patience of a man on a desert island."

Time: "Jayne Mansfield, cast as a swing-shift Susie whose hair is 'natural except for color,' and who appreciates a uniform 'to the fullest extent,' fills a disproportionate amount of screen time, not to mention space."

Variety: "And Jayne Mansfield wanders in and out to supply good humor, eye appeal and emphasis on war-weary pilots' inclinations in a good portrayal."

PUBLICITY PHOTO FOR *THE SHERIFF OF FRACTURED JAW* (1958).

THE SHERIFF OF FRACTURED JAW
20th Century Fox — 1958
110 minutes, Color

PRODUCER: Daniel M. Angel. DIRECTOR: Raoul Walsh. SCREEN-
PLAY: Arthur Dales. Based on the short story by Jacob Hay. MUSIC:
Robert Farnon. EDITOR: John Shirley. MAKE-UP: George Partleton.
PHOTOGRAPHY: Otto Heller. SOUND: Winston Ryder & Dudley
Messenger.

CAST: Kenneth More *(Jonathan Tibbs);* Jayne Mansfield *(Kate);* Henry
Hull *(Major Masters);* Bruce Cabot *(Jack);* Ronald Squire *(Toynbee);*
William Campbell *(Keeno);* Sidney James *(Drunk);* Robert Morley
(Uncle Lucius); David Horne *(James);* Eynon Evans *(Mason);* Reed de
Rouen *(Clayborne);* Charles Irwin *(Luke);* Tucker McGuire *(Luke's Wife);*
Nicholas Stuart *(Feeney);* Sheldon Lawrence *(Johnny);* Susan Denny
(Cora); Nick Brady *(Slim);* Gordon Tanner *(Wilkins);* Charles Farrell
(Bartender); Donald Stewart *(A Drummer);* Clancy Cooper *(Barber);*
Larry Taylor *(Gun Guard);* Jack Lester *(Coach Driver);* Chief Jonas
Applegarth *(Running Deer);* Chief Joe Buffalo *(Red Wolf);* Al Mulock
(Henchman); Margaret Hinxman *(Towns Woman);* Steven Berkoff *(bit
part);* Mary Reynolds *(bit part).*

English gun salesman Jonathan Tibbs leaves London in the late 1800's
to sell his arms in the Wild West of the United States. During his journey he is attacked by Indians, but then saves the life of their Chief. The
Indians declare Tibbs as family now.

When he arrives at the little town of Fractured Jaw, he rents a room in
Kate's Saloon. Every cowboy listens to Kate; she sets the rules. She treats
Tibbs the same way as the other men in Fractured Jaw; firm and strict.
One of the rules of her establishment reads: "The girls in this saloon are
ladies. Treat them that way unless they say you don't have to." As a true
Englishman, Tibbs treats Kate as a lady even though she acts cool with
him.

Through a series of misunderstandings Tibbs brings law and order to
the town and becomes its sheriff. Eventually the two declare their love
while Kate is giving Tibbs shooting lessons in the valley. There's a thrilling
finale with Tibbs' opponents trying to kill him, but they surrender with
the aid of the Indians. All ends happily when Tibbs marries Kate with
the Indian Chief as their witness.

In the summer of 1958 Jayne travelled to Great Britain to start filming at the famous Pinewood Studios. The exterior scenes of this production were filmed in Spain. The frontier town of Fractured Jaw was prefabricated in Hollywood and then shipped to Europe. Jayne was on location in England for three months and filmed one month in Spain.

Dubbed by singer Connie Francis, Jayne performed three songs: "If

WITH KENNETH MORE IN *THE SHERIFF OF FRACTURED JAW* (1958).

the San Francisco Hills Could Only Talk", "Strolling Down the Lane with Bill" and "In the Valley of Love". Although being dubbed, Jayne was nominated for the 1959 Golden Laurel Award in the category of Top Female Musical Performance. She ended last of five nominees.[45]

Jayne's former movie *Kiss Them For Me* wasn't the successful film 20th Century Fox executives had hoped for. All the negativism on Jayne's movie character and the attacks that Jayne should stop wearing out her

45. Leslie Caron won the Award for her role in *Gigi*. Gwen Verdon, Shirley Jones and Hermione Gingold were also nominated.

gimmicks; especially being the Monroe copycat, made Fox decide to send her away to work on a picture in Europe.[46] Besides the bad publicity, Jayne's built-up as a sex symbol also failed when she decided — against Fox wishes — to marry Mickey Hargitay in January 1958.

At first British character actor Kenneth More (1914-1982) wasn't thrilled to hear his co-star would be the 'American Publicity Mad Blonde'.

WITH KENNETH MORE IN *THE SHERIFF OF FRACTURED JAW* **(1958).**

"I certainly won't be overshadowed by her. Jayne's is a role that is subsidiary to mine. She's the most unterrifying little girl I've ever met. I'd be far more scared of working with someone like Virginia McKenna."[47] Once filming commenced More's opinion of Jayne changed. Their collaboration was really pleasant, making *The Sheriff of Fractured Jaw* one of Jayne's most agreeable film-making experiences. "It was fantastic! Cowboys and Indians and all that. It is an English western shot in Spain. I play a very

46. Already after the release of *The Girl Can't Help It* the press criticized Jayne's duplicating of Marilyn Monroe. *"There's an awful lot of Jayne Mansfield in "The Girl Can't Help It," on release this week. Most of it's bright, bubbling and new. I wanted to see more. But I couldn't because Marilyn Monroe keeps getting in the way. Mostly it's Mansfield's fault. Because there's too much of the copycat in this new sex kitten. Aping Monroe might be amusing in one film — deadly if repeated. She'd better forget those sex tricks, Marilyn was glad to drop them. Mansfield will be, too."* Stewart, Jane. *Picturegoer*, March 16, 1957.

47. Feeney Callan, Michael. *Pink Goddess — The Jayne Mansfield Story*. London: W.H. Allen, 1986.

different kind of girl. This is completely different from the things I've done so far. She governs the little city from her saloon!"

Jayne was paid a salary of $2500 a week. Kenneth More, however, made a better deal. He got 5 percent of the film's profits. The British media were enthusiastic about this film, in the States the press was divided.[48] Nevertheless *The Sheriff of Fractured Jaw* is a pleasant and entertaining

THE SHERIFF OF FRACTURED JAW (1958).

western comedy. It could easily have been Jayne's return film as a respected actress, after the disastrous experience of *Kiss Them For Me*.

Although More is the star of this movie and Jayne's part is build around his, she makes the most of her scenes. She dropped the come-hither poses and she sounds more genuine in her Texas accent, especially because there's no cooing and squealing on her part. The part of Saloon owner Kate gives Jayne the chance to shrug off the lewd characters she played before. This girl has to be tough in a time when women had to stand up for themselves if they wanted to achieve some status.

The western theme was new to Jayne. Wonderfully costumed, she blends in perfectly as the bawdy but soft-hearted entertainer and

48. *"Maybe Britain can't make a good Western! But with The Sheriff of Fractured Jaw we made the best satire on a Western the screen has ever produced — admittedly with a little help from veteran Western director Raoul Walsh."* Hinxman, Margaret. *Picturegoer Film Annual 1959-1960.*

temporary sheriff. *The Sheriff of Fractured Jaw* mixes comedy with action, which gives Jayne the opportunity to give some depth to the role of Kate. She's funny and witty when she first encounters Mister Tibbs. Later on she doubts his motives and keeps him at distance, although she knows she's grown affected by him. Finally Kate shows her vulnerability when she tells Tibbs she is in love with him.

THE SHERIFF OF FRACTURED JAW (1958).

Among the cast members are versatile US and UK actors like: Bruce Cabot (1904-1972), who became famous as the hero who rescues damsel in distress Fay Wray in the all time classic *King Kong* (1933). Prior to *The Sheriff of Fractured Jaw* he travelled to Italy to participate in *La Ragazza Del Palio* (1958) with Britain's own blonde bombshell Diana Dors. Ronald Squire (1886-1958), was trained at the Royal Academy of Dramatic Art (RADA) in London. He played on stage besides appearing in films. Another RADA student, Robert Morley (1908-1992), made his Broadway debut as the lead in the play *Oscar Wilde* in 1938. In 1960 he played the same role in the film version of that play. In all probability he met Jayne again later in his career on the set of *The Loved One* (1965). Hollywood veteran Raoul Walsh (1887-1980) was the famed director of Forties classics like *High Sierra* (1941) with Humphrey Bogart and *White Heat* (1949) with James Cagney. *The Sheriff of Fractured Jaw* was one of his last films, he retired from film making in 1964. Howard Dimsdale (1914-1991) wrote the screenplay under the pseudonym Arthur Dales because he was blacklisted by communist hunter Senator McCarthy. He wrote the scripts for a couple of Abbott & Costello pictures and turned to television once banned by McCarthy.

In the USA and Australia the film was cut down to 102 minutes. *The Sheriff of Fractured Jaw* was released in November 1958 in Great Britain. It reached number 7 of the ten top attractions at the UK box-office for 1959. US picture goers had to wait until January 1959 to see Jayne in her first — and last — western.

U.S. POSTER FOR *THE SHERIFF OF FRACTURED JAW* (1958).

REVIEWS

Hollywood Reporter: "Under Walsh's direction Miss Mansfield has dropped the squeals and other mannerisms she acquired from Marilyn Monroe and has made a welcome return to her native Texas accent."

Picturegoer Film Annual 1959-1960 (GB): "Whoever first thought of teaming Kenneth More and Jayne Mansfield deserves a bonus."

Variety: "Not to be missed. Whoever greenlighted the starring combo of Jayne Mansfield and Kenneth More has done themselves and filmgoers a good turn. These two effervescent personalities merge like bacon and eggs, and the result is a wave of yocks…Miss Mansfield gives More hearty support, looks attractive in a big bosomy way and sings two or three numbers very well."

New York Times: "Miss Mansfield is present in person — and considerable person it is, too — but her interest in or understanding of the proceedings appear suspiciously remote. Most of her time on screen is spent trying to strike grotesque attitudes in her fancy Mae West get-ups."

Motion Picture Exhibitor: "And whoever had the idea of obtaining the services of Jayne Mansfield to enact the dance hall girl the hero falls in love with deserves an extra month's vacation with pay. Miss Mansfield, who could become the Mae West of her generation, uses her Amazonian proportions to create a hilarious caricature (rough exterior, heart of gold within) of all the flashy females who ever flounced around in frontier saloons on the screen)."

Los Angeles Mirror News: The sex has been somewhat de-emphasized this time with Jayne. For once she gets away from the dumb blonde caricature to portray a free-wheeling frontier doll, as handy with a pair of six-guns as her teasing eyes."

TOO HOT TO HANDLE (1959).

TOO HOT TO HANDLE
(AKA PLAYGIRL AFTER DARK)
Associated British Productions — 1959
105 minutes, Color

PRODUCERS: John Evans, P. Hamilton Marshall & Ronald Rietti. DIRECTOR: Terence Young. SCREENPLAY: Herbert Kretzmer. Based on a story by Harry Lee. MUSIC: Eric Spear. EDITOR: Lito Carruthers. MAKE-UP: Stuart C. Freeborn. PHOTOGRAPHY: Otto Heller, B.S.C. SOUND: Charles Knott.

CAST: **Jayne Mansfield** *(Midnight Franklin)*; Leo Genn *(Johnny Solo)*; Carl Boehm *(Robert Jouvel)*; Danik Patisson *(Lilliane Decker)*; Christopher Lee *(Novak)*; Kai Fischer *(Cynthia)*; Patrick Holt *(Inspector West)*; Martin Boddey *(Mr. Arpels)*; Sheldon Lawrence *(Diamond Dinelli)*; Barbara Windsor *(Stephanie Swanson aka Pony Tail)*; John Salew *(Moeller)*; Tom Bowman *(Flash Gordon)*; Ian Fleming *(Pawnbroker)*; Penny Morrell *(Terry)*; Katherine Keeton *(Melody)*; Susan Denny *(Marjorie)*; Judy Bruce *(Maureen)*; Elizabeth Wilson *(Jacky)*; Shari Khan *(Jungle)*; Bill McGuffie *(pianist)*; Michael Balfour *(Tourist Guide)*; Larry Taylor *(Mouth)*; June Elvin *(Hostess)*; Morton Lowry *(Dinelli's Driver)*; Martin Sterndale *(Editor)*; Harry Lane *(Muscles)*; Robin Chapman *(Priest)*; Monica Marshall *(Dancer)*; Tonie Palmer *(Dancer)*; Lou Eather *(Dancer)*; Brian Tucker *(Dancer)*; Boyd MacKenzie *(Dancer)*; Ken Martyne *(Dancer)*.

Jayne Mansfield plays nightclub entertainer Midnight Franklin who is the star attraction of the Pink Flamingo nightclub in Soho, London. Johnny Solo is the owner of the club as well as Midnight's love interest. The plot revolves around him and his battles with rival club owner Diamonds Dinelli and the police. When the two tough entrepreneurs start getting threats and demands for protection, Solo and Dinelli fight back.

Midnight, concerned, wants to get Solo out of the business. She helps in Dinelli's plan to handover the 'protection' money, so Solo's men can catch the blackmailers. The plan fails, or so it seems, because Dinelli and Solo's speaker Novak are double crossing him. When they open the briefcase to get out the money, all they find are star photos of Midnight. As a result Solo was beaten up by Dinelli's men and his club trashed.

The competition between the two clubs heats up. Solo becomes an unknowing instrument in the death of underage chorus girl Pony Tail. When everyone connected with the Pink Flamingo has arrived for police questioning, only journalist Jouvel and showgirl Lilliane have the courage to tell the truth. Although Midnight's faith in Johnny has been badly shaken, she can't find it in her heart to be disloyal to him.

It is only when she discovers a gun concealed in his office after he had given her his word that he had no intention of murdering Novak and Dinelli, that she sees Johnny's true worth. For her own peace of mind

WITH LEO GENN IN *TOO HOT TO HANDLE* **(1959).**

and the ultimate good of the man she loves, she informs police inspector West about her lover. The final scene of the movie shows Jayne all by herself in the empty nightclub. She's in tears over her lost love as she walks out of the club.

The plot of *Too Hot to Handle* involves blackmail and murder, but the main focus is on minimal clothed showgirls, including Jayne in a transpar-

TOO HOT TO HANDLE (1959).

ent dress.[49] Solo's one-time friend and now opponent Dinelli, tells Jayne: "That's a very nice dress you nearly got on."

Jayne was pleased with her performance in this film: "In this picture I am the star of a night club in London and I have the opportunity to sing and dance and at the same time have some very dramatic scenes." Jayne sang two songs in this film: "Too Hot to Handle" and "You Were Made for Me".

Years later actress Barbara Windsor (b. 1937) said that Jayne disliked her and was aloof to her while filming. In one scene Jayne warns her for the promises men make to lure a girl into sin. "I know. I even know the

---

49. *"After their Miami honeymoon, Jayne and Mickey hit Las Vegas for a six-week engagement at the Tropicana. This was the debut appearance of Jayne's breathtakingly transparent net sequined dress, later adapted for her film Too Hot To Handle."* Sullivan, Steve. *Va Va Voom — Bombshells, Pin-ups, Sexpots and Glamour Girls.* Los Angeles: General Publishing Group, 1995.

dialogue. 'Baby I can get you a spot in a movie' or 'Baby you'll be nice to me and I'll fix it so you get to be the leading lady in the promised land'. And the next morning they hand you your taxi fare and it's 'Don't call us, we'll call you'." Windsor asks Jayne why she never left the club after all she had said about the seedy side of the nightlife scene. "Well I guess that's the 64 dollar question kid", Jayne answers despondently. Even at

TOO HOT TO HANDLE **(1959).**

this point in her career Jayne herself experienced these disappointments several times.

The film was originally filmed in colour, but it's hard to find the original print today. Most DVD copies are in black and white.[50] I think this makes the film less effective. When one watches the colourful trailer, the scenery might be a bit kitschy but it works well for the setting in a Soho Strip club. Although there are many ingredients that would have ranked this film as an A-movie, it just doesn't work. Jayne's acting is not bad. Her dramatic scenes are plenty, but are overshadowed by her performances which were considered just too vulgar. Jayne's co-star Leo Genn (1905-1978) was

50. *"Instead of re-filming the sequence, the foreign production decided to strip the negatives of the color process to make it black and white. By doing this, they could "paint" a white bikini over each frame of her number in which she was wearing the scandalous outfit."* Ferruccio, Frank & Santroni, Damien. *Did Success Spoil Jayne Mansfield?* Denver: Outskirts Press, Inc., 2010.

a respected English actor who made his acclaimed US stage debut on Broadway in 1939. Among his movie credits are classics like: *The Miniver Story* (1950), *Quo Vadis* (1951) and *Moby Dick* (1956). The presence of actor Karlheinz Böhm (b. 1928) — billed as Carl Boehm — was well chosen because he was the beloved lead in the Romy Schneider *Sisi* films and had just made the well received picture *Peeping Tom* (1959). Here he

U.S. POSTER FOR *TOO HOT TO HANDLE* (1959).

plays a staff reporter on a leading continental magazine, who has been assigned to write a feature on the boom in London strip clubs.

Still all these elements didn't guarantee *Too Hot To Handle* to be a success. The direction of Terence Young[51] promised more than he delivered. He would later make the first Bond film *Dr. No* (1962) with more success. If only he would have used Jayne as the first Bond girl! (The actor Ian Fleming [1888-1969] in the cast, is not to be confused with the other Ian Fleming, writer of the James Bond stories.)

Too Hot To Handle was originally scripted to be a dramatic film. But after completion it was edited and publicized as a sensational girlie

51. Terence Young (1915-1994) is mostly remembered for the three James Bond films he directed. He made his directorial debut in 1948. His best work occurred in the sixties when he directed Sean Connery in *Dr. No* (1962), *From Russia With Love* (1963) and *Thunderball* (1965), Kim Novak in *The Amorous Adventures of Moll Flanders* (1965) and Audrey Hepburn in *Wait Until Dark* (1967).

picture. That meant that with the US release, the picture could only be shown in the art house circuit. Although *Too Hot to Handle* was filmed in the summer of 1959 it was not distributed in the United Kingdom until October 1960. In the US the censors found Jayne's costumes too revealing, so the movie was cut back to 92 minutes and not released until January 12, 1961. US audience saw the film as *Playgirl After Dark*.

LOBBY CARD FOR *TOO HOT TO HANDLE* (1959).

Jayne explained to her fans in a newsletter why the film's release was delayed: "*Too Hot to Handle* is now owned by a New York millionaire. Allied Artists Pictures is trying very hard to get the rights on this. I believe they will be successful. If so, then you will be seeing it on the screen shortly thereafter."

Jayne's days as a celebrated movie star seemed over. She didn't want to be loaned-out and leave the country for England again. On January 13, 1960 she visited the army base in Alaska and appeared on 'Bob Hope's Buick Christmas Show'. In the sketch he asked Jayne what she was doing in England, to which she answers: "I was making a picture called *Too Hot To Handle*, but I guess in the United States it will be called *Midnight*. Wait till you see it, it's in Wide-Screen." "Sure it is!" Hope replies, resulting in a huge applause and a lot of wolf whistles from the army men.

Jayne's agent at the time, Bill Shiffrin described why Jayne's career came into decline: "I think she was a better actress than Novak or Monroe. She had a heart. She had emotions. She should have stressed her acting and not her personality. She had talent but after all her tomfoolery no one would buy her."[52]

The actor who would later become world famous as Count Dracula, Christopher Lee (b. 1922) remembered in a 1983 interview how pleasant working with Jayne Mansfield was: "Jayne Mansfield — the greatest sex symbol of her day — came on and went through all her acts, which formed part of the picture. It was a lot of fun. She was a charming and delightful woman; so quiet and shy. I've still got the silver ashtray she gave me. She gave it to people at the end of the film. She was charming and worked real hard; a real pro."

REVIEWS

Variety: "Jayne Mansfield made a 6,000 mile journey to make this British meller, but the trip hardly seems worth it. It will need all her marquee value to sell this dubious and seamy piece of entertainment which is set among the flashy backgrounds of Soho's strip-tease joints. A fair example of the Mansfield superstructure is displayed. She also sings a couple of undistinguished numbers adequately, but in a far from pulse-stirring fashion."

Monthly Film Bulletin: "This is the kind of immoral film which exploits the vices it pretends to condemn. Purporting to lift the lid off the strip-tease club underworld, it does so only to give the audience a titillating glimpse of nudity and brutality."

New York Times: "...rotten, hilarious British gangster film."

Films and Filming: "Everyone plays the material for what it's worth, and the result is a series of engaging cartoon-like exaggerations. The most wholly satisfying thing about the film is Otto Heller's striking colour photography."

52. Saxton, Martha. *Jayne Mansfield and the American Fifties.* Boston: Houghton Miffin Company, 1975.

WITH CARL MOHNER IN *THE CHALLENGE* (1959).

THE CHALLENGE
(AKA IT TAKES A THIEF)
Alexandra Productions — 1960
89 minutes, Black and white

PRODUCER: John Temple-Smith. DIRECTOR: John Gilling. SCREEN-PLAY: John Gilling. Based on the story by John Gilling. MUSIC: William McGuffie. EDITOR: Alan Osbiston & John Victor Smith. MAKE-UP: Stuart C. Freeborn. PHOTOGRAPHY: Gordon Dines. SOUND: Norman Savage & Dave Goghan.

CAST: Jayne Mansfield *(Billy Lacrosse)*; Anthony Quayle *(Jim Maxton)*; Carl Möhner *(Kristy)*; Peter Reynolds *(Buddy)*; Barbara Mullen *(Ma Piper)*; Robert Brown *(Bob Crowther)*; Dermot Walsh *(Inspector Willis)*; Patrick Holt *(Max)*; Edward Judd *(Sergeant Gittens)*; John Bennett *(Spider)*; Lorraine Clewes *(Mrs. Rick)*; John Stratton *(Rick)*; Peter Pike *(Joey)*; Marigold Russell *(Hostess)*; Liane Marelli *(Striptease Artiste)*; William McGuffie *(Pianist)*; John Wood *(School Inspector)*; Richard Shaw *(Lorry Driver)*; Bryan Pringle *(Sergeant)*; Bill Shine *(Farm Labourer)*; Wally Patch *(Ticket Collector)*; David Davenport *(Policeman)*; Victor Brooks *(Foreman)*; Arthur Brough *(Landlord)*; Lloyd Lamble *(Dr. Westerly)*.

Billy Lacrosse leads an English gang of burglars. Jim Maxton, who's in love with Billy, is talked into helping with a robbery. He agrees to drive the car with the loot into the country, then hide it and wait for the police investigations to end. When he returns home, the police are waiting. He is tried, convicted and sentenced for eight years in prison. When he is released after five years, he discovers that Billy is now living with Kristy, the new leader of the gang. Together they had turned Jim into the police in a failed attempt to claim the money for themselves. Kristy decides to kidnap Jim's son to find out where the hidden loot is. With the help of Billy, Maxton rescues his son. But at the same moment Scotland Yard arrests the gang members, including Billy. She goes to jail, but Maxton vows that he will wait for her.

Jayne sang one song (dubbed by singer Joan Small), namely "The Challenge of Love", in an outrageous dress that emphasized her hour glass figure, in her own 'Harlequin Club'.[53] As in previous films Jayne's physique was accentuated by most of her costumes. She wears dresses

---

53. Originally Jayne sang two songs. The song called "Love's Right Under Your Arms", was cut from the final version of the movie. A single version of "The Challenge of Love" was planned but never released.

with plunging necklines and a very tight fitting black evening dress, in which she is explicitly filmed from the side.

The film opened with Jayne as a brunette. We see a seedy bedroom, an open window with neon lights outside and we hear a wild Jazz orchestra playing and Jayne talk to Anthony Quayle while we see her legs, she's adjusting her stockings. She begs Quayle to let her make the call to

PIN UP FROM *THE CHALLENGE* (1960).

Kristy, telling him that Quayle is joining them in the planned robbery. Then the films makes a leap in time of five years, and Jayne has changed into a stunning blonde. When accused by Quayle of having an affair with Kristy while he was inside, she snaps "Would you expect me to be a nun?!" But that's about as tough as we see her in the rest of the film. Her love for Quayle is so strong that she betrays Kristy, gets shot in a fight and is sentenced to doing time in prison.

The movie also marks Jayne's first topless scene. Although it's not full frontal nudity, Jayne eagerly informed the press that: "they had to talk to me for three hours to persuade me to do a bedroom sequence without wearing a bra for *The Challenge*."[54] Working on this production wasn't a

54. The scene was cut out of the British and US prints of the film. It was supposedly shown in South America and some countries in Europe. It seems there are no more prints of this uncensored scene today.

happy experience for Jayne. Working days of sixteen hours were common. Jayne found out she was pregnant, but miscarried. According to Raymond Strait, Jayne was in the worst physical condition she had ever been in. "She didn't even feel like getting out of bed in the morning, much less spending long hours under hot lights on a set making a picture she couldn't stand."[55] Jayne had good support of two well trained actors. Sir Anthony

WITH ANTHONY QUAYLE IN *THE CHALLENGE* **(1960).**

Quayle (1913-1989) was a renowned British actor of stage and screen during 6 decades. Among his pictures are Alfred Hitchcock's *The Wrong Man* (1956), *The Guns of Navarone* (1961) and *Lawrence of Arabia* (1962). Austrian born actor Carl Möhner (1921-2005) played in many international productions. He starred in German, Italian, French, English and American movies. Among his films are: *Du Rififi Chez les Hommes* (1955) which is still played to full (art) houses in the United States and elsewhere in the world, and *The Camp on Blood Island* (1958), a stark World War II drama about the Japanese invasion of Malaya.

Director John Gilling (1912-1984) was a screen writer, assistant director and producer before he started to direct in 1948. He had just finished

55. Strait, Raymond. *The Tragic Secret Life of Jayne Mansfield.* London: Robert Hale & Company, 1976.

directing *The Flesh and the Fiends* (1960) when he started on *The Challenge*. Just like the latter, this film also contained semi nude scenes — of barmaids with their tops slipping down exposing their breasts — for the Continental version. In the sixties he directed many chiller movies for the famous Hammer Films company.

Jayne's role in *The Challenge* seems exactly the opposite of her earlier

WITH CARL MOHNER IN *THE CHALLENGE* (1960).

part in *Too Hot to Handle*, where she played a girl who dislikes the mafia practises that she is confronted with through her lover. In *The Challenge* Jayne herself heads a gang of crooks. But what the two girls have in common is that they both make up for their own or their loved ones' mistakes. Billy confronts Kristy that she will expose him, because she doesn't agree with the kidnapping of Maxton's son. But unlike Midnight losing her love with this action, Billy does get the man she desires in the end. Jayne has a couple of scenes where she is confronted with her past and the effect it has on her present life. All she wants is to break free from her underworld connections and built up a normal life with Jim Maxton and his son. In contrast to the gang leading hellcat is the blonde nightclub owner/singer Jim meets when he is released from prison.

As the blonde Billy, Jayne's part in the film's story is less effective. As far as the British press boys were concerned Jayne failed to impress: "The only good thing about this film is the performance of Anthony Quayle," was a much read review. And indeed it was Quayle's part the movie was built up around. Then again, Jayne also has a couple of scenes which showcase her talent. Especially in the first half hour of the film Jayne is quite good as the brunette tough girl. When Kristy introduces Billy to the rest of the — male — gang members, they are confused she's not a

WITH CARL MOHNER IN *THE CHALLENGE* (1960).

man. "My folks had a kind of last minute recap," she tells them with a cigarette dangling in the corner of her mouth. And later on, when the gang has successfully robbed a money van, she shakes off a police car in a wild car chase. "I always wanted to crash a police car," she tells the boys in the backseat. Why Billy is such a tough girl the film leaves unanswered.

Before filming commenced, Jayne told the British press: "I have had to cancel long-standing cabaret engagements on the Continent to make this film, but this part is one I can't miss. It gives me great dramatic scope, and that is exactly what I want. Recently I said that I've done so many comedies that I want a chance to prove myself in strong dramatic roles, and since I said that offers have been coming in from all over the world. They've been wonderful offers, and it was only after a great deal of consideration that I accepted *The Challenge*."

The Challenge was released in the UK in May, 1960. In the United States the film was released as *It Takes a Thief* on August 14th, 1963.

REVIEWS

New York Times: "*It Takes a Thief* gives the singularly untalented Jayne Mansfield a chance to mastermind a gang of thugs and make an emotional wreck of Anthony Quayle. Miss Mansfield is still Miss Mansfield and then some — undulating beneath a brunette wig and snarling like a fury."

Monthly Film Bulletin: "The sight of Jayne Mansfield as the brains, doing the books by day in horn-rims and black wig, slinking about in sequins by night and entertaining her guests with little songs, provides at least one good laugh."

Variety: "This is a fairly conventional melodrama but, though it won't advance Jayne Mansfield's career over much, her presence in the cast, together with Anthony Quayle, Carl Mohner and some reliable British stock, should make it a useful box office prospect. Miss Mansfield does little for her role, though she seems happier in the latter sequences than as a tough gang leader. It isn't easy to see why Miss Mansfield should have elected to stay on in Britain to appear in this film."

Motion Picture Herald: "Miss Mansfield emerges as a dramatic actress of considerable impact here; she has a role into which she can finally project far beyond the previous Mansfield showings. She manages to convey the necessary urgency, piquancy and subtlety. Direction is taunt, studied and suspenseful."

BELGIAN POSTER FOR *THE CHALLENGE* (1959).

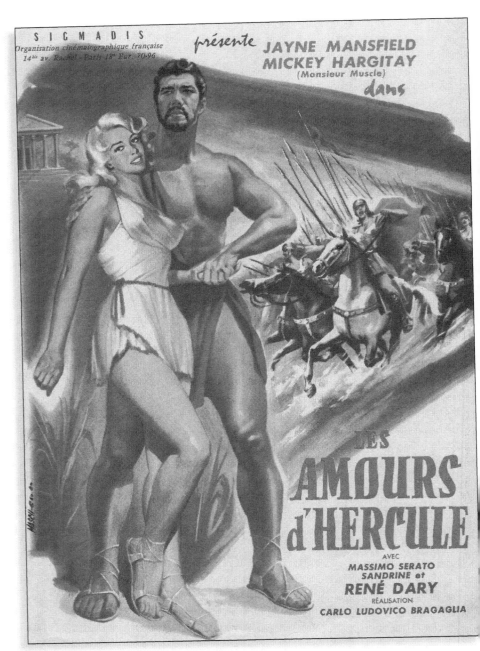

FRENCH POSTER ART FOR *GLI AMORI DI ERCOLE* (1960) SHOWS A BLONDE JAYNE.

GLI AMORI DI ERCOLE
(AKA THE LOVES OF HERCULES)
Grandi Schermi Italiani — 1960
105 minutes, Color

PRODUCER: Alberto Manca. DIRECTOR: Carlo Ludovico Bragaglia. SCREENPLAY: Allesandro Continenza & Luciano Doria. Based on the story by Alberto Manca. MUSIC: Carlo Innocenzi. EDITOR: Renato Cinquini. MAKE-UP: Amato Garbini & Duilio Scarozza. PHOTOGRAPHY: Enzo Serafin. SOUND: Renato Cauderi, Luigi Puri & Pietro Spadoni.

CAST: Jayne Mansfield *(Dejaneira/Hippolyte)*; Mickey Hargitay *(Ercole)*; Massimo Serato *(Lico)*; Moira Orfei *(Némée)*; René Dary *(Il Generale)*; Gil Vidal *(Achilles)*; Arturo Bragaglia *(King Uritho)*; Olga Solbelli *(Maga)*; Tina Gloriana *(Hippolyte)*; Rossella Como *(Elleia)*; Giulio Donnini *(Iarchus, Head Priest)*; Sandrine *(Mecara)*; Lidia Alfonsi *(The Oracle)*; Aldo Pedinotti *(Halcyone)*; Andrea Aureli; Andrea Scotti; Giana Loti; Barbara Florian; Giovanna Galletti; Antonio Gradoli; Cesare Fantoni; Sergio Calò.

When the son of Jupiter, Hercules, returns from one of his adventures, he finds his wife Mecara and his friends murdered by the army of Alcalia. On his way to avenge his wife's death, Hercules meets princess Dejaneira, who is the daughter of his enemy king Uritho. The king's cruel counsellor Lico murders the king and he wants the princess to marry him. Hercules falls in love with Dejaneira. Because Hercules won't take his revenge on her, for what her father did to him, the Gods demand Dejaneira to be put on trial. Hercules is the only one who can save her through a test of throwing daggers to the bound Princess. Almost losing his life in a fight with the Hydra, Hercules is saved by Hippolyte, queen of the Amazons. To seduce him, she drinks a magic potion which makes her look like Dejaneira. With the help of Amazon Némée, Hercules sees through her scheme and returns to the real Dejaneira. When he finds that she is kidnapped by Lico he pursues them. He finds Dejaneira in the cave of hairy giant Halcyone. This Bigfoot has killed Lico and attacks Hercules, who kills him and rescues Dejaneira.

Fifteen minutes after the start of the film Jayne appears when Hercules forces his way in to her city. In comparison to her slender ladies in waiting Dejaneira looks a bit bloated. Jayne was four months pregnant with baby Miklos at the start of filming; and it showed. She's quite dull as the antagonized crown princess of Alcalia. Her acting is limited to portraying distress, astonishment and fear most of the time and fainting at the sight of Hercules killing a bull (which keeps on breathing after being killed!) Her best scenes are as evil Amazonian queen Hippolyte. She seduces Hercules and lures him to stay with her forever. "Gaze at me. Caress me, kiss me. My lips are yours, I'm all yours" she whispers to a hypnotized Hercules.

GLI AMORI DI ERCOLE (1960).

Jayne and Mickey left for Italy in January 1960. Originally 20th Century Fox was opposed to Jayne's wish of having Mickey as her leading man, but she held on firmly and won. Jayne received a fee of $75,000. While filming, Leona Goldring, Jayne's friend and wife of her business manager, was amazed at Jayne's patience. "In one scene Mickey was supposed to fight a lion for Jayne. The lion would only lie down and go to sleep when heavily tranquillized. They had to go over scenes repeatedly to get any action. Jayne never objected, no matter how many times she was requested for retakes."[56]

Jayne wore huge falsies in this picture. Never before had her figure been more exaggerated than in this film. Her pregnancy was concealed by letting her wear a restricting corset, designed with metal boning.

56. In the movie there's no scene where Mickey fights a lion. The animal he does fight is a bull. Mann, May. *Jayne Mansfield: A Biography.* New York: Drake, 1973.

When the film was almost completed, production had to be shut down because the Italian film company had used all of their budget. "Jayne yelled and screamed on the phone to 20th Century Fox, demanding that they get involved since they contracted her out to do the movie. Fox reluctantly sent money to finish the film and bring home their troubled star."[57]

Italian film productions had brought renewed fame and acclaim for

WITH MASSIMO SERATO IN *GLI AMORI DI ERCOLE* (1960).

other actresses who found their careers in decline or who wanted to break free from restricting Hollywood film studios. But Jayne's 'sword and sandal' movie wasn't anything like Federico Fellini's *La Dolce Vita* (1959) which starred Anita Ekberg, nor even Mamie Van Doren's *Le Bellissime Gambe di Sabrina* (1959). Jayne's Italian adventure landed her with what probably is one of the most shabby and badly produced films in her career.

Mickey Hargitay wasn't a trained actor, and playing the lead was just too much for him.[58] The special effects are enormously cheap and

57. Ferruccio, Frank. *Diamonds to Dust, The Life and Death of Jayne Mansfield.* Denver: Outskirts Press, Inc., 2007.

58. Mickey Hargitay (1926-2006) had played two small parts in Hollywood before he starred in *Gli Amori di Ercole.* From the mid-sixties until the early seventies he played in a couple of Italian B-movies.

incredibly fake. There are two different English language versions of this movie. The European one has Mickey and Jayne's real voices, but in the Italian and the English version Jayne and Mickey were dubbed atrociously.[59] American born actress Carolyn De Fonseca lives and works in Italy and although *Gli Amori di Ercole* was post-synchronized, she dubbed Jayne's voice in the English version of the film. Subsequently, De Fonseca

WITH MICKEY HARGITAY IN *GLI AMORI DI ERCOLE* (1960).

would go on to dub Jayne's voice in all of her European films, such as *Dog Eat Dog* (1963) and *L'Amore Primitivo* (1964). She also provided Jayne's voice in *The Wild, Wild World of Jayne Mansfield* (1968).

The English language version was directed by Richard McNamara. McNamara was born in the USA, but after serving in World War II he remained in Italy. He acted in several films, but above all he worked as a dubber — specialized in dubbing American characters with an English accent in Italian-language movies. The other cast members were famous names, but most of them in Italy only. Character actor Arturo Bragaglia (1893-1962) was the one-year-older brother of the film's director Carlo Ludovico Bragaglia. He started his acting career in the late 1930's. *Gli*

59. *"The movie is dubbed in a variety of accents so that Mickey delivers Shakespearean English, Jayne West Coast American and the others sounds indigenous to locales between Los Angeles and London."* Saxton, Martha. *Jayne Mansfield and the American Fifties.* Boston: Houghton Miffin Company, 1975.

Amori di Ercole was one of his last films. A year earlier he had acted in *Nel Segno di Roma* with Hollywood blonde Anita Ekberg. Massimo Seratto (1916-1989) was the only native actor in the cast who had acted in American movies: *The Naked Maja* (1958) and *55 Days at Peking* (1963), both with Ava Gardner. French born actor René Dary (1905-1974) started acting at the age of five, appearing in such short movies as *Bébé* (Baby) until 1913. He returned to the big screen as an adult in 1934, playing parts in French and Italian productions.

Gli Amori di Ercole was released on December 23, 1960, in Europe. "*The Loves of Hercules* that Mickey and I made in Italy together is very much involved in legal difficulties over the title and the release date is still very indefinite. At the moment we can only assume that it will be resolved to everyone's satisfaction and eventually released." Despite Jayne's hopes it was not until 1966 that American audiences had a chance to see the film, when it was distributed by Walter Manley Enterprises. In the English markets the film was released as *The Loves of Hercules* and *Hercules and the Hydra*.

REVIEWS

There are no contemporary American reviews known to the author. The following reviews are ones from the last three decades.

The Motion Picture Guide: "Another film in the 'so bad it's good' category. Mansfield plays a dual role of an innocent queen who meets Hercules and the evil Amazon who wants Hargitay for her own."

The Psychotronic Encyclopedia of Film: "Jayne Mansfield in two roles, and her strongman husband Mickey Hargitay as Hercules! Funnier than *The Three Stooges Meet Hercules*."

IT HAPPENED IN ATHENS (1960).

IT HAPPENED IN ATHENS

20th Century Fox — 1960
100 minutes, Color

PRODUCER: James S. Elliott. DIRECTOR: Andrew Marton. SCREEN-
PLAY: Laslo Vadnay. MUSIC: Manos Hadjidakis. EDITOR: Jodie
Copelan. MAKE-UP: Marrico Spagnoli. PHOTOGRAPHY: Curtis
Courant. SOUND: Claude Hitchcock & Derek Leather.

CAST: Jayne Mansfield *(Eleni Costa)*; Trax Colton *(Spiridon Loues)*;
Maria Xenia *(Christina Gratos)*; Nico Minardos *(Lt. Alexi Volakos)*; Bob
Mathias *(Coach Graham)*; Lili Valenty *(Mama Loues)*; Ivan Triesault
(Granpa Loues); Bill Browne *(Drake)*; Brad Harris *(Garett)*; Paris
Alexander *(Nico Loues)*; Marion Sivas *(Maria Loues)*; Titos Vandis
(Father Loues); Charles Fawcett *(Ambassador Cyrus T. Gaylord)*; Todd
Windsor *(Burke)*; Titos Vandis *(Father Loues)*; Jean Murat *(Decoubertin)*;
Gustavo De Nardo *(George, newspaper man)*; Roger Fradet *(Dubois)*;
Paul Muller *(Priest)*; Denton De Gray *(O'Toole)*; John Karlsen *(King of
Greece)*; Benn Bennett *(Connolley)*; George Stefan *(Fat Man)*; George
Graham *(Announcer)*; Alan Caillou *(Narrator)*; Paris Alexander *(Nico
Loues)*; Stylianos Hionakis *(Marathon Runner)*; Mickey Hargitay Jr.
(Baby); Anna Karen *(bit part)*.

In 1896 the Olympic Games are held in Athens, Greece. Glamorous
actress Eleni Costa, who announces that she'll marry the winner of the
twenty-six mile marathon, is confident that her lover lieutenant Volakos
will win the race. On her way to Athens, Eleni and her maid Christina,
meet the young shepherd Spiridon. He falls in love with Christina. He
also decides to run the marathon and becomes the winner! Luckily for
Eleni, he wants to marry Christina, so the actress can marry her true love
Volakos. The movie was based on the true event of the participation of
an untrained young Greek shepherd, who defeated all the athletes in the
Olympic marathon of 1896.

It Happened in Athens was filmed almost entirely in Greece. Some
sources mention shooting took place in Rome, Italy, in 1960. 20th Century
Fox didn't release the movie until June 1962. Although Jayne looked gorgeous, it wasn't one of her best appearances. Jayne commented on her part:
"This particular actress I play had platinum hair because she had been to
Paris and is up on the latest fashions among film actresses. Well, what
she had done is copy Jean Harlow and Mae West. Oh dear, well I don't

know who was around then, but let's face it — none of the pictures today follows history closely. It's good to put glamour in a picture!"[60]

In September 1960, Jayne, Mickey, daughter Jayne Marie, sons Miklos and Zoltan together with two Chihuahuas, departed Los Angeles International Airport for Athens. Raymond Strait remembered in his book that the then head of 20th Century Fox, Spyros Skouras, personally

IT HAPPENED IN ATHENS (1960).

came over to Greece to visit the shooting location. His presence on the set should have reassured Jayne that Fox really had the intention to invest in her to become and stay a bigger star than Marilyn Monroe.[61] Of course that was not Skouras's main purpose, because when the film was finished Fox kept loaning her out until her contract expired in 1962. Grecian born Spyros Skouras was often accused of having artistic pretensions as well as having fondness for banality in his script choices.[62]

60. Saxton, Martha. *Jayne Mansfield and the American Fifties.* Boston: Houghton Mifflin Company, 1975.

61. Strait, Raymond: *The Tragic Secret Life of Jayne Mansfield.* London: Robert Hale & Company, 1974.

62. *"The depth of his banality was probably reached in two 1962 pictures, It Happened in Athens and The 300 Spartans, which were not so much released, as leaked."* Gussow, Mel. *Don't Say Yes Until I Finish Talking — A Biography of Darryl Zanuck.* New York: Doubleday & Company, Inc., 1971.

It Happened in Athens is a movie that was quickly forgotten. Still it isn't a bad movie. It does have its charming moments. The only reason why it is remembered now is because of Jayne Mansfield's part in its production. Jayne gives a delightful tongue-in-cheek performance. Some critics though don't credit Jayne as a factor in the film's appeal. "The film is interesting when focusing on the events, especially in the final marathon,

WITH TRAX COLTON IN *IT HAPPENED IN ATHENS* (1960).

but sags in credibility when Jayne Mansfield appears as a Greek movie star ready to marry the winner as a publicity stunt".[63]

Jayne Mansfield is the only big name in the whole cast. She is star billed, but actually plays a minor part in the story. She, again, plays a famous and sexy actress (of the stage) who wants to gain publicity by promising to marry the race's winner. She tries to tempt and seduce

IT HAPPENED IN ATHENS (1960).

Spiridon, even though she is really in love with Lieutenant Volakos. The character of Eleni was the weakest clone of Rita Marlowe Jayne played in her career. Eleni coos and whispers to the Greek shepherd boy Spiridon, but to much less effect than Miss Marlowe once did in *Will Success Spoil Rock Hunter?* On November 15, 1962 the *New York Times* published an article in which they described Jayne's acting as follows: " …and a famous actress, whom Miss Mansfield plays like a combination of Shirley Temple and Mae West."

63. Thomas, Tony & Solomon, Aubrey. *The Films of 20th Century Fox.* Secaucus, N.J.: Citadel Press, 1985.

In one scene she attends a race with Volakos. A journalist asks her what she thinks of his chances. "His chances with me or in the marathon race?" she replies wittily. She then remarks that she hasn't got a write up in the newspapers since the Olympics started. And while waiting for the winner of the marathon race, an announcer in the stadium informs the audience who's in the lead. When he announces that a Hungarian runner

IT HAPPENED IN ATHENS **(1960).**

is in first position, Jayne sighs in disbelief "A Hungarian?!". Of course her real life husband was Hungarian.

While filming, Jayne fell in love with Trax Colton. Colton was a contract player at 20th Century Fox in the early sixties. Fox hoped that he would be some kind of Rock Hudson, but he failed to impress the public and he quit acting after this movie. Bob Mathias (1930-2006) had a short career as an actor. He originally was a sportsman who had won a gold medal in the decathlon at the 1948 Olympic Games in London and in the decathlon at the 1952 Olympic Games in Helsinki. In his memoirs[64]

64. Mathias, Bob & Mendes, Bob. *A Twentieth Century Odyssey: The Bob Mathias Story.* Champaign, IL: Sports Publishing LLC, 2001.

he remembers Jayne as a pleasant person: "Even though most people thought of Jayne's life as a perpetual press release, she was a warm, intelligent person and genuinely cared for those she knew." Director Andrew Marton (1904-1992) was the director of MGM films like *King Solomon's Mines* (1950), *The Devil Makes Three* (1952) and *Green Fire* (1954) with Grace Kelly. In the late 1960s he mostly directed television series. *It Happened in Athens* was his first major picture that he had directed in six years.

Jayne's sons Miklos and Zoltan had cameo parts in the film. "He [Miklos] plays the brother of a little shepherd boy. He has the title of Baby Loues. In one scene he throws soup in his Grandfather's face. I had

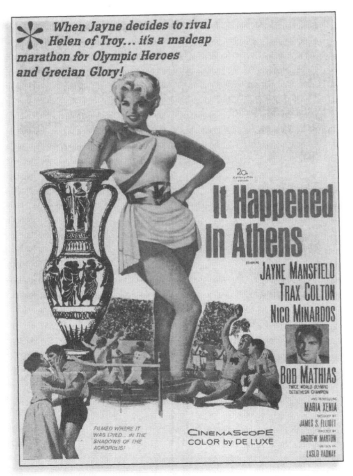

U.S. POSTER FOR *IT HAPPENED IN ATHENS* (1960).

a hard time getting him to throw the soup because he has always been trained not to do naughty things. Now, I have a hard time getting him not to do it, because he thinks it is the right thing to do!"

In preview the film wasn't received well so 20th Century Fox decided to re-edit and cut thirteen minutes out of the original print. Why the studio decided to uphold the release for a year and a half is unknown.

REVIEWS

Variety: "Miss Mansfield, who does more posing than acting, spends most of the footage dressing or undressing. Sometimes the story pauses just to watch pointedly as she begins peeling. This can be viewed as a diversion, and male audiences won't mind, but it does not say much for Andrew Marton's direction."

New York Times: "*It Happened in Athens* means the Olympics and — hold your breath — Jayne Mansfield. Yes, what a combination! Anyway, it did happen yesterday on a double bill circuit, in this friendly, simple minded tribute to sportsmanship, Greek hospitality and Miss Mansfield's chassis, in about that order. Twentieth Century-Fox photographed the venture entirely on location, and the color panoramas of Athens and the countryside couldn't be more fetching."

Box-office Magazine: "Jayne Mansfield — the only marquee name — acts as voluptuous window dressing, although her platinum hair and revealing costumes scarcely fit into the 1896 period. Except for the actual Olympic scenes, the film receives almost a tongue-in-cheek treatment from director Andrew Marton, especially whenever Miss Mansfield undulates into the scene using a breathless Marilyn Monroe-style delivery."

WITH RAY DANTON IN *THE GEORGE RAFT STORY* (1961).

THE GEORGE RAFT STORY
Allied Artists — 1961
105 minutes, Black and White

PRODUCER: Ben Schwalb. DIRECTOR: Joseph M. Newman. SCREEN-PLAY: Crane Wilbur. Based on the life of George Raft. MUSIC: Jeff Alexander. EDITOR: George White. MAKE-UP: Norman Pringle. PHO-TOGRAPHY: Carl E. Guthrie. SOUND: Ralph Butler.

CAST: Ray Danton *(George Raft);* **Jayne Mansfield** *(Lisa Lang);* Julie London *(Sheila);* Barrie Chase *(June);* Barbara Nichols *(Texas Guinan);* Frank Gorshin *(Moxie Cusack);* Margo Moore *(Ruth);* Brad Dexter *(Bennie Siegel);* Neville Brand *(Al Capone);* Robert Strauss *(Frenchie);* Herschel Bernardi *(Sam);* Joe De Santis *(Frankie);* Jack Lambert *(Fitzpatrick);* Argentina Brunetti *(Mrs. Raft);* Robert H. Harris *(Harvey);* Jack Albertson *(Milton);* Pepper Davis *(Comedy Team);* Tony Reese *(Comedy Team);* Cecile Rogers *(Charleston Dancer);* Murvyn Vye *(Johnny Fuller);* Tol Avery *(Wilson Mizner, the Wit);* Richard Bermudez *(Castro Officer);* J. Edward McKinley *(Studio Head);* John Clark *(Producer);* Art Lewis *(Emmett);* John Bleifer *(Mr. Raft);* Wally Brown *(Mike Jones);* Roy Jenson *(Biggie);* Tenen Holtz *(Doctor);* Patricia Casey *(Night Club Dancer);* Carol Russell *(Nightclub Dancer);* Joyce Rees *(Nightclub Dancer);* Robert Christopher *(Character);* Myron Healy *(Creelman);* Joseph J. Greene *(Fat Man);* Max Mellinger *(Fat Man);* George Cisar *(Markham);* Seamon Glass *(Jack McGurk);* Ernie Freeman *(Jose);* Joseph Forte *(Clerk);* John Close *(Plainclothesman);* Try Melton *(Truck Driver);* Marvin Willens *(Truck Driver);* Wally Rose *(Truck Driver);* Andy Romano *(Actor playing Capone);* Joe Quinn *(Gateman);* Emile Meyer *(Detective Captain).*

Biographical film about actor George Raft. We see dancer/actor Raft making his start in the world of show business as a dancer at the Dreamland Casino in New York, in the 1920's. His friend Moxie Cusack introduced him to night club owner Frenchie and soon Raft is not only dancing at Frenchie's club, but also takes on illicit jobs with his gangster mob delivering bootleg liquor. Through his connections with bootleggers and the mob, such as Bugsy Siegel,[65] he finally lands in Hollywood where he finds stardom playing a gangster in *Scarface* (1932).

65. In the film called Bennie Siegel.

In Hollywood Raft is constantly watched by the police, always suspected when crimes are committed. Raft becomes an established star, but his quick temper often gets him in trouble and on some occasions almost wrecks his career. He finds a new love interest in the voluptuous star Lisa Lang, makes big money and spends big money. He lives and entertains on a lavish scale, even by Hollywood standards, and soon

WITH RAY DANTON IN *THE GEORGE RAFT STORY* (1961).

becomes involved once more with the underworld.

Because of his mob connections Raft's career declines and he has to give up his lavish lifestyle. He leaves for Havana to participate in a hotel/casino venture, but he has to flee Cuba when the Castro revolution breaks out. The film ends when Raft is offered a comeback role in Marilyn Monroe's *Some Like it Hot* in 1959; as a gangster. "A gangster," he smiles sardonically, "That's the story of my life!"

Throughout his life George Raft had many affairs with beautiful women. One of them was actress Lisa Lang, played by Jayne, a character based on real life actress Betty Grable. Other girls in his life were singer Sheila (Julie London), dancer June (Barrie Chase), cigarette girl Ruth (Margo Moore) and entertainer Texas Guinan (Barbara Nichols). Jayne had more screen time than the other female parts. The other girls were just passing-by girlfriends, while his affair with Lisa Lang/Betty Grable was one of the most serious in his life.[66] "Betty had stopped dating Victor Mature and was again seeing George Raft, whom she had first met in the mid-1930s. Then trumpeter-band leader Harry James entered her life. Later when James was appearing in Hollywood at a local nightclub, he and Raft got into a big fistfight over Betty."[67]

It looked like Jayne didn't play the Lang character with Betty Grable in

WITH ROBERT STRAUSS, RAY DANTON AND FRANK GORSHIN IN *THE GEORGE RAFT STORY* (1961).

mind. Where Grable was the fresh faced chorus girl/starlet, Jayne transformed Miss Lang into a glamorous and sometimes demanding movie star. Jayne and Ray Danton have a couple of scenes together where Jayne is allowed to express different emotions. Especially her last scene in the movie, where she is mad at Raft because she thinks he's double-crossing her with another girl, is played quite effectively by Jayne. Annoyed that nobody told her that Raft had to leave Hollywood, she starts and

66. Betty Grable (1916-1973) was 20th Century Fox reigning blonde star from the 1940's until 1953. She first encountered George Raft on the set of *Palmy Days* (1931) while she was still a struggling starlet under contract to United Artists. The *George Raft Story* focuses on their relationship during the 1940's. George was still married at the time. In 1943 Betty's relationship with Raft ended when she married Harry James.

67. Parish, James Robert. *The Fox Girls*. New York: Arlington House Publishers, Inc., 1972.

6104-119

PUBLICITY PHOTO FOR *THE GEORGE RAFT STORY* (1961).

argument with him. "Why did you leave in such a hurry?" Raft: "I just spoke to Moxie, didn't he tell you?" Lisa: "Moxie told me quite a few things in one time or another to cover up for you." When Raft tells her his mother is sick and he's going to visit her, she becomes even more infuriated. "I don't believe you. You'd lie about the time of day. You don't know what truth is, you used to be nothing but a cheap crook. You told

WITH RAY DANTON IN *THE GEORGE RAFT STORY* (1961).

me so yourself and you still are!" When the phone rings and interrupts their quarrel, she even pesters him more by shouting: "You're one habit I'm going to kick." Raft replies that she should just do that and that he never wants to see her again, adding "My mother is dead," leaving Jayne behind with an confused expression on her face.

Even though Jayne was star-billed in this production, her actual screen time is limited to 20 minutes. She first enters the film an hour in the story. Although Jayne did quite well with the material she was given, it still doesn't rate her part of movie star Lisa Lang among one of her best. Given the fact that *The George Raft Story* was a cardboard quickie with one-dimensional characters, Jayne's just as good as the rest of the cast. A cast with familiar names; Ray Danton (1931-1992) who was under contract to Universal in the fifties. In the early sixties he became adept in playing gangsters in films like *The Rise and Fall of Legs Diamond* (1960) and *Portrait of a Mobster* (1961). In 1987 Danton directed Jayne's daughter Mariska in her first TV series, *Downtown*.

Sultry singer and actress Julie London (1926-2000) started her movie career in the mid forties. Jayne had met her earlier on the set of *The Girl Can't Help* It (1956), in which Miss London played a small part. After

JAYNE AND RAY DANTON IN *THE GEORGE RAFT STORY* (1961).

The George Raft Story she turned to television, appearing in many popular series. Fellow blonde bombshell Barbara Nichols (1928-1976) started her movie career around the same time as Jayne did. She was quite a good actress who supported the stars of many quality films of the fifties and sixties. She was Doris Day's co-worker in *The Pajama Game* (1957) and Sophia Loren's friend in *That Kind of Woman* (1959). In *The George Raft Story* she has a sing and dance routine in the dress Marilyn Monroe had worn in *Some Like it Hot* (1959).

George Raft was still alive when this movie was made (he died in 1980, at age 79). "The bio gives the impression that Raft went from stardom to obscurity. In real life he had roles in '50s films...Raft also had a production company that produced his television show, *I'm the Law...*"[68]

68. Fusco, Joseph. *The Epitome of Cool: The Films of Ray Danton.* Albany, GA: BearManor Media, 2010.

THE GEORGE RAFT STORY (1961).

WITH J. ARTHUR McKINLEY AND ROBERT STRAUSS IN *THE GEORGE RAFT STORY* (1961).

20th Century Fox was now constantly loaning Jayne out to whoever needed her services. *It Happened in Athens* was not put out when Jayne started working on *The George Raft Story*. Jayne wore a wig in her scenes, because her hair was severely damaged from the peroxide bleaching over the years. On August 4, 1961 Jayne finished her contract obligations for Allied Artists.[69] Jayne depended on diet pills to keep her perfect form

JAYNE AND PRODUCER BEN SCHWALB ON THE SET OF *THE GEORGE RAFT STORY* (1961).

while filming. Besides that, she started drinking heavily, changing her otherwise sunny but strong-willed character into an annoyed and tumultuous person to deal with most of the time.

Jayne said of the film: "I think this is a good movie, a different movie, and I'm proud of my work in it." She attended the movie's premiere in Chicago on November 22nd, 1961. In the UK the movie was re-titled *Spin of a Coin* and in other countries as *The Women in My Life*.

---

69. Earlier that year Allied Artists Picture Corporation had produced a movie with Jayne's *The Burglar* co-star, Mickey Shaughnessy. His character receives a 'Jayne Mansfield Hot Water Bottle' in the film called *Dondi*. In 1957 Poynter Products Inc., produced this 22 inches tall, three dimensional Jayne Mansfield hot water bottle.

REVIEWS

Variety: "Five women are shown involved in Raft's life — each a shallow, shadowy, inconclusive interlude. (Her role enables) Miss Mansfield to display her astonishing physique...."

New York Times: "Miss Mansfield appears later, briefly, as a spoiled movie queen, wriggling around like a high-school Mae West."

Film Daily: "Jayne Mansfield is ...well, Jayne Mansfield."

BELGIAN POSTER FOR *THE GEORGE RAFT STORY*.

PANIC BUTTON (1962).

PANIC BUTTON
Gorton Associates — 1962
90 minutes, Black and white

PRODUCER: Ron Gorton. DIRECTOR: George Sherman. SCREEN-
PLAY: Hal Biller. Based on a story by Ron Gorton. MUSIC: Georges
Garvarentz. EDITOR: Gene Ruggiero. MAKE-UP: Giuseppe Peruzzi.
PHOTOGRAPHY: Enzo Serafin. SOUND: Enzo Silvestrito.

CAST: Maurice Chevalier *(Philippe Fontaine);* Jayne Mansfield *(Angela);*
Michaels Connors *(Frank Pagano);* Eleanor Parker *(Louise Harris);* Akim
Tamiroff *(Salvatore aka Pandowski);* Carlo Croccolo *(Guido);* Vincent
Barbi *(Mario);* Mel Welles *(Enrico Pagano Sr.);* Angelo Dessy *(Carlo);*
Kenny Delmar *(voice);* Leopoldo Trieste *(Allesandre);* Walter Coy *(Mr
Green);* Aldo Silvani *(Rocco);* Charles Fawcett *(Gino);* Alberto Rabagliati;
Paula O'Neil; Annette Andres; Harriet Medin; Luciano Bonanni;
Danielle Vargas; Angela Cavo; Amos Davoli ; Anna Maria Surdo; Mino
Doro; Bianca Maria Roccatani; Attilio Dottesio; Loris Gizzi; Rosalba
Grottesi; Margaret Rose Keil; Aldo Pini; Mirella Piglio; Jerry Chierchio.

Pagano Enterprises, faced with a heavy income tax return unless the
firm loses a half-million dollars in a business venture, decides to make
a deliberately bad TV pilot film of *Romeo and Juliet.* Pagano executive
Frank hires French seventy years old has-been film star Phillipe Fontaine
and Angela, a voluptuous wannabe actress with no talent, to star in the
production and asks deceitful and vain dramatic coach Pandowski to
direct it. Pagano has no intentions of showing the film once completed
and when Fontaine finds out he steals the film. Pagano confronts him
and demands to return the film. But Fontaine, his ex-wife Louise and
her employee Guido dress as nuns to secure the movie's theatrical release.
They smuggle it to Venice, where the finished film is shown at the
Venice Film Festival. It is mistakenly considered as a witty parody on the
play *Romeo and Juliet* and awarded a Golden Lion. Frank has fallen in
love with Angela and becomes the head of a film production company
specialized in Shakespeare themed television plays with Angela as the
leading lady.
Panic Button could have been a really good movie. It's reminiscent of
other sixties comedy *The Producers* (1968), directed by Mel Brooks. Many
later-day critics compared the two movies, acclaiming *The Producers* to
be the better one. It is also comparable to the sixties comedies of director

Billy Wilder. Would he have been the director, this movie could have been a top money making box-office hit. All the potential is there; a good cast and a funny original script, but George Sherman's directing lacks the boldness and pizzazz of Wilder's comedies like *Some Like it Hot* (1959) or *Kiss Me, Stupid* (1964). The script produced some witty moments, with Chevalier living among all those sexy bikini clad starlets in his ex wife's

WITH MICHAEL CONNORS IN *PANIC BUTTON* (1962).

'women only' hotel and the fact that Parker assumes that Pagano thinks she runs a brothel, but they could have been put to much better use if directed in Wilder's style.

Sherman (1908-1991) was assigned for this production, because he was to make another production in Italy that same year. It was one of the last films of French born Hollywood actor Maurice Chevalier (1888-1972). He sang two songs in this film: "Un Clochard Ma'Dit" and "L'Amour is Wonderful."[70] When asked at the time, how he liked working with Jayne Mansfield, Chevalier said: "It was most enjoyable. Some smart producer should exploit her comedy potential because she really has a flair for outré

70. Some sources mention that Chevalier sang "I Can't Resist the Twist", but in most copies of the movie this performance is deleted. In those copies the scene were Jayne dances with Chevalier and twists to the beat of a Jazz orchestra is also cut.

humor. There's nothing phony about it either. When we were rehearsing a dance scene where we do the twist — now that's a dance that's ruined people half my age — her bra broke. She stopped to make adjustments, looked around, and said to me, 'Things like this happen to me all the time. And always at rehearsals — damn it.'"[71]

Forty year old actress Eleanor Parker (b. 1922) found her career in

WITH AKIM TAMIROFF IN *PANIC BUTTON* (1962).

motion pictures almost over after this movie, but had the luck to be cast in blockbuster movie *The Sound of Music* (1965), which prolonged her career as a television actress until the 1990's. The actor who received the best reviews in this production was Russian born Akim Tamiroff (1899-1972). He had just finished *Romanoff and Juliet* (1961) a comedy with a Romeo & Juliet theme also.

Jayne looks ravishing. She appears in a couple of scenes but her total screen time is negligible. After twenty-five minutes she first enters the film, when she is telephoned by her cousin Mario, Frank Pagano's right hand, to be the star in Pagano's film. Angela makes a living with entertaining

71. Ringgold, Gene & Bodeen, DeWitt. *Chevalier — The Films and Career of Maurice Chevalier.* Secaucus, N.J.: Citadel Press, 1973.

men and studies drama with acting teacher Salvatore. In one scene he has her play a deer. Dressed in a black leotard and with her hands on her head as antlers, she asks her teacher: "Signor Salvatore, are you sure I'll learn to be an actress by practising to be a deer?" He then makes the instruction more complicated by having her imagine chased by a hunter. "You gonna have to keep one thing in mind, I'm not under contract to

WITH MICHAEL CONNORS IN *PANIC BUTTON* (1962).

Walt Disney!" Angela tells him while galloping away. It's a funny scene with Jayne at her best as a dumb broad.

Although Angela appears to be a confident, self assured girl, she easily falls for the charms of Pagano. Jayne's screen time is too limited to completely answer the question if she's just using her charms to prosper her acting career or if she is a typical dumb starry-eyed blonde. Two of Jayne's other scenes hint that Angela is not so dumb as she seems. First we see Angela studying some books in the library wearing black glasses, making speaking notes and later, while visiting the beach with Pagano, she asks his advice on investing. Again the film leaves unanswered if she is serious about her business inquiries or is just trying to impress Frank.

As so many times before in her career, it looked like Jayne had been cast for decoration purposes only. Chevalier sums it up quite directly in a scene where Jayne enters a nightclub: "Excellent architecture...but the structure is too distracting."

Jayne had a brief romantic involvement with co-star Michael Connors[72] before she started a much more serious love affair with the Italian producer Enrico Bomba. This affair was well publicized and almost caused a breakup with husband Mickey Hargitay. At the time she told her friend May Mann:

LOBBY CARD FOR *PANIC BUTTON* (1962) WITH MAURICE CHEVALIER.

"You should meet my producer. He's Enrico Bomba — the most exciting, suave, attractive man! It's love at first sight — me and Rome and Bomba."[73]

While filming Jayne wrote to her press agent Raymond Strait: "*Panic Button*, my picture, is going just beautifully. The rushes look great. Chevalier and I get along real swell. I've been offered five new pictures every week. This town is the busiest! It really swings at night and so do I — along the Via Veneto."[74]

The loan-out contract to Seven Arts-Yankee Productions was signed on April 16, 1962. Her salary was set at $1500 per week for a period of ten working weeks (minus two free weekends). Jayne and her family arrived

72. Michael Connors (1925) is best remembered as TV's *Mannix* which ran from 1967-1975.

73. Mann, May. *Jayne Mansfield: A Biography*. New York: Drake, 1973.

74. Strait, Raymond: *The Tragic Secret Life of Jayne Mansfield*. London: Robert Hale & Company, 1974.

IN ROME TO FILM *PANIC BUTTON*, 1962.

in Italy May 8, 1962. *Panic Button* was filmed on location in Venice and Rome. In July 1962 Jayne and Mickey returned to Hollywood. During filming Jayne got the news that 20th Century Fox had decided not to renew her five year contract. "I feel free as a bird. I'm happy with my new picture, Panic Button. I have offers from Germany's "Elvis Presley" singing star to co-star with him in a movie and eight more offers as well."[75] [76]

Panic Button had no major release in the United States. It wasn't released until April 1964 in the Los Angeles area, shown on the lower half of a double bill. It was trade shown in New York and there reviews were favourable. In Italy the film was released as *Panic Button-Operazione Fisco*. The US reissue title is *Let's Go Bust*.

REVIEWS

Variety: "Statuesque Jayne Mansfield is the amateur thespian enlisted to co-star with Chevalier in the tele short. In her few love scenes with Michael Connors she does surprisingly well, and, of course, looks her usual self in a bikini. The camera is flattering to neither Miss Mansfield nor Chevalier."

Los Angeles Bridge News: "If you rummage through enough double bills you occasionally run into a pleasant surprise. *Panic Button* is one of them. Casting Maurice Chevalier, the youngest leading man I can think of, as a washed-up actor and buxom Jayne Mansfield in a comedy about making Romeo and Juliet into a TV pilot is a moderately funny idea to which, bless my soul, even Miss Mansfield contributes a couple of deliciously amusing bits."

Motion Picture Herald: "This is an enjoyable comedy loaded with the ingredients that make for effective traffic at the box-office. It contains a splendid cast, a zany story embellished with music, and a well mounted production encompassing some fine scenes in Rome and Venice."

Film Daily: "A zany comedy on picture making in Italy that bubbles with humor. *Panic Button* gallops merrily along, turning up bursts of comedy amid touches of corn."

75. Mann, May. *Jayne Mansfield: A Biography.* New York: Drake, 1973.

76. "Germany's Elvis Presley" was singer-actor Freddy Quinn and the film Jayne mentions is *Heimweh nach St. Pauli* (1963).

U.S. POSTER FOR *PROMISES! PROMISES!* (1963).

PROMISES! PROMISES!

Noonan-Taylor Productions — 1963
75 minutes, Black and white

PRODUCER: Tommy Noonan & Donald F. Taylor. DIRECTOR: King
Donovan. SCREENPLAY: William Welch & Tommy Noonan. Based
on the play *The Plant* by Edna Sheklow. MUSIC: Hal Borne. EDITOR:
Edward Dutko. MAKE-UP: Sidney Perell. PHOTOGRAPHY: Joseph
Biroc. SOUND: Frank McWorther & Harry M. Leonard.

CAST: Jayne Mansfield *(Sandy Brooks)*; Tommy Noonan *(Jeff Brooks)*;
Marie McDonald *(Claire Banner)*; Mickey Hargitay *(King Banner)*; Fritz
Feld *(Ship's Doctor)*; T.C. Jones *(Ship's Hairdresser, Babbette)*; Claude Stroud
(Steward); Marjorie Bennett *(Mrs. Snavely)*; Eddie Quillan *(Bartender)*;
Vic Lundin *(Gigolo)*; Eileen Barton *(Girl in Doctor's Office)*; Pat O'Moore
(Ship's Captain); Imogene Coca *(Herself)*; Richard Dawson *(bit part)*.

Television writer Jeff Brooks and his wife Sandy want to become pregnant. Jeff seems impotent, and to relieve the pressure between the two,
they decide to go on an ocean cruise. Hoping that a restful trip will solve
the problem, Jeff consults the ship's doctor, who gives him aspirin in the
guise of a fertility pill. The Brooks befriend the couple in the cabin next to
them; King and Claire Banner. When Jeff and Sandy have had a romantic
dinner they end the evening drinking with the Banners. The next morning they find themselves with each other's spouses. To make things even
more confusing, Claire and Sandy find out that they're both pregnant!
Jayne sings "Lu-lu-lu-lu, I'm in Love" in the bathtub and "Promise
Her Anything" on the deck of the ship for all the passengers and crew.
The ship that was partially used in some scenes was the *S.S. Independence*,
an ocean liner built in 1951. The working title for this production was
Promise Her Anything. It was produced by Tommy Noonan for an alleged
$80,000. Filming started on January 10, 1963 and *Promises, Promises!* Was
released in Los Angeles on August 2, 1963.
In one scene Sandy has a baby shower. All guests are females except for
one. The ship's barber Babette joins in on the fun doing an impersonation
of Tallulah Bankhead, Bette Davis and ...Jayne Mansfield. Sandy stands
up and says "I can do her too," and she and Babette play Jayne Mansfield
while the guests are cheering them on.
Jayne had two nude scenes. One was in the bathroom and the other
was a bedroom scene with Noonan. Playboy magazine ran a feature article

about these scenes under the title *The Nudest Jayne Mansfield*. It is still the largest selling issue, with 2,000,000 copies, of the magazine to date.[77] One must remember that the footage is tame to today's standards, but in the early 1960's it was quite shocking to most people. About the scenes Jayne said to *Playboy* magazine: "One thing I want to stress is that this is the first time I've ever posed completely nude. It was art for art's sake —

WITH TOMMY NOONAN IN *PROMISES! PROMISES!* (1963).

my theme for the future."[78] Upon the news that the film was banned in Cleveland because of these scenes, Jayne commented in her famous witty way: "There are two scenes in which I appear nude for a brief moment. The only objections I've heard are that the scenes are not long enough."[79]

Many biographers explain Jayne's decision to do these scenes lay in the fact that Jayne was proud of her body in an exhibitionistic way. "...what is apparent in these shots is Mansfield's obvious erotic pleasure at her open and cinematic display of her body. She appears to exult in the cinematic

77. *"Hugh Hefner was arrested in Chicago for this issue of his world-famous magazine, charged with it being lewd and indecent."* Ferruccio, Frank & Santroni, Damien. *Did Success Spoil Jayne Mansfield?* Denver: Outskirts Press, Inc., 2010.

78. *Playboy* magazine, June 1963.

79. Saxton, Martha. *Jayne Mansfield and the American Fifties.* Boston: Houghton Mifflin Company, 1975.

display and gaze at her nudity in a way that seems less like acting than a true sense of enjoyment."[80]

Jayne wore her own dresses in this movie. They were designed for her by designer and fashion critic Richard Blackwell (1922-2008). He was the creator of the *Ten Worst Dressed Women List*, an annual awards presentation he unveiled in January of each year.[81] Mr. Blackwell was not amused that

WITH MICKEY HARGITAY, MARIE MCDONALD AND TOMMY NOONAN IN
***PROMISES! PROMISES!* (1963).**

Jayne had used his creations in this nudie picture, so in January 1964 he announced Jayne to be one of the worst *undressed* women of the last year.

Jayne had hoped that *Promises! Promises!* Would put her back in the major league of film making, but the result was the opposite. Hollywood totally lost its interest in her and Jayne left for Europe to star in a string of European co-productions to which her name was probably an asset. Maybe Jayne's participation in this production is better explained by the pay check she received. Jayne was paid $150,000 for the movie and

80. Jordan, Jessica Hope. *The Sex Goddess in American Film 1930-1965 — Jean Harlow, Mae West, Lana Turner, and Jayne Mansfield.* Amherst, New York: Cambria Press, 2009.

81. The first *Ten Worst Dressed Women* list premiered in 1960, but as the House of Blackwell became more successful, the list took off. By its third year every television and radio network and virtually all news services worldwide began to cover it. (Source: Wikipedia, the free encyclopedia on the internet).

$25,000 for the Playboy pictorial. Biographer and friend May Mann recounted Jayne telling her: "It isn't the kind of movie I want. But I've got to keep the money coming in."

Promises, Promises! Is the first feature length movie to display full nudity by a well known Hollywood star.[82] Hollywood moguls in the fifties had always considered nudity as a forbidden subject. Of course The

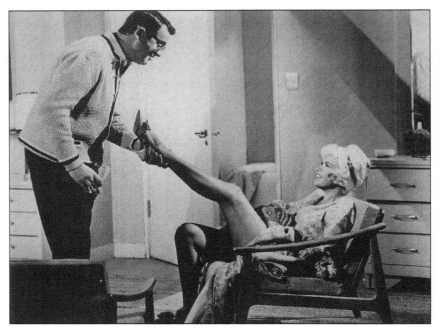

WITH TOMMY NOONAN IN *PROMISES! PROMISES!* (1963).

Catholic Legion of Decency and The Hays Code censored Hollywood's output by keeping close contact with the film's distributors. The fifties society's morals were changing with the coming of an new era. The swingin' sixties were on their way. Eventually meaning the end of the huge influence these censorship boards had on Hollywood productions." The nudist-camp genre rapidly fizzled out as equivalent amounts of flesh began to be exposed aesthetically in mainstream features. There were attempts to find another formula for the gratuitous presentation of nudity, including hooking otherwise forgettable movies on to the impressive physiques of big-name sex stars like Jayne Mansfield and Mamie Van

82. Marilyn Monroe's nighttime skinny-dipping scene in a backyard pool would have been the first nude scene in an American film by a major star, but the movie we're talking about, *Something's Got To Give* (1962), was never completed.

Doren. But although these films were successful at the box-office, not even Jayne or Mamie could thereafter claim special mammary attention in an increasingly topless world."[83]

Due to Jayne's persistence Mickey Hargitay got a part in the movie. Producer and actor Tommy Noonan was against the casting of wife and husband. He probably was worried to find another obstacle in his way,

WITH MICKEY HARGITAY IN *PROMISES! PROMISES!* (1963).

talking Jayne into doing her nude scenes, when her husband was constantly around. Of course Mickey was against these scenes, but Jayne prevailed — as always — and agreed to do the scenes on a closed set.

Noonan (1921-1968) was a bespectacled comedy actor who reached his peak of fame in the 1950's. He had played with other famous blondes from that era, before he started producing a couple of exploitive softcore "comedy" movies.[84] King Donovan (1918-1987) was an actor turned

---

83. Pascall, Jeremy & Jeavons, Clyde. *A Pictorial History of Sex in the Movies*. London: The Hamlyn Publishing Group Limited, 1975.

84. Noonan played Marilyn Monroe's boyfriend in *Gentlemen Prefer Blondes* (1953) and was in *How to Be Very, Very Popular* (1955) and *The Best Things in Life Are Free* (1956) with 20th Century Fox's Sheree North. In the early sixties he produced and played in *3 Nuts in Search of a Bolt* (1964) in which Jayne's rival Mamie Van Doren had her famous nude beer bath scene. Originally he offered the Marie McDonald part in *Promises, Promises!* to Mamie Van Doren. She declined because Jayne would be paid more.

director. *Promises, Promises!* Was the only Cinema released motion picture he directed. In 1960 he married television star Imogene Coca, who played a small part in the film. German born character actor Fritz Feld (1900-1993) played small parts in hundreds of movies and teleplays. He's the ship's doctor who provides Noonan with potency pills which are actually placebos.

JAYNE WITH MARIE MCDONALD AND T.C. JONES IN *PROMISES! PROMISES!* (1963).

Jayne's co-star Marie 'The Body' McDonald (1923-1965) was a popular pin-up model and actress in the 1940's. In the fifties she turned to television. *Promises, Promises!* Was her last motion picture. She dated — and later married — the film's producer Donald F. Taylor at the time, causing her to get special treatment while filming. Jayne was annoyed by this, therefore the women's relationship during filming was cold. In 1965, McDonald was found dead of a drug overdose. Three months after her death, her sixth husband, Donald F. Taylor also committed suicide. Other cast members of *Promises, Promises!* Also met untimely deaths. Female impersonator T.C. Jones died at age 50 from cancer, the same disease that took the life of Tommy Noonan, who only reached the age of 46.

REVIEWS

Variety: "The only excuse for this shabby, sex-propelled contrivance is that obviously there is an audience waiting to devour it. Several glimpses of a bare-breasted Jayne Mansfield and one of her derriere-in-the-buff figure to satisfy the Peeping Toms, Dicks and Harrys who frequent those

WITH TOMMY NOONAN IN *PROMISES! PROMISES!* (1963).

off-beat, anatomical "art" houses where this attraction is apt to be distributed. But beyond the occasional vicarious sensual thrill it affords the ogle-happy denizen of these cinematic flesh palaces, there is nothing in *Promises, Promises!* Her tape-measure performance can be summed up in the phrase, 'thanks for the mammary.'"

Los Angeles Herald-Examiner: "Although as a movie it's a bust, it does keep its promise to reveal more of Mansfield ...it's vastly overrated. Miss Mansfield does considerable talking, little acting, and even sings (???) the title tune."

Playboy: "It is therefore fitting and proper that the trail from 'nudie' to 'straight' films be blazed by none other than the undisputed champion of the in-the-altogether brinkmanship, Miss Jayne Mansfield. Jayne now proudly heads the scant list of authentic Hollywood heroines whose feats of bearing go beyond the call of duty."

U.S. POSTER FOR *SPREE* (1963).

SPREE
United Producers Releasing Co. — 1963
84 minutes, Color

PRODUCER: Carroll Case & Hal Roach Jr. DIRECTOR: Mitchell Leisen & Walon Green. SCREENPLAY: Sydney Field. MUSIC: Remo Usal. EDITOR: Roy Livingston & Edward A. Biery. PHOTOGRAPHY: Alan Stensvold. SOUND: Dick Peck.

CAST: Vic Damone; **Jayne Mansfield**; Juliet Prowse; Mickey Hargitay; Constance Moore; Rosana Tapajós; Clara Ward Singers; Barkley Shaw; Sydney Field *(narrator)*.

This exposé featured as a documentary on Las Vegas was filmed primarily at the Tropicana and the Dunes Hotels. Entertainers who were highlighted in the Las Vegas shows include Vic Damone, Juliet Prowse doing a Cleopatra takeoff and Constance Moore. Jayne Mansfield performs a striptease or rather a 'satire on a strip', as Jayne called it herself. She sings "Promise Her Anything" to Mickey Hargitay. (Reminiscent of the scene as used in *Promises! Promises!*). And she performs an acrobatic

SPREE (1963).

dance with Mickey Hargitay where he lifts Jayne high up in the air. The film also contains scenes of the gambling casinos, clandestine cock fights and bare-fisted boxing.

Vic Damone and Juliet Prowse sued the producers and distributing company to have their names, voice, and likeness deleted from the film and its advertising. Both performers stated that they made wholesome

SPREE (1963).

film appearances that the film company distorted.[85] The film's posters and lobby cards were all censored with stickers over the faces of Damone and Prowse. Jayne Mansfield and Mickey Hargitay did not file legal action.

Jayne's striptease act first saw the light of day in mid-1963. Jayne headlined a burlesque act that toured throughout the United States. Jayne 'costumed' in a net bra, pasties and a rhinestone G-string, performed her teasing strip show to enthusiastic audiences. The burlesque show finally reached Las Vegas, where it was filmed for this documentary. Jayne commented on her act in an interview: "What I sell is not pure sex, but a satire on it. I always ask the wives present if I can play with their husbands for

85. Faris, Jocelyn. *Jayne Mansfield. A Bio-Bibliography.* Westport: Greenwood Press, 1994.

a minute, and I only kiss a few bald heads. Everyone seems to enjoy it, as they are all part of it."[86]

Spree was produced in 1962 and 1963 with the working title *Las Vegas By Night*. Eight days before Jayne's death, on June 21, 1967 the film was distributed, but it did not premiere until February 15, 1968 in Los Angeles.

WITH MICKEY HARGITAY IN *SPREE* (1963).

REVIEWS

Box-office Magazine: "...performing in various nightclubs are ...the late Jayne Mansfield and her husband at the time, Mickey Hargitay. Miss Mansfield is not shown to much advantage in an embarrassing strip act."

Variety: "Jayne Mansfield strips in this exploitation film which makes a pitch via sensational display ads for current local engagement. What comes out on screen in poor color and static handling is a pseudo-travelog through Las Vegas casinos, niteries, party palaces et al, without any of the spectacular overtones promised."

86. Sullivan, Steve. *Va Va Voom — Bombshells, Pin-ups, Sexpots and Glamour Girls.* Los Angeles: General Publishing Group, 1995.

BELGIAN POSTER FOR *HEIMWEH NACH ST. PAULI* (1963).

HEIMWEH NACH ST. PAULI
(AKA HOMESICK FOR ST. PAUL)
Constantin Productions — 1963
104 minutes, Color

PRODUCER: Wolf C. Hartwig. DIRECTOR: Werner Jacobs. SCREEN-
PLAY: Gustav Kampendonk. Based on the musical by Gustav Kampendonk.
MUSIC: Lothar Olias. EDITOR: Klaus Dudenhofer. SOUND: Hans Ebel
& Werner Pont. PHOTOGRAPHY: Heinz Pehlke. MAKE-UP: Gerda &
Walter Wegener.

CAST: Freddy Quinn *(Hein Steineman aka Jimmy Jones)*; Jayne
Mansfield *(Evelyne)*; Ullrich Haupt *(Bob Hartau)*; Joseph Albrecht
(Theo Steineman); Erna Sellmer *(Mutter Steineman)*; Christa Schindler
(Rosie Becker); Beppo Brem *(Seppl)*; Hein Riess *(Kuddel)*; Bill Ramsey
(Manager Jack); Heiner Holl *(Manager Harry Hayes)*; Charles Palent
(Rotkappchen); Addi Münster *(Wirt)*; Nelson Sardelli *(Chorus Boy)*; Peter
Mosbacher; Joseph Offenbach; Rudolf Platte; Heinz Reincke; Marisa
Solinas.

Former sailor Hein from Germany, has become the well-known singer
Jimmy 'The Lonesome Star' Jones in America. He performs his songs
on a TV variety program, of which entertainer Evelyne is the sexy star.
Looking at the show, one of Jim's old sea pals (Haupt) discovers that
Jimmy is his long lost buddy Hein Steineman. The pair meet each other
and while talking and re-connecting, Jimmy becomes homesick for St.
Pauli, Hamburg. When Evelyne leaves for Hamburg for a singing engagement, he decides to follow her to Germany. While Evelyne dates his pal
Bob, Jimmy makes up with his estranged parents, finds true love with a
girl called Rosie and decides that he likes being a sailor more than a singer
and takes a job on a ship.

The film opens with a view of the sky line of New York. The Statue
of Liberty is shown and the first interior shots are that of a TV studio
were Freddy Quinn is performing. Quinn gets to sing the title song
and a couple of other songs in German. For the opening scene he is
surrounded by showgirls and wearing a silver suit, imitating the Elvis
Presley pelvis shakes while he sings in English: "I've got everything,
suede shoes, purple suit, diamond ring, golden guitar. They're callin'
me the Lonesome Star!" Jayne's two musical numbers are: "Wo ist der
Mann" ("Where is the Man") and the incredibly titled "Schnicksnack

Schnukelchen", which means as much as 'a tramp' (literally: nonsense sweetheart). She used her own voice for the songs, but her speaking voice was dubbed in German.[87]

Again Jayne was cast as the temperamental star; this time for the medium of television. She hates to do the program's sponsors' commercials in between her shows. Announced as Sexy Hexy she promotes the

HEIMWEH NACH ST. PAULI (1963).

healthy cigarette Nofum, "a cigarette even a four year old can smoke" as Evelyne claims. Jayne secured a small part as a chorus boy for her lover, singer Nelson Sardelli.[88] He, of course, was the man who got her in the final of the musical number "Wo ist der Mann".

Jayne left for Europe in the summer of 1963. Filming in Germany began as a happy experience for Jayne. She had taken her two sons, Miklos and Zoltan, with her and enjoyed her time off picnicking, fishing and

87. US *Billboard* music magazine ran an article on Jayne's singing. It also mentioned the plans for a TV production with Jayne during her stay in Hamburg. July 6, 1963.

88. Brazilian born Sardelli (1934) was the son of an Italian immigrant who settled down in South America. He first met Jayne in early 1963. Although both were married at the time, Jayne and Sardelli had a well publicized affair; it was he — not Hargitay — who joined her in Hamburg, Germany while filming *Heimweh nach St. Pauli*. Sardelli is still active in showbiz today. Remarkable enough he doesn't mention anything about his connection with Jayne Mansfield on his website *nelsonsardelli.com*.

sailing with them. Raymond Strait also mentions that she laid off the booze during her whole stay in Germany. When she caught the flu it complicated the production schedule. A conflict with her parents left Jayne feeling that her parents lacked understanding for her feelings. Combined with every day morning sickness because of her two month pregnancy, and Jayne almost miscarrying because of all this tension, Jayne

WITH FREDDY QUINN IN *HEIMWEH NACH ST. PAULI* (1963).

lapsed deeper into depression. Still she managed to finish the picture and received a letter from the American Consulate upon returning to the United States, expressing thanks for her contribution to good relations between the two countries and stating that she had set a fine example of an American in Europe.[89]

Jayne's co-star Freddy Quinn[90] was a very popular singer in Europe

HEIMWEH NACH ST. PAULI **(1963).**

at the time. He had played the lead in the very successful stage musical of *Heimweh nach St Pauli* in 1962. In 1967 the show was revived. Again Quinn starred as the singing sailor. US Billboard magazine mentioned that the musical was Germany's most successful stage show.[91] By co-starring with Jayne, Freddy Quinn hoped to become more famous overseas. This never happened, because the film was never released nationwide in the US.

89. Strait, Raymond: *The Tragic Secret Life of Jayne Mansfield.* London: Robert Hale & Company, 1974.

90. Freddy Quinn (1931) was born in Austria. His parents moved to the US when he was little. He returned to Europe in his teens. Quinn was a famous singer and actor in Germany and made several movies. In 1964 he starred with another Hollywood blonde, namely Jayne's long time rival Mamie Van Doren, in *Freddy und das Lied der Prärie aka The Sheriff was a Lady.*

91. *"The musical played 199 performances in Hamburg and 64 in Vienna, where it broke all records for a foreign production."* Billboard magazine, January 21, 1967.

Quinn told how he got Jayne to do the film: "When the musical was filmed, the producer wanted to have Barbara Valentin[92] as my leading lady, but I wanted Jayne Mansfield, at that time Hollywood's number one sexbomb. I called her from a bar in Hamburg and I said: 'This is Freddy Quinn,' and she responded 'Hi Anthony.' I could convince her to do the film by telling her how poor the German movie industry was. She agreed to do the film for $25,000 although her original fee would have been ten times higher. I paid her salary myself, and therefore received 10 percent from the profit of the foreign showings. What would a movie with Barbara Valentin have earned in foreign showings?" Although Quinn mentions her fee being $25,000, Jayne received a salary of $35,000 for this movie.

The only other American in the cast, besides Jayne, was the singing actor Bill Ramsay (b. 1931). He served for The United States Air Force and was stationed in Germany in 1952 during the Korean War. He continued singing in clubs and was spotted by a German talent scout who gave him his first movie part in 1955.

The 60s proved to be the darkest decade in the history of the postwar commercial German cinema. Many production companies closed while survivors struggled to maintain their share of the market, now seriously eroded by American competition and the growth of television. Initially, the crisis was perceived as a problem of overproduction. Consequently, the German film industry cut back on production. 123 German movies were produced in 1955, only 65 in 1965.

Heimweh nach St. Pauli had its premiere on August 29, 1963 in Hamburg. The film received a very limited American release in New York City, and was mostly seen by the German and Polish descendants from the town of Yorktown, which lays 35 miles from New York City.

REVIEWS

New York Times: "...*Homesick for St. Pauli*, which starred Jayne Mansfield as a denizen of Hamburg, Germany's night-strip district, and Freddy Quinn, Germany's leading recording star. . ."

Variety: "...Freddy must have an American co-star for the simple reason that he [the producer] hopes to increase the picture's gross in the U.S. market."

---

92. Austrian born actress Barbara Valentin (1940-2002) was called Germany's answer to Jayne Mansfield in the 1960s.

EINER FRISST DEN ANDEREN (1964).

EINER FRISST DEN ANDEREN
(AKA DOG EAT DOG!)

Ajay Film Co. — 1964
84 minutes, Black and white

PRODUCER: Ernst Neubach. DIRECTOR: Gustav Gavrin. SCREEN-PLAY: Robert Hill & Michael Elkins. Based on the novel by Robert Bloomfield. MUSIC: Carlo Savina. EDITOR: Gene Ruggiero. MAKE-UP: Attilio Camarda & Franco Corridoni. PHOTOGRAPHY: Ricardo Pallottini.

CAST: Jayne Mansfield *(Darlene)*; Cameron Mitchell *(Lyle Corbett)*; Isa Miranda *(Madame Benoit)*; Elisabeth Flickenschildt *(Xenia)*; Ivor Salter *(Dolph Kostis)*; Aldo Camarda *(Livio Morelli)*; Pinkas Braun *(Yannis, The Butler)*; Dodie Heath *(Sandra Morelli)*; Werner Peter *(Detective Gino)*; Siegfried Lowitz *(Gangster)*; Ines Taddio *(Hotel Americano's Singer)*; Robert Gardett *(Detective Reno)*.

Bad girl Darlene, Dolph Kostis, her gangster boyfriend, and Lyle Corbett have robbed a US navy ship of one million dollars it was carrying. Jayne and her lover stay, under the aliases Mr. and Mrs. Smithopolous, at the Americano hotel. Intent on keeping the money for himself, Kostis tries to kill Corbett, but he fails. The hotel manager (Aldo Camarda), finds out they are the robbers and decides to take the money for himself. When he and his sister Sandra try to sabotage the gangster's boat, Sandra is caught by the crooks.

When Kostis flees with Darlene to their villa hideout on a neighboring island, Corbett catches up with them to take revenge. Mistrustful, but still bound by the money, the whole group takes to the sea to make their getaway. Together they flee to an island in the Adriatic Ocean where they are to be picked up. The hotel manager follows to free his sister and lay his hands on the money. On the island they encounter the owner of an old brothel, a demented older woman named Madame Xenia, and her butler Yannis.

There are numerous intrigues when each person tries to get his/her hands on the money. At the end of the film, the crooks, the hotel manager and his sister and the balding butler are dead and the stolen money floats all over the Adriatic, watched by the insane Madame Benoit. In the final shot, Darlene dies too. She drowns when she wants to collect the money from the ocean.

Jayne played a good part as the sluttish bad girl, nymphomaniac Darlene, who is complaining most of the movie that she needs a new lipstick and some clean panties. Darlene's favorite word seems to be 'Crackers', for she starts almost every sentence with this filler. We see Jayne at the opening of the film, lying in bed in her nightie fondling, kissing and throwing the stolen money in the air. We see Jayne in a catfight

EINER FRISST DEN ANDEREN LOBBY CARD, WITH IVOR SALTER.

with Dodie Heath on a small sail boat; biting her hands, scratching and pulling her hair. When Corbett overpowers her boyfriend Kostis, Darlene puts her attention to Corbett and tries to seduce him. "With this kind of dough, two's company but three's really a crowd." To which Corbett replies by pushing her away quite aggressively. When Darlene tries to get close to him later in the movie and he declines her advances again, she throws herself at Morelli. Morelli's sister is appalled by Darlene's manners, to which Darlene remarks: 'What's the matter sweetie, shock you? Oh you good girls, you hang on to it too long and when you do finally decide to let go, you're surprised nobody wants it anymore."

Jayne was four months pregnant while filming this picture, the costumes she wore tried to conceal her negligee. Jayne Mansfield was very pleased with her performance and the movie itself: "*Dog Eat Dog* is my biggest film opportunity. Heavy drama and suspense. I've even heard I might be nominated for an Oscar" she wrote her press secretary Raymond Strait.[93] It's guessing who informed her about this; of course Jayne Mansfield was never nominated for an Academy Award. Although the movie is far from a master piece, some scenes and performances are quite effective. Jayne's acting isn't as bad as most reviews describe. Jayne manages to look and act natural underneath that huge pile of blonde

EINER FRISST DEN ANDEREN LOBBY CARD, WITH CAMERON MITCHELL.

hair, the corky dialogue and wearing nothing more than a negligee most of the time.

Michael Arthur Productions (with Albert Zugsmith as the director) was originally credited for this movie, but an Italian/German film company did the actual filming. Yugoslavian — now Croatia — born producer, writer and director Gustav Gavrib (1906-1976) seems to be the legitimate director of this production. Ray Nazarro, and Richard E. Cunha are also named in some filmographies as the directors. Nazarro is credited as director in official Italian and UK records, Cunha was credited for the shorter and different cut English dubbed version. The movie was filmed in and around the former Republic of Yugoslavia. Jayne's own voice isn't heard also, although the dubbed voice comes close to Jayne's.

93. Strait, Raymond: *The Tragic Secret Life of Jayne Mansfield.* London: Robert Hale & Company, 1974.

WITH CAMERON MITCHELL IN *EINER FRISST DEN ANDEREN* (1964).

There's one curious moment in the film where Darlene sits outside and talks to Yannis, the bald butler. He says that she can't imagine how life is on a deserted island. To which Jayne/Darlene answers: "Don't kid yourself honey. I know what life is like everywhere. Have you ever been to Biloxi, Mississippi? Now there's a town for you." Of course, four years after shooting this scene, Jayne was killed near Biloxi.

EINER FRISST DEN ANDEREN LOBBY CARD, WITH PINKAS BRAUN.

Rugged American actor Cameron Mitchell (1918-1994) played in many Hollywood B-grade action movies. In the 1960's he went to Italy where he appeared in a string of C-grade action and epic productions. Italian born film diva Isa Miranda (1905-1982), played the hotel's proprietress. Miranda was a huge star in Europe in the 1930's. In 1939 Paramount Studios brought her to Hollywood to star in two of their productions, probably because their former European diva Marlene Dietrich, was released from her contract that same year. Miss Miranda never reached the same star status in Hollywood as Dietrich. She returned to Europe in 1940. Popular singer Ines Taddio (b. 1928) sings a German schlager in the hotel's bar/dining room.

Strangers When We Meet was the reissue title, also the title of the novel by Robert Bloomfield on which the film was based. The film was shot in August and September 1963. The movie had its premiere in West

GERMAN POSTER FOR *EINER FRISST DEN ANDEREN* (1964).

Germany in June 1964. The Italian title is *La Morte Vestita di Dollari*. The New York premiere of the film, re-titled *Dog Eat Dog!* Was on July 13th, 1966.

REVIEWS

There are no contemporary American reviews known to the author. The following reviews are ones from the last three decades.

The Psychotronic Encyclopedia of Film: "Jayne Mansfield and Cameron Mitchell together! In a nihilistic tale of greed, madness, and murder! Obviously an important statement involving two of our most enduring stars."

Leonard Maltin's Movie and Video Guide 1992: Low level, unintentionally funny potboiler with lust, greed and depravity, with various characters intent upon making off with a stolen million dollars. A highlight: Jayne's constant complaining about her need for clean panties."

New York Times — Dave Kehr (03/14/2006): "[A] compellingly strange and sordid crime film...."

L'AMORE PRIMITIVO (1964).

L'AMORE PRIMITIVO
(AKA PRIMITIVE LOVE)
Italian International — G.L.M. — 1964
83 minutes, Color

PRODUCER: Dick Randall, Joel Holt, Fulvio Luciano & Pietro Paulo Giordani. DIRECTOR: Luigi Scattini. SCREENPLAY: Luigi Scattini & Amadeo Sollazzo. Based on the story by Luigi Scattini & D.M. Pupillo. MUSIC: Coriolano Gori. EDITOR: Otello Colangeli. PHOTOGRAPHY: Claudio Racca.

CAST: Jayne Mansfield *(Dr. Jayne)*; Franco Franchi *(Franco, Hotel Porter)*; Ciccio Ingrassia *(Ciccio, Hotel Porter)*; Carlo Kechler *(The Professor)*; Mickey Hargitay *(Hotel Bell Captain)*; Luigi Scattini *(Commentator)*; Lucia Modungo *(The Maid)*; Alfonso Sarlo; Eugenio Galadini; Riccardo Cucciolla; Agata Flori.

The film opens with Jayne — playing an anthropologist — checking into a hotel, the soundtrack playing the famous strains of Italian song "Bella Come Te". Within five minutes she comes up with at least ten different excuses to disrobe, shower and prance around almost naked in her hotel room. Italian comic duo Franco Franchi and Ciccio Ingrassia (the latter is the tall one with the mustache) play two bungling hotel bellhops, spying on Jayne's every move. At the time they were Italy's top funnymen. Mickey Hargitay plays their boss.

Jayne, the anthropologist, has made a film on the subject of the universal primitiveness of love, but one professor to whom she shows it in Rome is left unconvinced. About halfway through the film, Jayne invites the bald and very square looking professor into her hotel room to view her new documentary/shock-u-mentary. Jayne starts narrating the action as the screen unfolds to show topless Filipino rice paddy women, topless African women, a live pig sacrifice, interracial sex and oriental cock-fighting, a gator hunt, witch doctors and Hong Kong hookers. Suddenly a witch doctor pounds the drums while a bevy of young girls do the topless Temptation Dance. Then the movie within a movie veers off into a dream sequence, in which Jayne appears in a grass skirt,[94] dancing in front of the drum pounding Franco and Ciccio (while Annette Funicello is heard singing "Date Night In Hawaii") in the lobby of the hotel.

---

94. In some publicity stills Jayne wears a brunette wig, but in the film she is seen with her blonde hairdo.

When asked about the validity of all this wild documentary footage, filmmaker Jayne defines that all men, deep down inside, are actually primitive lusting animals. In the explosive finale, she proves her point by performing a striptease for the professor. She happily continues the strip tease even after she uncovers the two bellboys Franco and Ciccio spying on her. The bellhops go berserk and the professor turns into a

L'AMORE PRIMITIVO (1964).

drooling, sex-crazed maniac.

The hotel scenes were actually filmed at the Hilton hotel were Jayne and Mickey were staying during their time in Italy. The scenes of Jayne judging a beauty contest, going to a nightclub and visiting a massage parlor, were later used again in *The Wild, Wild World of Jayne Mansfield* (1967). Both movies consisted of scenes with Jayne and documentary style input. These films were known as 'Mondo' films. They showed unusual customs from around the world. "1964's L'Amore Primitivo actually used a fictional framework to surround its mondo scenes, having Jayne Mansfield, playing herself, show mondo footage to a college professor who was also a werewolf."[95] Jayne's friend May Mann states in her book, that *L'Amore Primitivo* was originally titled *Jayne Mansfield Reports*.[96]

Sicilian born Franco Franchi (1922-1992) and Ciccio Ingrassia (1922-2003) were each struggling entertainers/ballad singers when they met in 1954. In 1955 they formed a pair and acted in low-class stage shows until they were discovered by movie director Mario Mattoli, who used them

L'AMORE PRIMITIVO (1964).

in *Appuntamento a Ischia* (1960). Besides their popular quickie comedies they worked with famous Italian directors like Federico Fellini and Pier Paolo Pasolini. Together they made over 100 films.

Director Luigi Scattini (1927-2010) had previously built up a reputation as an accomplished documentary filmmaker, with award winning titles like *La Via del Carbone* (1962), and *La Vergine di Caacupé e Puerto*

95. Romanski, Phillipe & Sy-Wonyu, Aïssatou. *Trompe(-)l'oeil: imitation & falsification*. Rouen, France: Publications Univ Rouen Havre, 2002.

96. She also stated that Jayne had just married Matt Cimber. And that they flew back to Italy after their wedding to complete the second part of the picture. The author assumes that this so called 'second part' finally became *The Wild, Wild World of Jayne Mansfield*. This hypotheses is justified because Jayne originally left for Italy with her former husband Mickey Hargitay in May 1964. Hargitay also played a part in the film. Besides this statement Jayne Mansfield had married Cimber on September 30th, 1964 while *L'Amore Primitivo* was already released in August that same year.

Sastre (1963). After *L'Amore Primitivo* he worked with comedy duo Franchi and Ingrassia again in a much better film, *Due Marines e un Generale* (1966), which also featured Buster Keaton and Hollywood blonde Martha Hyer. About Jayne's striptease scene in *L'Amore Primitivo* he commented on his weblog: "The final scene, for example…lasted much longer than the version that ended up in the film. It was perhaps a bit

L'AMORE PRIMITIVO (1964).

too 'racy' for the time, with Jayne going topless, so we cut it out before anyone complained."[97]

Jayne Mansfield left the US in May 1964 to start filming *L'Amore Primitivo* in Rome. On August 17, 1964 the film had its world premiere in Italy. The film was released in the United States on November 3, 1966 under the name *Primitive Love*. In 1967 it was distributed in France as *L'amour Primitif* and in Germany as *Primitive Liebe*.

WITH CICCIO INGRASSIA IN *L'AMORE PRIMITIVO* (1964).

REVIEWS

There are no contemporary American reviews known to the author. The following reviews are ones from the last three decades.

The Psychotronic Encyclopedia of Film: "Jayne Mansfield in another of her obscure European comedies. She plays Jayne, an anthropologist who had made a film showing that love is universally primitive."

Des Moines Register: "Low budget film made by Jayne Mansfield after her United States career went into decline."

97. *www.luigiscattini.wordpress.com*

THE LOVED ONE
MGM — 1965
122 minutes, Black and white

PRODUCER: John Calley & Haskell Wexler. DIRECTOR: Tony Richardson. SCREENPLAY: Terry Southern & Christopher Isherwood. Based on the novel by Evelyn Waugh. MUSIC: John Addison. EDITOR: Hal Ashby & Brian Smedley-Aston. MAKE-UP: Emile La Vigne. PHOTOGRAPHY: Haskell Wexler.

CAST: Robert Morse *(Dennis Barlow)*; Jonathan Winters *(Henry Glenworthy)*; Anjanette Corner *(Aimee Thanatogenous)*; Dana Andrews *(Gen. Buck Brinkman)*; Milton Berle *(Mr. Kenton)*; James Coburn *(Immigration Officer)*; John Gielgud *(Sir Francis Hinsley)*; Tab Hunter *(Whispering Glades Tour Guide)*; Margaret Leighton *(Mrs. Helen Kenton)*; Liberace *(Mr. Starker)*; Roddy McDowall *(D.J. Jr.)*; Robert Morley *(Sir Ambrose Ambercrombie)*; Barbara Nichols *(Sadie Blodgett)*; Rod Steiger *(Mr. Joyboy)*; Lionel Stander *(The Guru Brahim)*; Roxanne Arlen *(Whispering Glades Hostess)*; Pamela Curran *(Whispering Glades Hostess)*; Claire Kelly *(Whispering Glades Hostess)*; Barbara Hines *(Whispering Glades Hostess)*; Eileen O'Neill *(Whispering Glades Hostess)*; Brenda Thomson *(Whispering Glades Hostess)*; Robert Easton *(Dusty Acres)*; Ayllene Gibbons *(Joyboy's Mother)*; Don Haggerty *(Haggerty)*; Asa Maynor *(Nikki, D.J. Jr.'s Secretary)*; Chick Hearn *(Announcer at Condor's funeral launch)*; Bernie Kopell *(Assistant to the Guru Brahim)*; Alan Napier *(English Club Official)*; Ed Reimers *(Minister at Whispering Glades)*; Reta Shaw *(Manager of the Zomba Café)*; Paul Williams *(Gunther Fry)*; John Bleifer *(Mr. Bernstein)*; Bella Bruck *(Mrs. Bernstein)*; Jim Brewer *(Jim)*; Jamie Farr *(Waiter at English Club)*; Gail Gilmore *(Girl in Funeral Home)*; Joy Harmon *(Miss Benson)*; Beverly Powers *(Orgy Dancer)*; Christopher Riordan *(Best Man)*; Martin Ransohoff *(Lorenzo Medici)*; Elizabeth Ann Roberts; Brad Moore; Warren Kemmerling; Dort Clark; **Jayne Mansfield** *(scene deleted)*.

Newly arrived in Hollywood from England, Dennis Barlow finds he has to arrange his uncle's interment at the highly-organized and very profitable Whispering Glades funeral parlor. But he has three problems — the strict rules of owner Blessed Reverend Glenworthy, the rivalry of embalmer Mr. Joyboy (Rod Steiger), and the shame of now working himself for *The Happy Hunting Ground* pets' memorial home.

WITH ROBERT MORSE IN *THE LOVED ONE* (1965).

ROBERT MORSE AND BARBARA NICHOLS IN *THE LOVED ONE* (1965).

Robert Morse (b. 1931) was already a celebrated stage actor, who had won the 1962 Tony Award as Best Actor for *How to Succeed in Business Without Really Trying*, before he starred in some comedies in the sixties. He was also the star of Jayne's last film *A Guide for the Married Man* (1967). Director Tony Richardson (1928-1991) was a representative of the British New Wave. In 1964 he received two Academy Awards for *Tom Jones*. He was married to actress Vanessa Redgrave from 1962 to 1967.

The promotional tagline for this satirical movie was "The motion picture with something to offend everyone!" Jayne played a travel receptionist, but her scene was cut out of the final print. The first assembly of the footage ran over five hours, so in the course of cutting the film down, several deletions had to be made. *The Loved One* was released on October 11, 1965. British author Evelyn Waugh (1903-1966) was opposed to the fact that his novel was re-written and placed in the current time when the film was produced. He wanted to have his name removed from the film's final print, but was too late to have that demand granted. The film opened in London only two weeks before Waugh's death in the spring of 1966.

REVIEWS

New York Times: "All in all, *The Loved One* is disastrous as trenchant satire but should do what its merchandisers say. It should offend a lot of people. Somehow people seem to like that."

New York Herald Tribune: "And yet there are some scathing vignettes, some sportive portraits by the unlikeliest of players and some ferocious fun."

London Times: "Poor Jayne, every curve and wiggle lies on the cutting room floor."

THE FAT SPY
Phillip/Magna Pictures — 1965
75 Minutes, Color

PRODUCER: Everett Rosenthal. DIRECTOR: Joseph Cates. SCREEN-
PLAY: Matthew Andrews. MUSIC: Joel Hirschhorn, Hank Hunter & Al
Kasha. EDITOR: Barry Malkin. MAKE-UP: Clay Lambert. PHOTOG-
RAPHY: Joseph C. Brun.

CAST: Phyllis Diller *(Camille Salamander aka Rapunzel Fingernail)*;
Jack E. Leonard *(Irving/Herman Gonjular)*; Brian Donlevy *(George
Wellington)*; **Jayne Mansfield** *(Junior Wellington)*; Jordan Christopher
(Frankie); The Wild Ones *(Themselves)*; Johnny Tillotson *(Dodo Bronk)*;
Lauree Berger *(Nanette)*; Lou Nelson *(Punjab, The Sikh)*; Toni Lee Shelly
(Mermaid); Penny Roman *(Secretary)*; Chuck Alden *(Treasure Hunter)*;
Tommy Graves *(Treasure Hunter)*; Linda Harrison *(Treasure Hunter)*;
Jeanette Taylor *(Treasure Hunter)*; Tommy Trick *(Treasure Hunter)*; Toni
Turner *(Treasure Hunter)*; Eddie Wright *(Treasure Hunter)*; Deborah
White *(Treasure Hunter)*; Tracy Vance *(Treasure Hunter)*; Adam Keefe
(Special Voice).

THE FAT SPY (1965).

ON LOCATION FOR *THE FAT SPY* (1965).

George Wellington, the president of a cosmetics company, is the owner of an island off the coast of Florida. He thinks that the Fountain of Youth is on that Island. His employee Irving Gonjular is sent to the island to protect the Fountain from teenage treasure hunters who want to find it for themselves. He also dispatches his daughter, Junior, to get rid of them. She's happy to go because her lover Irving is the island's only resident.

WITH JACK E. LEONARD IN *THE FAT SPY* (1965).

Junior sends Irving to spy on the kids to find out what they know. Because he's more concerned with nurturing his roses, Junior threatens Irving to shoot him in order to get him to elope with her.

Irving's twin brother Herman also arrives at the island. Herman is a major executive at Wellington's firm in love with rival cosmetic manufacturer Camille Salamander. He hunts through Wellington's computer to find the exact location of the fountain. He wants to provide Camille with this information, hoping she wants to marry him. Finally Camille and Herman find out that the secret of youth is contained in two black roses. When they eat one of the roses, they become little children again. In the end the ghost of medieval Spanish explorer Ponce de León[98] appears. When the two teenage turtledoves Frankie and Nannette eat the last black rose, Frankie's voice is transformed into Pontes'.

A lot of the film's 'jokes' are about Jayne's type mark giggling and squealing. In one scene Wellington tells his daughter: "Remember, Irving has been alone on a deserted island, for six months!" "Ooh Daddy"

WITH JACK E. LEONARD IN *THE FAT SPY* (1965).

Junior giggles and squeals. "If only she wouldn't giggle," Wellington says in the camera while Jayne leaves the office. Later on when Junior has joined Irving on the deserted island, she's overwhelmed with his present for her, an orange rose plant. She thanks him in the typical Jayne way, the frame freezes and Irving says "I wish she stopped that giggle".

A lot of song clips interrupt the story line. The songs are not bad, they're typical sixties teenage ballads, but they just don't mix in with the

98. Juan Ponce de León y Figueroa (1474-July 1521) became the first Governor of Puerto Rico by appointment of the Spanish crown. He led the first European expedition to Florida, which he named. He is associated with the legend of the Fountain of Youth, reputed to be in Florida. According to a popular legend, Ponce de León discovered Florida while searching for the Fountain of Youth. (source: Wikipedia, the free encyclopedia on the internet).

film's story. Although Jayne looks lovely in her sixties makeup, hairdo and dresses, that also just sums up all the best in Jayne's performance. She looked a bit on the heavy side, because she was five months pregnant with the last of her five children, son Antonio Raphael Ottaviano (aka: Tony Cimber). That's also the reason why Jayne isn't seen wearing a bikini or bathing suit the whole film. The teenagers are seen dancing and wandering through in trunks and bikinis, but Jayne wears baggy dresses and blouses to camouflage her pregnancy. The only sexy 'outfit' she is permitted to wear is a towel. In a very close shot we see her rubbing herself in with moisturizer while her 'lover' Irving is on the phone trying not to notice her.

While singing "I Like to be a Rose in Your Garden" to Irving, Jayne looks very happy and it's one of the most pleasant and watchable scenes of the entire film. One can see from her performance that Jayne tried hard to make it work, but the scenes and lines of dialogue she was given just didn't work. As a beach movie/teenage comedy the movie is just not good enough. It misses the fun, innocence and happy feeling like for example the movies of Frankie Avalon and Annette Funicello. Had American International Pictures been the producing company of this film, it would still be low budget, but the end result would have been, one would expect, much better.

Why these teen beach pictures were so popular in the early sixties was explained by author Alan Betrock: "Well, they moved fast and were escapist fun. There were no parents. They were ridiculous. They were, in spite of AIP's claims of cleanliness, sexy. All those bodies and bikinis churning away to twangy rock 'n' roll offered a fantasy vision of life without serious problems. And with the mid-sixties real world bringing youth such problems as assassinations, the Vietnam war, racial unrest, radical changes in clothes and hairstyles, drugs and the like, these pictures were a safe haven for a retreat to the status quo."[99]

The acting of all actors is feeble, not to say appalling. Jack E. Leonard (1911-1973) was a bald, bespectacled comedian in nightclubs and on television in the 1950's and 1960's. He appeared in only a few films (e.g. Jerry Lewis comedy *The Disorderly Orderly*, 1964) with *The Fat Spy* being his only starring role. Standup comedian and actress Phyllis Diller (b. 1917), started her film career in the 1960's. *The Fat Spy* provided her with her premiere as a leading actress. Luckily for her, her teaming up

99. Betrock, Alan. *The I Was a Teenage Juvenile Delinquent Rock 'n' Roll Horror Beach Party Movie Book — A Complete Guide to the Teen Exploitation Film: 1954-1969*. London: Plexus Publishing Limited, 1986.

with comedian Bob Hope was more successful. Well into her 90's, she still makes the occasional cameo appearances in films and on television today. In her autobiography Miss Diller describes Jayne as "overweight, hooked on pills and firmly on the skids."[100]

Actor Brian Donlevy (1901-1972), cast as Jayne's father, made one of his final film appearances in this production. He supported many great actors during the 1920's, 1930's and 1940's. His biggest role, and the one he's best remembered for by 1950 cult film fans, is as Professor Quatermass in *The Quatermass Experience* (1955) and *Quatermass 2* (1957). Just before he made *The Fat Spy*, he was seen in the equally appalling teenage beach party film *How to Stuff a Wild Bikini* (1965) with Annette Funicello.

Singer Johnny Tillotson (b. 1939) recalls: "The whole reason I took that film was I thought I'd get a chance to meet Jayne Mansfield. We shot it down in Florida. I went down a few days ahead of schedule, in order to meet Jayne Mansfield. I was so excited. I'd never been in a movie before. When I showed up a few days before my scenes were supposed to be shot, I asked around. 'Is Miss Mansfield here?' They said, 'Well, I'm sorry to tell you that Jayne shot all of her scenes last week. She's no longer here on the set. But we do have Phyllis Diller.'"[101]

Watching Jayne Mansfield in this film, one wonders if Jayne's Junior was meant to be a parody on Jayne the famous sexy movie star, or maybe Jayne the 'has-been' movie star? She plays a real dumb blonde, big busted, sun tanned and not unattractive. But in spite of her appealing features she just has eyes for a bald and obese man who never shows his affection for her, but rather studies and cuddles his cultivated plants. Is this were fifties fun loving but devoted dumb blondes like Jerri and Alice[102] ended up a decade later?

The end titles are about the funniest thing in the whole movie. Sentences, like "Will Junior bloom in Irving's garden?" and "See the following sequels: The Return of the Fat Spy. The Son of the Fat Spy. Bride of the Fat Spy," roll over the screen and almost tempt the audience to finally smile. *The Fat Spy* was filmed in June and July 1965 in Cape Coral, Florida. It had a floating release in late 1965, but the official date of release is May 11, 1966.

---

100. Diller, Phyllis. *Like a Lampshade in a Whorehouse — My Life in Comedy.* New York: J.P. Tarcher/ Penguin, 2005.

101. Interview by Mark Voger. www.nj.com.

102. Jeri Jordan from *The Girl Can't Help It* (1956) and Alice Krachner from *Kiss Them For Me* (1957).

REVIEWS

Variety: "Miss Diller has a few scenes in this pic but handles them credibly, while Leonard is strapped with a large share of this banal script. As for Donlevy and Mansfield, they were hopefully only passing through."

Los Angeles Herald-Examiner: "*Fat Spy* is a waste of time, talent. One of the things in this world which will remain a mystery to me is how it can be that motion pictures of the ilk of *The Fat Spy* spring into existence and are taking seriously by anyone, including the people who produce it and perform it."

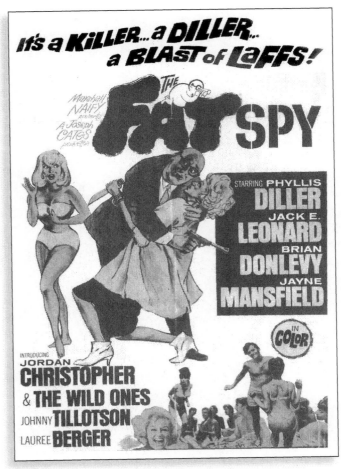

U.S. POSTER FOR *THE FAT SPY* (1965).

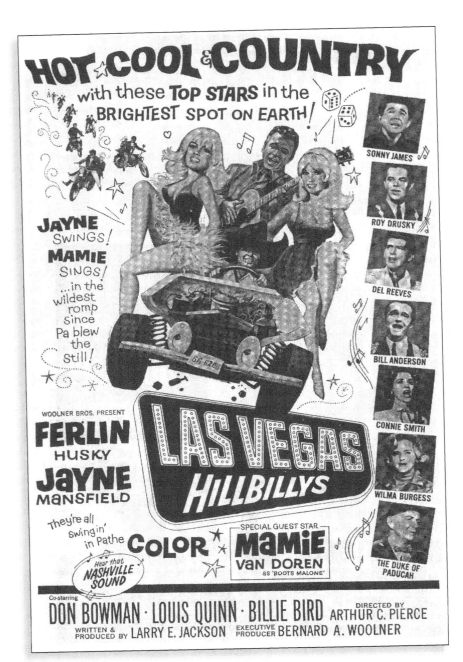

U.S. POSTER FOR *LAS VEGAS HILLBILLYS* (1966).

LAS VEGAS HILLBILLYS

Woolner Bros. — 1966
90 Minutes, Color

PRODUCER: Larry E. Jackson. DIRECTOR: Arthur C. Pierce. SCREEN-
PLAY: Larry E. Jackson. MUSIC: Dean Elliot. EDITOR: Roy V. Livingston
& Holbrook N. Todd. MAKE-UP: Mark Snegoff. PHOTOGRAPHY:
William de Diego.

CAST: Ferlin Husky *(Woodrow "Woody" Wilson Weatherby)*; Mamie Van
Doren *(Boots Malone)*; Jayne Mansfield *(Tawni Downs)*; Don Bowman
(Jeepers); Billie Bird *(Aunt Clementine)*; Louis Quinn *(Honest Harry Toolup,
Mortgage Holder)*; Richard Kiel *(Moose, Bodyguard)*; Arlene Charles *(Girl)*;
Helen Clark *(Girl)*; Christian Anderson *(Biker Boy)*; Robert V. Barron
(Donald); Bennett King *(Barman)*; Sonny James *(Himself, Singer)*; Del
Reeves *(Himself, Singer)*; Bill Anderson *(Himself, Singer)*; Wilma Burgess
(Herself, Singer); Roy Drusky *(Himself, Singer)*; Connie Smith *(Herself,
Singer)*; The Duke of Paducah *(Himself)*; Larry Barton; John Harmon;
Chuck Harrod; Theodore Lehmann; The Junior Caroline Cloggers
(Themselves); The Jordanaires *(Themselves)*.

Woodrow Wilson, a Hillbilly bootlegging wood hauler, inherits a
Las Vegas casino from his uncle. When he and his friend Jeepers leave
Tennessee to investigate the property, they encounter Tawni Downs, a Las
Vegas entertainer. She has run out of gas and the boys push her car to a
garage. She turns out to be Woody's dead uncle's 'protégé'. They learn that
their inheritance is nothing more than a rundown bar in a converted barn.
Besides that it also comes with a $38,000 debt and a couple of persistent
creditors. Only the bartender and the singer under personal contract to
his uncle, Boots Malone, are still around.

Woody sends for his Aunt Clementine, who has some ideas they hope
can turn the business around. She spends her savings to obtain some
famous country stars to perform in the casino. They put Boots in charge
of managing the 'Golden Circle Casino', and Tawni helps the pair out by
running the gambling operations. Woody's dream of becoming a country
& western performer has come true. The casino becomes a success and in
the end Woody and Boots fall in love.

Las Vegas Hillbillys was a sort of country music answer to the popular
sixties beach party flicks. While *Hillbillys* was produced, the popular CBS
series *The Beverly Hillbillies* ran for its fourth season. Maybe the producers

of *Las Vegas Hillbillys* tried to get a piece of the pie. To add some action to this Hillbilly musical comedy, a group of pot smoking teenagers on motor bikes show up to almost trash the place. To get them to calm down the band starts playing Dixie music, to which the gang immediately begins dancing.

Other musical numbers were provided by Ferlin Husky ("White Lightning Express", "I Feel Better All Over" and "Money Greases The Wheel"), Sonny James ("What Makes a Man Wander", "I'll Keep Holding On" and "True Love's a Blessing"), Del Reeves ("The Belles of Southern Belle" and "Women Do Funny Things To Me"), Bill Anderson ("Bright Lights and Country Music"), Wilma Burgess ("Baby, Sweet Sweet Baby"), Roy Drusky ("I Don't Believe You Love Me Anymore"), Connie Smith ("Nobody But a Fool"), Mamie Van Doren ("Fresh Out of Lovin'" and "Baby, Sweet Sweet Baby") and Jayne Mansfield ("That Makes It"). Her performance of the parody of the 1958 classic "Chantilly Lace"[103] is easily the movie's bright spot. Jayne 'dances' quite mechanically with a red couch and two chorus boys as her only props, while singing "I'm hip, Daddy. That makes it…ooh, that's so kinky" into a golden, and probably the first hands free, telephone! Too bad she didn't have a couple more numbers, or maybe even been in a couple more scenes.

Although star billed and introduced to Woody and friends as 'The Biggest Star in Las Vegas', she only has a handful of scenes. If she were edited out completely it would have changed nothing to the overall story. The scene where Jayne enters the film (twenty-four minutes after the start) and meets the boys for the first time is filmed in the studio with a fake backdrop of the desert and hills of Las Vegas. The scenery in the real outdoor footage is totally different than the studio backdrop. More than a half hour later in the film's proceedings, Jayne is featured again in Woody's dream performing "That Makes It".

Many sources mention that the shapeless sixties wardrobe had to hide Jayne's weight problems after the birth of her fifth child. This should be the main reason why Jayne didn't want to be filmed with long-time blonde rival Mamie Van Doren.[104] Still she looks appealing and glamorous in a

103. *Chantilly Lace* was the hit record of 'The Big Bopper' aka Jiles Perry "J. P." Richardson, Jr. (1930-1959). He was an American disc jockey, singer, and songwriter whose big voice and exuberant personality made him an early rock and roll star. Richardson was killed in a small-plane crash in Iowa, along with singers Buddy Holly and Ritchie Valens (Source: *Wikipedia*).

104. *There was a disagreement over Las Vegas Hillbillys billing but none of the overt hostilities were played up by the press at the time. "Mamie and Mansfield were cool to each other, brought on perhaps by the realization that they were the last of the bombshell dinosaurs." Lowe, Barry. Atomic Blonde — The Films of Mamie Van Doren.* Jefferson: McFarland & Company, Inc., Publishers, 2008.

scene with Billie Bird. Dressed in a tight fitting but still elegant soft pink blouse and skirt she looked quite elegant.

Jayne and Mamie hardly spoke to each other on the set either. Mamie recalls in her auto-biography: "There was a good bit of press at the time to the effect that Jayne and I fought all the time during the filming of 'Hillbillys'. The truth of the matter was that we only had one argu-

LAS VEGAS HILLBILLYS (1966).

ment — a habitual among performers: top billing. When a compromise was finally made giving us both top billing, Jayne and I didn't speak half a dozen words. We simply refused to be in the same room with each other if we could possibly avoid it."[105] In their scene together a double is used. The moment consisted of Boots entering the casino while Tawni chats with Woody on the parking lot. Boots greets Tawni and asks what's the purpose of her visit. "Hello Boots, darling. I thought it was about time to get acquainted with Woody. We're practically relatives you know" Tawni answers. Boots, looking haughty, replies: "You two kissin' cousins enjoy yourself. I've got work to do."

105. Van Doren, Mamie with Aveilhe, Art. *Playing the Field — My Story*. New York: G.P. Putnam's Sons, 1987.

Mamie Van Doren (b. 1931) was a popular pin up actress at Universal Studios in the early fifties. When her contract wasn't prolonged in 1956, she freelanced for various producers and film studios. Warner Bros. used her in cult classic *Untamed Youth* (1957), Metro Goldwyn Mayer starred her in rock 'n roll marihuana pic *High School Confidential* (1958), and Paramount provided her with a co-starring role in her only A-level

FERLIN HUSKY AND MAMIE VAN DOREN IN *LAS VEGAS HILLBILLYS* (1966).

movie *Teacher's Pet* (1958), with Clark Gable as her partner. In 1955 she had married band leader Ray Anthony, who had a small role in *The Girl Can't Help It* with Jayne. Mamie said no to the Broadway play *Will Success Spoil Rock Hunter?*, only to see Jayne triumph as Rita Marlowe and hailed as Hollywood's newest blonde sensation in the year her contract at Universal was resigned.[106] Although Jayne is star-billed and Mamie is billed as a special guest star, it's Mamie who has the lion share of scenes in the movie.[107]

106. *"I was still mad at Jayne for having taken the role in 'Rock Hunter' that I'd turned down, and becoming a star as a result. Besides that, she and Marilyn* [Monroe] *were my competition at the box office."* Van Doren, Mamie with Aveilhe, Art. *Playing the Field — My Story.* New York: G.P. Putnam's Sons, 1987.

107. *"The Las Vegas Hillbillys pairs Mamie Van Doren and Jayne Mansfield as Boots Malone and the larger-than-life Tawny. The former '50s rivals meet without doing any scenes together. It is the magic of editing and equal credits."* Fusco, Joseph. *The Films of Mamie Van Doren.* Albany, GA: BearManor Media, 2010.

Country singer and actor Ferlin Husky (1925-2011) had a few hit records in the 1950's and 1960's and as a result starred in a couple of films. After *Las Vegas Hillbillys* he made a sequel called *Hillbillys in a Haunted House* (1967) with fifties blonde starlet Joi Lansing. Screenwriter and occasional producer/director of science fiction films, Arthur C. Pierce (1923-1987) had studied drama and worked as an actor and stage manager in various stage productions, starting in 1948. In 1977 he wrote some episodes for the popular TV series *Fantasy Island*.

After the birth of her son (October 17), Jayne was depending on diet pills to lose the extra weight and she was drinking heavily again. Her marriage to Matt Cimber was falling apart. Close-ups of Jayne from this period show the signs it left on her face. She looks tired and washed out. *Las Vegas Hillbillys* is considered the most unflattering film appearance in Jayne Mansfield's career.

Las Vegas Hillbillys started filming in late 1965 under the working title *Country Music, USA* and the shooting was completed at the end of December 1965. The movie was first released in Fresno, California on May 11, 1966.

REVIEWS

Box-office Magazine: "A country music jamboree with two beauteous blondes, Jayne Mansfield and Mamie Van Doren, helping singer Ferlin Husky to carry the story line, this should please the fans of rural rhythm. This films is one of the best in its field and, with good promotional backing will garner excellent box office grosses."

Motion Picture Exhibitor: "Loaded with country or mountain music, this opus with a mighty thin plot has little less to offer. Singers and musicians they may be, but actors they certainly aren't. Jayne Mansfield is in for name value only and has little to do. The color is okay and enhances things. If you go for this type of music, this should be your dish."

**JAYNE WITH PRODUCER HUGO GRIMALDI ON THE SET OF *SINGLE ROOM FURNISHED*
(1967).**

SINGLE ROOM FURNISHED
Empire Film Studios — 1967
93 Minutes, Color

PRODUCER: Hugo Grimaldi. DIRECTOR: Matteo Ottavanio aka Matt Cimber. SCREENPLAY: Michael Musto. Based on the play by Gerald Sanford. MUSIC: James Sheldon, Raoul Kraushaar & Jaime Mendoza-Nava. EDITOR: Hugo Grimaldi. MAKE-UP: Edith McAfee. PHOTOGRAPHY: Leslie Kovacs.

CAST: Jayne Mansfield *(Johnnie, Mae, Eilene)*; Dorothy Keller *(Flo)*; Fabian Dean *(Charley)*; Billy M. Greene *(Pop)*; Terri Messina *(Maria Adamo)*; Martin Horsey *(Frankie)*; Walter Gregg *(Billy)*; Bruno VeSota *(Mr. Don "Quak Quak" Duck)*; Velia Del Greco *(Mrs. Adamo)*; Isabelle Dwan *(Grandmother)*; Jean London *(First Girl)*; Nancy Brock *(Second Girl)*; Margie Duncan *(Dancer)*; Ava Sheara *(Dancer)*; DeDe Lind *(Dancer)*; Michael Rich *(Grandchild)*; Elisa Rich *(Grandchild)*; Erie MacGruder *(Girl at Window)*; Robert Van Strawder *(Grocery Boy)*; Marty Levine *(Mr. Ferdente)*; Jana Pearce *(Waitress)*; Trevor Doughty *(Mr. Peabody)*; Lucille Ford *(Lucia)*; The Paris Sisters *(Themselves, Vocals)*; Jack Irwin *(Himself, Vocals)*; Walter Winchell *(Himself)*.

WITH WALTER GREGG IN *SINGLE ROOM FURNISHED* (1967).

299

The film centers on Maria, an unmanageable girl in her teens, and the life story of forlorn Johnnie. Pop tells Maria the story of Johnnie's lowly life, a poor Bronx teenager just out of school, whose young husband (Frankie) leaves her when she's pregnant, for the freedom of the Navy. Heartbroken, Johnnie looses the baby, takes on a new personality by becoming a brunette and changes her name to Mae. She takes a job as

WITH BILLY M. GREENE IN *SINGLE ROOM FURNISHED* (1967).

a waitress at a restaurant, where she falls in love with a friendly customer called Mr. Duck, but he leaves her just as they're about to get married. Mae finds consolation with her neighbor, Charley, who is so sympathetic that he proposes to her. However he breaks the engagement, and Mae changes her name to Eilene, turns blonde again and becomes a prostitute.

The most striking scene in the film is of Eilene lying on her bed with her face in front of the camera sharing with her lover Billy her sad life. Street-hardened she hints to the sort of 'work' she's done in the room. "Prostitute is a beautiful word," she mumbles, "compared to 'whore' and the others...." For a moment she gets caught up in the sailor's irrational plans to get married and live on an island together. But when he accidentally breaks a prized doll of hers given by Frankie, she turns on him and drives him away. He leaves and shoots himself. Eilene realizes that her fate will never change...

In most of her earlier films Jayne was all dressed up as the glamorous leading vixen, but here there's not much room to be attractive. And even when she plays the cartoon sexpot Eileen — exactly the same type she'd modeled on her many bimbo characters from *Female Jungle* through *A Guide for the Married Man* — she's a far cry from her early days at Fox. Still she gives a hauntingly poetic performance in a gloomy movie that

WITH BRUNO VESOTA IN *SINGLE ROOM FURNISHED* (1967).

could have been better with a more solid script. Jayne's performance wasn't bad, but her dramatic parts in *The Burglar*, *The Wayward Bus* and even *The Challenge*, were better examples of her attempt to become recognized as a serious actress. Then again, thirty-two year old Jayne Mansfield benefitted from the knowledge of life and knew something more of her character's sadness and loneliness than she could have known ten years earlier.

In her early thirties and with a changing attitude to sexuality, the sixties made her think about the image she had built up so successfully during the last decade. Jayne decided to play down on the glamour and invest on becoming a dramatic actress. Before filming commenced she announced: "My career is moving in a sensitive direction. I'm going to do a movie in which I portray three parts: a prostitute, a cripple and a pregnant unmarried...I want to make a big indentation on the world."[108]

In 1965 Jayne had formed her own production company, Jaynatt Productions, Inc., in which she was president and Matt Cimber was vice-president. Financing their first project was a problem, that's why portions of *Single Room Furnished* were produced sporadically over a three-year

AS A BRUNETTE IN *SINGLE ROOM FURNISHED* (1967).

period. (Her stormy relationship with Cimber, that would end in divorce in July 1966, made filming difficult also). Jayne insisted that Matt would direct her, although the film's producer was against it. As always Jayne prevailed. Filming started late 1965 and on April 19, 1966 (Jayne's 33rd birthday) the film's executive producer and scriptwriter Michael Musto, threw a completion party.

Columnist Dorothy Manners (1903-1998), was the assistant of feared gossip queen Louella Parsons for more than 30 years, when she took over after Parsons' retirement in 1965. On November 28, 1966 she wrote: "In

108. The part of the cripple is not shown in the final version of the film. It seems Jayne was mistaken by naming this character. Saxton, Martha. *Jayne Mansfield and the American Fifties.* Boston: Houghton Miffin Company, 1975.

Jayne Mansfield's first full-fledged drama, she'll play a teenager, a prostitute and a waitress in Single Room Furnished for producer Mike Musto. Should get in to real art when she plays the teenager!" Columnist and long-time friend of Jayne, May Mann recalled: "Jayne played three roles, giving her a wide dramatic range. The film proved unsaleable for lack of proper distribution. The few critics who saw it declare Jayne a magnificent

U.S. POSTER FOR *SINGLE ROOM FURNISHED* (1967).

actress. Strangely, the last scene showed Jayne looking in a mirror which shattered in her face as you heard a terrible crash of cars: it was almost like a warning of Jayne's own death to come."[109]

As May said, the movie failed to find a distributor and it finally premiered in Phoenix, Arizona, on August 21, 1968. It was distributed by Crown International Pictures on a double bill with the Danish sex comedy *Jag — en älskare* (1966) (English title: *I, A Lover*). Matt Cimber[110] added an extra storyline to bring the film up to feature length running time. These scenes about the tentative romance between plain Charley and Flo, Eilene's neighbors, have no connection with the original narration and slow down the storyline. Playwright Gerald Sanford sued Matt Cimber and the Mansfield estate for the illicit (mis)use of his story.[111]

Single Room Furnished was Cimber's debut feature film. He first met Jayne while directing the off-Broadway production of the play *Bus Stop* in 1964. There they fell in love and were married in Mexico on September 24 that same year. During their marriage Matt directed Jayne in other stage plays; after their divorce he would direct several soft-core B-movies.

The film's cast mostly consisted of television actors who were either at the end of their careers or just starting out. Old-stager Billy M. Greene (1897-1973) had played in many TV series in the fifties and made a handful of feature film appearances in the sixties. *Single Room Furnished* was one of his last. Terri Jean Messina (1946-2007) made her debut as the naïve and impressionable Maria. She was mostly seen on television and ended her career in the early 1970's. And sizeable B-movie actor Bruno VeSota (1922-1976) reunited with Jayne, after they played together in *Female Jungle* all those years earlier. He was a regular in many films by director/producer Roger Corman, earning him a modest cult status nowadays. He died from a heart attack at age 54, leaving behind his wife and six children. Appearing in a cameo part was 1967 Playmate of the month August, DeDe Lind (1947). She recalls working with Miss Mansfield as a pleasant experience: "I admired her a lot. She was very friendly on the set — not a prima donna at all — and very professional."[112]

109. Mann, May. *Jayne Mansfield: A Biography.* New York: Drake, 1973.

110. Matt Cimber (1936) was born of Italian ancestry as Thomas Vitale Ottaviano.

111. Saxton, Martha. *Jayne Mansfield and the American Fifties.* Boston: Houghton Miffin Company, 1975.

112. Sullivan, Steve. *Va Va Voom — Bombshells, Pin-ups, Sexpots and Glamour Girls.* Los Angeles: General Publishing Group, 1995.

Like many of her other works from the sixties, *Single Room Furnished*, once finished, was denied a nationwide US release. At first Jayne, disappointed with this, said: "If only someone somewhere would show it, if only they'd give it a proper release. It's not necessarily the greatest but I'm certain this picture would make people sit up and realize what I could do."[113] And later on, she exclaimed more annoyed: "It seems strange the public can't accept me as a serious actress. If *Single Room Furnished* ever gets released, that will be a surprise, I'm sure. It should bring me a whole new career. I didn't study acting, singing, dancing and going to college just to look good in bikinis."[114] Unfortunately Jayne never got the chance to regain her career and direct it towards a more serious acting future. *Single Room Furnished* was released after her death. Jayne's obituary is read in a 15 minute prologue by columnist and friend Walter Winchell[115] He also reviewed Jayne's performance in *Single Room Furnished* as follows: "Jayne Mansfield, a legend in her time, has left us a legendary character…in her last and finest performance."

REVIEWS

Los Angeles Times: "In her last film, *Single Room Furnished*, Jayne Mansfield played a fading forty-year-old prostitute …and a woman in her twenties."

113. Feeney Callan, Michael. *Pink Goddess — The Jayne Mansfield Story.* London: W.H. Allen, 1986.

114. Mann, May. *Jayne Mansfield: A Biography.* New York: Drake, 1973.

115. Walter Winchell (1897-1972) was a gossip columnist and radio commentator in the 1930s and 1940s. During the 1950s Winchell favored Senator McCarthy, who lead the communist witch hunt among Hollywood actors, producers, screen writers and directors. When the public turned against McCarthy, Winchell also lost in popularity. And when his home paper, the New York Daily Mirror, closed in 1963, Winchell faded from the public eye. Sharp tongued, but mostly in favor of Jayne, Winchell once commented: *"Jayne Mansfield is making a career of being a girl."* (source: Wikipedia, the free encyclopedia on the internet).

WITH TERRY-THOMAS IN *A GUIDE FOR THE MARRIED MAN* **(1967).**

A GUIDE FOR THE MARRIED MAN

20th Century Fox — 1967

89 Minutes, Color

PRODUCER: Frank McCarthy. DIRECTOR: Gene Kelly. SCREENPLAY: Frank Tarloff. Based on the book by Frank Tarloff. MUSIC: Johnny Williams. EDITOR: Dorothy Spencer. MAKE-UP: Ben Nye. PHOTOGRAPHY: Joe MacDonald.

CAST: Walter Matthau *(Paul Manning)*; Robert Morse *(Edward l. Stander)*; Inger Stevens *(Ruth Manning)*; Sue Ane Langdon *(Mrs. Irma Johnson)*; Jackie Russell *(Miss Harrins, Manning's Secretary)*; Claire Kelly *(Harriet Stander)*; Aline Towne *(Mrs. Mousey Man)*; Linda Harrison *(Miss Stardust)*; Elaine Devry *(Jocelyn Montgomery, a Rich Divorcee)*; Jason Wingreen *(Mr. Johnson)*; Heather Carroll *(Mrs. Miller)*; Eddie Quillan *(Cologne Salesman)*; Dale Van Sickel *(Stunt Driver)*; Mickey Deems *(Waiter)*; Chanin Hale *(Miss Crenshaw)*; Eve Brent *(Joe X's Blowzy Blonde)*; Marvin Brody *(Taxi Driver)*; Majell Barrett *(Mrs. Fred V.)*; Marian Mason *(Mrs. Rance G.)*; Tommy Farrell *(Rance G's Hanger-on)*; Fred Holliday *(Party Guest)*; Pat Becker *(Party Guest)*; Robert Patten *(Party Guest)*; Dee Carroll *(Party Guest)*; Ray Montgomery *(Party Guest)*; Jackie Joseph *(Janet Brophy, Party Guest)*; Heather Young *(Girl with Megaphone)*; Evelyn King *(Female Plaintiff)*; Nancy DeCarl *(Woman with Baby)*; Warrene Ott *(Woman with Gun)*; Michael Romanoff *(Maitre D'Hotel)*; Karen Arthur *(Lady Dinner Partner at Romanoff's)*; Damian London *(Lone Male Diner at Romanoff's)*; Hal Taggart *(Diner at Romanoff's)*; Julie Tate *(Woman in Bed at Banner Motel)*; George N. Neise *(Man in Bed at Banner Motel)*; Tim Herbert *(Shoe Clerk)*; Patricia Sides *(Mau Mau Dancer)*; Pat MacCaffrie *(Motel Clerk)*; Jimmy Cross *(Mr. Brown, Clara's Husband)*; Sharyn Hillyer *(Zelda, Girl in Bed)*; Virginia Woods *(Bubbles)*; Robert Aiken *(Ticket Clerk)*; Jutta D'Arcy *(Mother)*; Cherie Foster *(Mother in Toreador Pants)*; Maureen Gaffney *(Bridge Palyer)*; Joy Harmon *(Party Girl)*; Bobbie Jordan *(Waitress)*; Gregg Lally *(Ed's Son)*; Jeff Lally *(Ed's Son)*; MichaelMark *(Shoeshine Man)*; Walter Maslow *(Photographer)*; Gene O'Donnell *(Photographer)*; Dick McAuliffe *(Man in Tennis Club Locker Room)*; Leo Needham *(Studio Policeman)*; Larry McCormick *(Maitre D')*; Delores Wells *(Very Attractive Woman)*; Charles Wagenheim *(Man in Steam Room)*; Dale Van Sickel *(Driver)*; Corinna Tsopei *(Girl on Wilshire Blvd.)*; Angeline Pettyjohn *(Girl on Wilshire Blvd.)*; Rita Rogers *(Girl on Wilshire Blvd.)*; Paul Sorenson *(Detective)*; Darlene Tompkins

(Bosomy Blonde); and the *Technical Advisers*: Lucille Ball *(Mrs. Joe X.)*; Art Carney *(Joe X.)*; Jack Benny *(Ollie 'Sweet Lips')*; Polly Bergen *(Clara Brown)*; Joey Bishop *(Charlie)*; Sid Caesar *(Man at Romanoff's)*; Wally Cox *(Man married for 14 years)*; Terry Thomas *('Tiger' Harold)*; **Jayne Mansfield** *(Harold's Mistress)*; Hal March *(Man who loses Coat)*; Louis Nye *(Irving)*; Carl Reiner *(Rance G.)*; Phil Silvers *(Realtor)*; Ben Blue

A GUIDE FOR THE MARRIED MAN (1967).

(Shoeless Man); Ann Morgan Guilbert *(Charlie's Wife)*; Jeffrey Hunter *(Mountain Climber)*; Marty Ingels *(Meat Eater)*; Sam Jaffe *(Shrink)*.

Ed convinces his best friend Paul that he should fool around with other women in order to preserve his happy marriage. Ed illustrates his point with a series of vignettes acted out by a lot of famous celebrities. Paul tries to cheat on his sexy wife Ruth with the even more sexy and luscious Irma. The joke of it all is that Ruth is a beautiful woman. Ruth, clearly nude underneath her see-thru nightie, tries to entice Paul who prefers to lie in bed and read his book instead.

Jayne's two minute cameo with British comedian Terry-Thomas was one of the film's highlights. In a steam room Ed tells his friend Paul the story of Harold. A guy who broke the cheating husband guide's rule by taking his mistress to his home when his wife was away. We see this visualized by a car entering a street. Two 'men' get out and cross the street to enter a house. Inside they passionately kiss each other, to reveal one of

U.S. POSTER FOR *A GUIDE FOR THE MARRIED MAN* (1967).

them being a girl. After their rendezvous (which remains unseen) the mistress is missing her bra. "Are you sure you're wearing one?" the man asks her. "What kind of a girl do you think I am; of course I was," the busty blonde says, spilling out of her dressing gown. The cheating husband is afraid his

LOBBY CARD FOR *A GUIDE FOR THE MARRIED MAN*.

wife will find it eventually; but the girl simply answers: "She'll just think it's hers." He turns over to her, with her huge breasts right behind him, and says: "Don't be ridiculous!" In an attempt to find the bra, Thomas almost goes crazy by ransacking the bedroom, while Jayne couldn't care less and touches up her make-up before leaving the room without her brassiere.

Terry-Thomas, the gap-toothed comedian and Jayne were perfectly paired. Terry-Thomas (1911-1990) started his career in his native country England. He was adept at playing upper-class Englishman and he appeared in several Hollywood films in the 1960s. Terry-Thomas said of filming with Jayne: "I saw everything she had through a diaphanous pink negligee she wore in a bedroom scene with me. As I've always said, packaging is everything."[116]

Besides Jayne, another big busted blonde also appeared in *A Guide for the Married Man*. Linda Harrison (b. 1945) had earlier played in Jayne's

---

116. Ross, Robert. *The Complete Terry-Thomas*. Richmond, GB: Reynolds & Hearn Ltd, 2002.

The Fat Spy as a bikini clad treasure hunter and would become world famous as the brunette Nova in *Planet of the Apes* (1968). She was under contract at 20th Century Fox and married producer Richard D. Zanuck son of the man who contracted Jayne Mansfield in 1956, Daryl F. Zanuck. On the set of this movie she was reunited with Walter Matthau (1920-2000), the actor who had also played in the Broadway play *Will Success Spoil Rock Hunter?* all those years before.

Jayne's scene was shot under great personal distress. A few weeks earlier, her son Zoltan had been mauled by a lion at the Jungleland Park in Thousand Oaks, California. He was recovering from spinal meningitis at Conejo Valley Community Hospital, after undergoing brain surgery while Jayne was working on this film.

Jayne, like the other celebrities who did a cameo, was paid $10,000 for two days work. *A Guide for the Married Man* would also bring her back on the studio lot where it all started: 20th Century Fox. It would be the last film of Jayne Mansfield: it successfully restored her sexy dumb blonde image and, in the author's opinion, is an estimable farewell. The movie premiered on May 25, 1967 in New York.

REVIEWS

Variety: "Terry-Thomas and Jayne Mansfield, as a pair of philanderers, make the mistake of using his house for their trysting place. She is unable to find her brassiere and the horror of his wife's eventual discovery of it ages him overnight."

New York Times: "Of all these witty demonstrations I find most amusing the one in which Art Carney teams with Lucille Ball to demonstrate how a husband can break out of the domestic fold by taking an aggressive posture toward his wife, and another in which Jayne Mansfield loses her bra in Terry-Thomas' home — a contretemps proving that a husband should never take his inamorata to his own house."

ITALIAN POSTER FOR *THE WILD, WILD WORLD OF JAYNE MANSFIELD* (1967).

THE WILD, WILD WORLD OF
JAYNE MANSFIELD
South-Eastern Pictures — 1967
99 Minutes, Color

PRODUCER: Dick Randall. DIRECTOR: Arthur Knight, Joel Holt & Charles W. Broun Jr. SCREENPLAY: Charles Ross. MUSIC: Marcello Gigante. EDITOR: Manuela Folena & Artscope Ltd. PHOTOGRAPHY: Edwina Brown, Max Glenn, Claudio Racca & Henry Lange.

CAST: Jayne Mansfield *(Herself)*; Mickey Hargitay *(Himself)*; Miklos Hargitay *(Himself)*; Zoltan Hargitay *(Himself)*; Dick Randall *(Man on the Via Veneto)*; Joel Holt *(Man at the Trevi Fountain)*; Andre Dupont *(Male Nudist)*; Fernand Aubry *(Himself)*; Lila Solh *(Girl on Table)*; Lino Enners *(Judge at Bosom Contest)*; Bob Oliver *(Jury Member at Bosom Contest)*; Brigitt Hallberg *(Winner of Bosom Contest)*; Joan Parker *(Topless Ice cream seller)*; Anne Phillips *(Topless Shoe Polisher)*; Gloria Morris *(Topless Painter)*; Elvira Lake *(Topless Mechanic)*; Andrea Mason *(Topless Hairdresser)*; Jackie *(Topless Dancer in Cage)*; Fred Long *(Producer)*; The Ladybirds *(Topless All-Girl Band)*; Robert Jason; Rocky Roberts and the Airedales; Monte Duro; The Paparazzo's of Rome; Place Pigalle Can Can Girls; The International Transvestite Contest Winners.

Like Jayne's earlier documentary on Las Vegas night life, *Spree*, this production was a travelogue of Jayne's adventures in southern Europe. Mainly filmed in Italy, with side trips to Cannes, France and the United States; *The Wild, Wild World of Jayne Mansfield* takes a journey in the then popular *Mondo Cane*[117] style. Despite its claims of genuine documentation, certain scenes in the film are either staged or creatively manipulated in order to enhance the 'shock' effect.

Jayne takes us with her on a tour through Rome, where she shares a fantasy about Roman athletes. To illustrate her 'day dream' scenes from *Gli Amori di Ercole* are used. Then we travel with her to the 1964 Film Festival of Cannes. Jayne takes a side trip to the nudist colony on the Isle of Levant, where she almost kind of joins in. "Gee, I hope nobody's watching!" Jayne is heard saying.[118] Then it's off to Paris for a beauty treat-

117. Paolo CavaraGualtiero Jacopetti (source: Wikipedia, the free encyclopedia on the internet).

118. Jayne's narration was supplied by a voice double named Carolyn De Fonseca, an Italian actress who had appeared in many US/Italian co-productions in the early sixties.

ment in the Salon of Fernand Aubrey[119], where she is generously oiled down. In the evening she attends some racy dance revues. In New York and Los Angeles, she visits some topless clubs and listens to a topless all-girl pop band, The Ladybirds. This scene also contains topless go-go dancers to which Jayne remarks: "As for the girl in the cage, a little silicone will go a long, long way!" This scene was in the original print of the film only, in later showings the scene was deleted.

POSTER FOR *THE WILD, WILD WORLD OF JAYNE MANSFIELD* (1967).

Besides footage from *Gli Amori di Ercole*, the nude scenes from *Promises, Promises!* and the striptease from *L'Amore Primitivo* are used in this production to spice things up.

Overall it's a dull movie which probably never would have seen the light of day if Jayne hadn't met her untimely death. It was filmed mostly in 1964 during Jayne's time in Europe. She was filming *L'Amore Primitivo* in Rome at the time and was a guest at the French Film Festival in Cannes. Later on some footage was added when Jayne was back in the United States. Other footage, like the Drag Queen Beauty Contest, were believed to be put in after Jayne died to give the film the length it needed to be released to the theatres.

119. Fernand Aubry (1907-1973) was a famous Parisian hair stylist and makeup artist. His catch phrase was: *"There is no woman without beauty, but only hidden beauties who are not aware of it"*. Today there still are many Aubry beauty salons using his line of beauty products.

The final part of the film has Mickey Hargitay giving us a tour through the Pink Palace, playing the pink piano, and displaying the famed wall of magazine covers. While in the couple's bedroom the camera pans on a pair of Jayne's stiletto heels, we hear the narrator say: "A pair of shoes wait by the heart shaped bed. Who will fill those shoes?"

The film had three 'directors': Joel Holt, who was also the associ-

THE WILD, WILD WORLD OF JAYNE MANSFIELD (1967).

ate producer of *L'Amore Primitivo*; Arthur Knight (1919-1991), who was a film historian and anti-censorship crusader, is best known for his pioneering history of the cinema, *The Liveliest Art: A Panoramic History of the Movies* (1957) as well as for his long running column in Playboy magazine, called *Sex in the Cinema*; and Charles Wood Broun Jr. (1924-2001) who also produced the exploitation quickie *She-Man* (1967). A mediocre trio who put *The Wild, Wild World of Jayne Mansfield* together for theatrical release.

The film's producer, Dick Randall (1926-1996) also gave us the awfully wonderful *Cottonpickin' Chickenpickers* (1967) with busty Danish pin-up blonde Greta Thyssen and *Casa D'Appuntamento* aka *The French Sex*

PHOTO MONTAGE FROM THE GERMAN PROGRAM FOR
THE WILD, WILD WORLD OF JAYNE MANSFIELD.

Murders (1972) with Anita Ekberg. In January 1965 Randall announced that Jayne would be making a movie called *Feast of the Vampires*. It was never made. He also was the producer of the 1965 stage play *The Rabbit Habit*, directed by Matt Cimber and with Jayne in the lead.

Distributed by Blue Ribbon Pictures, the movie had its US release on April 18, 1968, in New Orleans.

REVIEWS

There are no contemporary American reviews known to the author. The following reviews are from the last two decades.

Movieline: "...deliriously demented 1968 travelogue. In Rome Jayne is pinched by hired extras on the Via Veneto, runs from hired paparazzi, and has 'silly, wicked daydreams.' Jayne also visits a French nudist colony, knocking down locals with her 40" breasts. The only question remaining is, is this video so funny it's sad, or so sad it's funny?"

Psychotronic: "If you haven't seen this brilliant fascinating fake documentary masterpiece, it's about time! Jayne conducts a mondo tour of strip clubs, a nudist colony and a drag fashion show. Sometimes Jayne "remembers" scenes from some of her movies. The editor deserved an Oscar."

WITH LEW GALLO IN *WILL SUCCESS SPOIL ROCK HUNTER?* (1955).

The Plays

Jayne Mansfield made her stage debut on September 21, 1951 at the Austin Civic Theatre, in *Ten Night in a Bar Room*. She played Fanny Morgan, the spouse of an alcoholic husband and had her one scene in the last act of the play. At that time she was still in College. When she joined her husband Paul at Camp Gordon, Georgia in 1952, she appeared in small roles in several stage productions. Her biggest part was the lead in *Anything Goes*. Paul went to war and Jayne moved back to Dallas where she joined the Dallas Institute of the Performing Arts. On October 22, 1953, Jayne was seen in Arthur Miller's Pulitzer Prize winning drama *Death of a Salesman*. Jayne played the part of Miss Forsythe. Reporter Bob Brock, of the *Daily Time Herald*, wrote a couple of lines about Jayne in his review of the play: "Jayne Mansfield is perfect as a girl of the night."

This chapter summarizes the major plays Jayne Mansfield appeared in. Her big break came in 1955 with *Will Success Spoil Rock Hunter?* That play made her name and was her ticket to success in Hollywood. When Jayne's film career was sagging in the early sixties, she went back to the stage. Her performances in *Bus Stop* and *Gentlemen Prefer Blondes* were not bad, but the remaining of Jayne's stage aspirations are to be neglected.

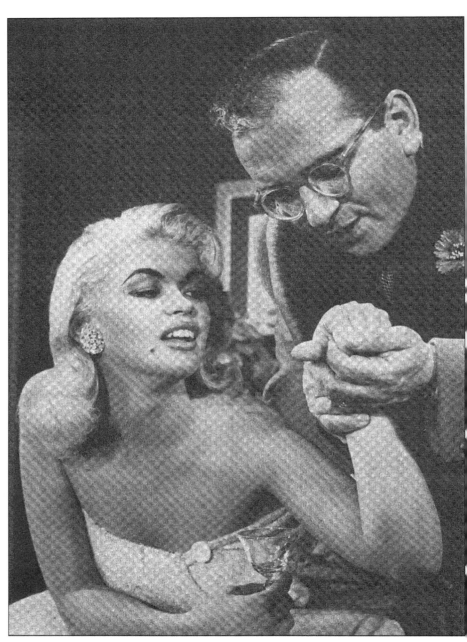

WITH MARTIN GABEL IN *WILL SUCCESS SPOIL ROCK HUNTER?* (1955).

WILL SUCCESS SPOIL ROCK HUNTER?
1955

PRODUCER: Jules Styne. ASSISTANT PRODUCER: Sylvia Herscher. DIRECTOR: George Axelrod. WRITER: George Axelrod. PRODUCTION STAGE MANAGER: David Kanter. STAGE MANAGER: Pat Chandler & Michael Wettach. COSTUMES: Jane Derby. WARDROBE MISTRESS: Rose Caully. HAIR STYLES: Larry Mathews.

CAST: Jayne Mansfield *(Rita Marlowe)*; Orson Bean *(George MacCauley)*; Walter Matthau *(Michael Freeman)*; Martin Gabel *(Irving LaSalle)*; Harry Clarke *(Harry Kaye)*; Lew Gallo *(Masseur)*; Carol Grace *(Secretary)*; William Thourlby *(Bronk Brannigan)*; David Sheiner *(Bellman)*; Tina Louise *(Swimmer)*; Michael Tolan *(Chauffeur)*.

The play is a comedy about fan magazine writer MacCauley who sells his soul to the Devil, who is disguised as Hollywood literary agent LaSalle, to become a successful screenwriter. La Salle asks ten percent — of MacCauley's soul — as a fee for his services. When George visits blonde sex goddess Rita Marlowe in her New York hotel room, he fantasizes about a romance with her. And when Rita reveals her attraction to him, he can't belief how powerful his success has become. The Second Act takes place in the office of Rita Marlowe Productions in Hollywood. While writing a screenplay for LaSalle about the romance of a prostitute and a psychiatrist, George finds out that his girlfriend is still married to Los Angeles Rams football star Bronk Brannigan. In Act Three George has won an Oscar for his screenplay. When Brannigan appears on the scene and starts fighting with him, he seeks the help of LaSalle who, for another ten percent, enables George to get the better of the football player.

In the final scene George begins to doubt his agreement with LaSalle. Each of his wishes has cost him a piece of his soul and now there's only ten percent left. In the final confrontation with LaSalle, fellow playwright Michael Freeman comes to the rescue and tricks the Hollywood agent to sign him and release MacCauley from his contract. LaSalle grabs the offer but soon realizes it was a bad trade, because Freeman is completely happy with his life as it is and has no intention of selling off the remaining ten percent.

In the First Act Rita is supposed to be interviewed by George MacCauley. He hasn't got a chance to ask any questions, because the movie star just rattles on and keeps pronouncing his surname wrong in every sentence. "You may not believe this, Mr. Coleman, but I never *wanted* to be a sex symbol. You know what the funniest thing about me is? In person, I'm not really sexy at all. Honest I'm probably the least sexy person you know! I mean really I am! And I'm just terrible in bed. Everybody says so!"[1] According to the opinion of Jayne's third husband Matt Cimber, this quote was quite relevant to Jayne as a private person. "Everybody said 'Boy, she really must be a hot number'. I didn't think so. I know more secretaries who were hotter than…you know. Not to negate what she had as a sex symbol, but when you say Sex Symbol, what does that mean? Jayne was never more to me than a pin-up."

Jayne's pin-up status annoyed her co-star Martin Gabel (1912-1986), who was a renowned actor, director and producer who had appeared on Broadway as early as 1934. He ignored Jayne most of the time and said degrading things about her behind her back. In an interview Orson Bean described what Jayne had to endure: "I remember one time he [Gabel] was waiting to go on and his opening line was 'My dear, how are you?' But before he'd go on he'd be gassing his teeth, pacing back and forth and I'd been standing there listening to him muttering 'To think that I, who have played Cassius with Orson Welles, should be reduced to appearing in this tawdry comedy with that cunt!' He'd then walk on all smiles and bellow out 'How are you my dear!'"[2] According to Bean, Jayne affronted Gabel by upstaging him, which infuriated him even more. Years later Jayne met Gabel again when he was a panelist on TV's *What's My Line?*[3]

With the success of his former Broadway production *The Seven Year Itch*, George Axelrod had become an overnight sensation. The rights of this play were sold to 20th Century Fox and they starred Marilyn Monroe in their successful film version of 1955. Because Axelrod's story had been so heavily altered, he was inspired to write another play about a playwright who refused to compromise to Hollywood's standards. Walter Matthau played the playwright who remained true to himself by declining the Hollywood offers. Ironically, *Will Success Spoil Rock Hunter?* was again bought by Hollywood studio 20th Century Fox, who completely

1. Axelrod, George. *Will Success Spoil Rock Hunter?* New York: Bantam Books, Inc., 1957.

2. *Jayne Mansfield fan club newsletter*, spring 1991.

3. Jayne appeared as the mystery guest for the third time on May 24, 1964 (the others occurred in 1956, 1957 and her last appearance would be in 1966). When Gabel is confronted with Jayne as the mystery personality, he seems bemused. When the host remarks that she baffled Mr. Gabel, Jayne answers: *"I didn't think Martin Gabel could ever be baffled."* To which Mr. Gabel just looks bewildered and seems speechless.

re-wrote the story and kept just one character from the original play, namely Rita Marlowe. The character of Rita Marlowe is a parody on Marilyn Monroe and sex symbols like her. The star's surname is an homage to 16th Century playwright Christopher Marlowe, who wrote the play *The Tragical History of Doctor Faustus*; which plot served as the inspiration of Axelrod's play. Originally Axelrod wanted to call his play

WITH ORSON BEAN AND WILLIAM THOURLBY IN *WILL SUCCESS SPOIL ROCK HUNTER?* (1955).

Will Success Spoil Rock Hudson? When Hudson's agent threatened with a law suit, the title was changed.

Starring with Jayne were Orson Bean (b. 1928) and Walter Matthau (1920-2000). Opposite to Jayne, Bean was brought to Hollywood to star with Betty Grable and Sheree North in 20th Century Fox' *How to Be Very, Very Popular* (1955) before he starred in *Will Success Spoil Rock*

WITH ORSON BEAN AND LEW GALLO IN *WILL SUCCESS SPOIL ROCK HUNTER?* (1955).

Hunter? Hollywood blacklisted him for his outspoken liberal views in the early 1950s, so Bean was mostly seen on television and on the stage. About working with Jayne he has said: "I found her to be one of the most delightful people that I ever met and I was very close with Jayne for the entire run. She was totally guileless. She was crazy like a fox and knew exactly what she wanted. She never, ever, ever, once schluffed off a performance. She always gave 101% and it came out of that knowledge, that absolute knowledge that all eyes were on her." Actresses Carol Grace (1924-2003) and Tina Louise[4] (b. 1934) were Jayne Mansfield's understudies. On October 4, 1955, Dorothy Killgallen wrote in her column: "Jayne Mansfield, Tina Louise and Carol Saroyan[5] are all imitating Marilyn Monroe, probably by direction. It gets a bit repetitious in that department." Another observer commented: "This girl has absolutely no acting technique and she never will have. But of course she doesn't want to be an actress — she wants to be a star. I think she'll make it." But most reviewers were positive about Jayne's portrayal. Columnist Walter Winchell led the critics' acclaim: "She's as beautiful as Marilyn Monroe (in every department) and she effortlessly delivers the most devastating impression in years." *The New York Daily News* wrote: "Miss Mansfield is splendid as a sexy but typically dumb blonde." When Warner's released Jayne Mansfield from her film contract, she was asked to audition for *Will Success Spoil Rock Hunter?*: "I didn't want to audition for it. I didn't want to do a play, but he [Bill Shiffrin] insisted I try for it, so on my way to Philadelphia I stopped off in New York and read for the part. And I got it." In her autobiography, Jayne talks in a rather positive way about the play and describes she was quite eager to get the part of Rita Marlowe: "From the first day of rehearsal I became Rita Marlowe. The role gave me a chance to act on stage the way I would like to behave off stage. Rita was refreshing, honest, direct, funny and not entirely oblivious of her bombshell of a body thinly camouflaged from admiring males."[6]

4. Tina Louise's career resembled Jayne's. She started out as a pin up model, appeared in several plays on Broadway before finding fame in Hollywood, did two Playboy pictorials and also was considered a sex symbol. In 1964 she took the part in a television show that Jayne had turned down because she felt the role was the kind of stereotype from which she wished to distance herself. After three seasons Tina quit playing Ginger Grant in the sitcom *Gilligan's Island.* Although she was afraid that the part typecasted her as a sex doll, the role did make her a pop icon of that era instead. One wonders what it would have done to Jayne's career if she had done it.

5. Carol Grace was married to playwright William Saroyan at the time of Killgallen's column. In August 1959 she married *Will Success Spoil Rock Hunter?* co-star Walter Matthau.

6. Mansfield, Jayne and Hargitay, Mickey. *Jayne Mansfield's Wild, Wild World.* Los Angeles: Holloway House Publishing Company, 1963.

But that was in retrospect and with the knowledge that this play started her movie career as a Hollywood star. In 1955 Jayne still wanted to be a movie star more than to do a play on Broadway. "It was a real temptation for me to get out of it. I wanted to stay in pictures. But Gregg [Bautzer, Jayne's lawyer] and my agent convinced me to stick it out, telling me it would be a big break for me. So I took a chance, went against my judgment, and stayed in the play." *Will Success Spoil Rock Hunter?* opened on October 13, 1955 at the Belasco Theater, and closed November 3, 1956, after 444 performances.

BUS STOP
1964

PRODUCER: Matt Cimber. DIRECTOR: Matt Cimber. ASSISTANT DIRECTOR: Marty Levine. WRITER: William Inge. WARDROBE MISTRESS: Jackie Reed. HAIR DRESSER: Tony Pazzuello.

CAST: Jayne Mansfield *(Cherie, singer);* Stephen Brooks *(Bo Decker, cowboy);* Ann B. Davis *(Grace Haylard, restaurant owner);* Charles Caron *(Dr. Gerald Lyman, former college professor);* Mickey Hargitay *(Carl, bus driver);* Elizabeth Hartman *(Elma Duckworth, waitress);* Robert Jackson *(Virgil Blessing, ranch hand).*

The play is set in a diner about thirty miles west of Kansas City in early March 1955. A snowstorm has halted the progress of a bus, and the eight characters (five on the bus) have a weather-enforced layover in the diner from approximately 1 to 5 a.m. Among the bus passengers are a young rancher called Bo Decker and blonde Cherie, a barroom chanteuse. Cherie is kidnapped by Bo, who wants to take her to Montana to marry her. At first Cherie tries to get rid of her suitor, but eventually she falls in love with him and accepts to marry him.

Bus Stop took Jayne on tour from May 26 through June 14, 1964 to Yonkers, New York and, after an intermission, from September 1 through September 14, 1964 to Warren, Ohio and Detroit, Michigan. The cast consisted of the regular members, as listed above, and was added with local actors and actresses to fill in the smaller parts.

While rehearsing for *Bus Stop* Jayne fell in love with her director Matt Cimber and when the tour ended Jayne married him. The excellent cast included actor Stephen Brooks (1942-1999), who graduated from the American Academy of Dramatic Arts in 1960 and had made a name for himself in the television series *The Nurses* (1963). He died of a heart attack at age 57.[7] Ann B. Davis (b. 1926) was cast as Schultzy, Bob Cummings' secretary, in the very popular fifties comedy show *The Bob Cummings Show* (aka *Love That Bob)* from 1955-1959. In the seventies she played another beloved character on a TV hit show: housekeeper Alice Nelson in *The Brady Bunch.*

---

7. Originally Mickey Hargitay wanted to play the part of Bo Decker. But because Cimber had already cast Brooks to play that part, Hargitay settled with the part of the bus driver. "Matt handled it by declaring that cowboys didn't have Hungarian accents and that the bus driver could be one hell of a good part if he played it right." Strait, Raymond. *The Tragic Secret Life of Jayne Mansfield.* London: Robert Hale & Company, 1976.

Tragic and talented Elizabeth Hartman (1943-1987) was an up and coming actress at the time she appeared in *Bus Stop*. After the play she was screen-tested by MGM and Warner Bros. In the autumn of 1964 she was cast for the leading part opposite Sidney Poitier in MGM's *A Patch of Blue* (1965). For her portrayal of the blind Selina she won the 'Golden Globe Award for New Star of the Year'. In her

THE CAST OF *BUS STOP* (1964).

later years she suffered from depression and was believed to have committed suicide, when she fell to her death from the window of her apartment. Raymond Strait remembers Jayne's anger when she heard that Mickey was making a pass at Hartman. She had taken a liking to the girl and — unknown to Elizabeth — had a guard put on her dressing room to keep Hargitay out. "She's a nice girl, and I'll not have that bastard messing with her. He'll just fuck up her life like he has mine."[8] Hartman stayed neutral in the tensions that surrounded Mickey and Jayne, and was respected by the whole crew because of her energetic dedication to her part and the play.

The *Detroit Daily Press* reviewed that "Miss Mansfield doesn't give her 'all' to the characterization, but it was certainly all her, in contrast, her

8. Strait, Raymond. *The Tragic Secret Life of Jayne Mansfield*. London: Robert Hale & Company, 1976.

characterization was a wisp — too light, almost removed from the scene. But she comes up with some pretty good lines. The play will satisfy all those who want to see if all the things they've heard about its star are true. Believe me, it's the naked truth."[9]

9. Faris, Jocelyn. *Jayne Mansfield — A Bio-bibliography.* Westport, CT: Greenwood Press, 1994.

AT THE STAGE DOOR, *GENTLEMEN PREFER BLONDES* (1964).

GENTLEMEN PREFER BLONDES
1964/1966

PRODUCER: Matt Cimber. DIRECTOR: Matt Cimber/Peter Conlow. WRITERS: Anita Loos & Joseph Fields. MUSIC: Jules Styne, Leo Robin. CHOREOGRAPHY: Nancy Lynch. MUSICAL DIRECTOR: Charles Jaffe. ASST. MUSICAL CONDUCTOR: Don Shrimpton.

CAST: Jayne Mansfield *(Lorelei Lee);* Mickey Hargitay *(Josephus Gage).*

Famous story about two girlfriends who travel to Paris to find themselves a husband on the way. The two showgirls Lorelei Lee (Jayne) and Dorothy Shaw travel to Europe by boat. Lorelei will visit her fiancée, millionaire Augustus Esmond, and will marry him without his father's interference. But the Esmond family hires a private detective, Josephus Gage, to spy on Lorelei. Gage falls in love with Dorothy. Lorelei also gets in trouble with the law over a supposedly stolen tiara, but the matter is settled in court. All ends well when Dorothy marries Ernie and Lorelei says yes to Augustus.

Jayne and Mickey were the only two regulars in the play. All the other parts were played by local actors and actresses. Kelly Brytt played Lorelei's friend, Dorothy Shaw, in the 1964 run of the play. Robert Gallagher (b. 1920), Hildegarde Halliday (1902-1977), John Cecil Holm (1904-1981) and Ray Malone (b. 1925) also appeared in the play in 1964. Gallagher played small parts on television and in the movies since the early fifties. In the play he was Lorelei's fiancé Gus Esmond. Hildegarde Halliday played Mrs. Ella Spofford and John Cecil Holm played millionaire Sir Francis Beekman, who has his eye on Lorelei. Ray Malone acted and danced in musicals and TV shows since 1943 and appeared as himself, a dancer.

Jayne started touring with the play on June 20, 1964 in Framingham, Massachusetts. She performed there for one week. She played Warwick, Rhode Island from June 29 thru July 4. This was followed by 12 days in Anaheim, California on August 18. Two years later Jayne went back on tour with the play.[10]

Jayne's opening night reviews were flattering. The *Los Angeles Herald* said: "Jayne a Hit as Blonde in Anaheim." However, the *Anaheim Bulletin* wrote how Jayne was totally wrong as the Twenties flapper Lorelei Lee:

10. From June 6 through June 13, 1966 she was in Long Island, New York. On June 14, she played at the Painters Mill Music Fair in Pikesville, Maryland. From July 11 through July 18, 1966 she performed at the Storrowtown Music Fair in West Springfield, Massachusetts. And she ended her tour on July 26, 1966 after a week, in Westbury, New York. Faris, Jocelyn. *Jayne Mansfield — A Bio-bibliography.* Westport, CT: Greenwood Press, 1994.

"But when Miss Mansfield is in vague contact with Lorelei, she asserts a vigorous comic-erotic authority as herself." After having played saloon singer Cherie so well in *Bus Stop*, Jayne decided to do another play that featured a persona that was made famous by Marilyn Monroe in the film version. Maybe Marilyn is the ultimate Lorelei Lee, but Jayne had quite some success with her version also. She sang "Diamonds are a Girl's Best Friend" and "It's Delightful Down in Chile". (The latter was not heard in the 1953 film version). Originally Jayne would have worked with another director, but she insisted that Cimber would be assigned for the job. On the Rhode Island program, Peter Conlow[11] is credited as the play's director.

---

11. Actor, choreographer, director Peter Conlow (1929) had appeared on Broadway as an actor as well as a dancer. He co-choreographed some shows and directed off Broadway plays.

CHAMPAGNE COMPLEX
1964/1965

PRODUCER: Laurence Feldman. DIRECTOR: Matt Cimber. WRITER: Leslie Stevens.

CAST: Jayne Mansfield *(Allyn Macy);* Douglas Marland *(Helms Fell Harper);* Matt Cimber *(Dr. Carter Brown).*

Champagne Complex, a three-act farce, is about Allyn Macy, a lovely young girl who is engaged to a serious and pompous young business executive. The tycoon, called Helms Fell Harper, has a hard time smoothing relations between the carefree girl and his stuffy family especially after that night at a champagne reception when she started to disrobe. Allyn's worried beau calls in his psychoanalyst bachelor uncle, Dr. Carter Brown. Instead of relieving her from her 'champagne complex', Brown falls in love with her. The treatment reveals that the girl wants the analyst himself as Cupid to her psyche. When Harper finds out that his uncle is having an affair with his fiancée he is not amused and the men start a fight. It seems that, deep down inside, the girl does not love her stuffy fiancée; hence her champagne complex.

PROGRAM FOR *CHAMPAGNE COMPLEX* (1965).

In the show two of Jayne's Chihuahuas were seen with her. She was quite upset when one, Galena, died while the show was in Milwaukee, Wisconsin in 1964.[12] Just like Jayne's earlier plays, *Bus Stop* and *Gentlemen Prefer Blondes,* the cast was completed by local talent. The *Milwaukee Journal* was not impressed with the play nor Jayne's performance: "As an actress, Miss Mansfield leaves something to be desired — namely, acting. She strides about constantly, giggles, pouts, says 'Eeek!' talks baby talk to her dog." The other complaint was that the play lasted too long; that

12. Faris, Jocelyn. *Jayne Mansfield — A Bio-bibliography.* Westport, CT: Greenwood Press, 1994.

is to say, almost three hours. Jayne tried to get her long-time friend Bob Hope to star with her in the film version of *The Champagne Complex*, but that plan never materialized.

Douglas Marland (1934-1993) who played the part of Harper, began his career as an actor for the stage and television. However, he became more successful as the head writer of television soaps like *General Hospital*, *Guiding Light* and *As the World Turns*. He won three Emmy Awards. His death was caused by complications from abdominal surgery.

The Champagne Complex played in Milwaukee from October 27 through November 7, 1964 and then went to the East Coast from January 19 through January 30, 1965, where it was seen in Long Island, New York.

NATURE'S WAY
1965

PRODUCER: Eddie Rich. DIRECTOR: Matt Cimber. WRITER: Herman Wouk. ADVANCE DIRECTOR: Howard Miller. PRODUCTION STAGE MANAGER: Thomas McKeehan. PRODUCTION DESIGNER: Charles Brandon.

CAST: Jayne Mansfield *(Maggie Turk)*; Matt Cimber *(Billy Turk)* Charles Caron *(Butler)*; Arch Allen *(Mr. Chaney)*; Vanda Barra *(Nadine Fesser)*; Peter Harris *(Vivian Voles)*; Grant Gordon *(Gilbert Price)*; Elizabeth Kerr *(Mrs. Fawcett)*; Mel Haynes *(Dr. Bacher)*; Neal Thorpe *(Rip Vorhees)*; Pamela Harrison *(Mrs. Vorhees)*; Martin Levine *(Dr. Blimber)*; Robert Koesis *(The Waiter)*; Andrew Green *(The Musician)*.

Billy and Maggie Turk have been married for five months. Maggie is pregnant. Billy is a highly successful songwriter and the couple live in an expensive Park Lane penthouse. Their future seems bright, but then the mother-in-law arrives, followed by a huge tax bill. Then playwright Vivian Voles whisks Billy off to Europe. Secretly in love with Maggie, he plans to break up the marriage by introducing Billy to an European princess.

Jayne and Matt Cimber played *Nature's Way* from August 17 until August 22 in Canada. The play closed after 8 performances. Local actors completed the supporting cast. Jayne

PROGRAM FOR *NATURE'S WAY* (1965).

didn't have to pretend playing a pregnant woman; she was almost seven months pregnant with her son Tony Cimber, while appearing in the play.

A comedy in two acts and three scenes, *Nature's Way*, had opened on Broadway in 1957. Wouk situated the play in the early sixties. Orson Bean (who played with Jayne Mansfield in *Will Success Spoil Rock Hunter?*) and Betsy von Furstenberg starred in the original play. Playwright and novelist Herman Wouk (b. 1915) had won the Pulitzer Prize for Fiction for his novel, *The Caine Mutiny* (1951). *Nature's Way* was his second and last story written especially for the stage.

THE RABBIT HABIT
1965

PRODUCER: Dick Randall. DIRECTOR: Matt Cimber. Writer: Rex
Carlton. ADDITIONAL DIALOGUE: Ken Callender. STAGE MAN-
AGER: Richard B. Shull. GENERAL MANAGER: Lee Hewitt. SCENIC
DESIGNER: Henry E. Lowenstein. WARDROBE MISTRESS: Marjorie
Simon. HAIR DRESSER: Kitty Burke.

CAST: Jayne Mansfield *(Jill Marlowe/Neilson, the wife)*; Hugh Marlowe *(Dr.
John Neilson, missile scientist/the husband)*; Alex D'Arcy *(Professor Hartoonian,
an astrologer)*; Joan Shawlee *(Doris, the secretary)*; Jadeen Vaughn *(Dr. Valerie
Swanson, Ph.D. in public relations)*; Marjorie Bennett *(Kate, the maid)*.

Chorus girl Jill Marlowe has given up her career to marry a missile
scientist. When the couple can't get pregnant, they seek the help of an
astrologer. When he suggests to sleep with Jill himself, that almost ruins
her marriage.

This two-act play opened in Denver, Colorado on December 1, 1965
— a month and a half after the birth of Jayne's fifth child — and closed
after only five nights on December 5. The entire action takes place in
the fashionable residence of the Neilson's, near a missile base at Cape
Kennedy, Florida. The play was intended to open on Broadway on
February 14, 1966. The production was capitalized at $37,000, but lost
$60,000 due to operating deficits, closing expenses and various incidental
liabilities. Jayne's character was originally named Miko Marlowe; however the name 'Miko' was changed to 'Jill'. The photos that were used in
the theatre programs for *the Rabbit Habit* were the publicity stills that
were originally taken for Jayne's German movie *Heimweh nach St. Pauli*
(1963).

The Rabbit Habit mostly received poor reviews, although Jayne's share
in the play was reviewed less harshly. *Variety* wrote: "Though Jayne
Mansfield has comic possibilities, the listless direction by Matt Cimber
fails to help a helpless script."

Jayne appeared alongside Hollywood actors Hugh Marlowe (1911-
1982), Alex D'Arcy (1908-1996) and Joan Shawlee (1926-1987), who had
in common that they all had played in a movie with Marilyn Monroe.[13]

---

13. Hugh Marlowe played in *All About Eve* (1950), Alex D'Arcy in *How to Marry a Millionaire* (1953)
and Joan Shawlee was the bandleader in Monroe's *Some Like it Hot* (1959).

Actress Marjorie Bennett (1896-1982) who played the house maid in this play, had played the role of Miss Snavely in Jayne's movie *Promises! Promises!* (1963).

Playwright Rex Carlton wanted Jayne to star in his upcoming film project *Blood of Dracula's Castle* (1969), but she denounced the offer.

PROGRAM FOR *THE RABBIT HABIT* (1965).

After Carlton (1915-1968) had written the screenplay for the science fiction-thriller *The Unearthly Stranger* (1964), he began an association with director/producer Al Adamson, for whom he wrote the screenplay for *Blood of Dracula's Castle*. When this film ran into post-production legal problems that delayed its release, Carlton panicked. It is said that he couldn't pay back the money he had lent from the mob to finance this project. On May 6, 1968, Carlton shot himself in the head.

In January 1966, Jayne also experienced money trouble when her agency withheld $500 in commissions against Jayne's account from *The Rabbit Habit*. It was explained to her that the producer's cheques had bounced, but she was never credited or given a refund.

JAYNE WITH JACK BENNY, 1956.

Television Appearances

Hollywood was experiencing a difficult period in the early fifties. The new medium of television became a bigger threat than expected. As of January 1, 1946, there had been only about 10 thousand TV sets in the entire United States. Five years later, 12 million sets were operating throughout the country and NBC had began coast-to-coast operations with 61 stations.[1] Definitely, television had become popular in the 1950s.

People were staying home from the movies. Receipts were tumbling. Movie houses all over the country closed their doors and opened again as supermarkets. Since WW II, 51 cinemas closed down in New York, 64 in Chicago and 134 in Southern California.[2] Columnist Hedda Hopper, farsighted warned the Hollywood community: "Television is the one medium that I don't believe Hollywood can't give the old run-around; so we might as well take the TV producers by their hot little hands and cooperate."[3] The very structure that had created the mammoth studio control over its star system was heading for collapse. By 1957 all the major film companies, with the exception of Paramount, had sold all their output prior to 1948 to their arch-enemy. Most of the studios were making fewer films, and some of them (e.g. Republic and RKO) were shut down entirely and transformed in television studios.[4]

---

1. Settel, Irving.New York: Frederic Ungar Publishing Co., 1983.

2. Pye, Michael. London: Orbis Publishing Limited, 1982.

3. The Hollywood Reporter, May 1950.

4. RKO was sold to Desilu in 1957, the company of Lucille Ball and Desi Arnaz. The Republic lot was sold to CBS. The studios were used for the production of television programs.

THIS IS YOUR LIFE WITH RALPH EDWARDS (1962).

Jayne Mansfield's first professional job for television was a ten line part on the Lux Video Theater in October 1954. Many sources state that actor/ director Jack Webb had used Jayne for a walk-on on his TV series *Dragnet*. But the episode she appeared in stays untitled, because she is not credited for any of the episodes in 1954 or 1955. About her television debut, she told *TV Guide* magazine in a 1956 interview: "I was very thrilled about it, at last I was acting for money. I got $300. My second TV show was just last month — *The Bachelor*, an NBC spectacular — and it was the first time I'd ever had a singing role. I did appear on some interview shows and on *Person to Person*, but they don't count. My agent tells me what to do, so now audiences will only see me on big, exploited, planned TV shows."

Jayne Mansfield regularly appeared on game shows like *Talk it Up*, *Down You Go* — for which she was a regular panelist in 1956 — *The Match Game* and *What's My Line?* In December 1960, Jayne was the main guest on *This is Your Life*. Many times she was the comic foil for comedians like Jack Benny (1956, 1957, 1963), Bob Hope (1958, 1960, 1961, 1962, 1966), Steve Allen (1959, 1960) and Milton Berle (1966). In 1965 Jayne's own production company Jaynatt Productions, produced a television pilot for *The Jayne Mansfield Hour*. The pilot was made for NBC but was never shown on television. Jayne would have played a character called Jayne Marlowe, obviously a referral to the character Rita Marlowe from *Will Success Spoil Rock Hunter?* [5]

Featured in this chapter are Jayne Mansfield's most noteworthy dramatic and comedy appearances on the small screen.

AN ANGEL WENT AWOL
NBC — 60 minutes, B&W
Original air date: October 21, 1954.

DIRECTOR: Earl Eby. TELEPLAY: Winifred Wolfe & Jack Gordun.

CAST: Joanne Dru *(Polly)*; George Nader *(Jeremy)*; Angela Stevens *(Christy)*; Charlotte Knight *(Lucy Gilind)*; Robert Jordan *(Boy at Piano)*; Jayne Mansfield *(Girl at Piano)*; Margaret Lindsay *(Intermission Guest)*.

In this romantic fantasy, a struggling young actor figures out that his recent success is due to his wife. He sees her as his guardian angel. Jayne's

5. The pilot was directed by Mervin Nelson and also featured Eric Rhodes, Ronnie Cunningham, Matt Cimber and Craig Timberlake. Jackson, Jean-Pierre & Françoise. **Jayne Mansfield** Paris, Edilig, 1984.

WITH CAROL HANEY AND HAL MARCH IN "THE BACHELOR" (1956).

tiny part gave her ten sentences of dialogue. Two years later Jayne would make a cameo appearance in Joanne Dru's *Hell on Frisco Bay.*

SUNDAY SPECTACULAR: "THE BACHELOR"
NBC — 90 minutes, Color
Original air date: July 15, 1956.

DIRECTOR: Joseph Cates. TELEPLAY: Coleman Jacoby & Arnie Rosen.

CAST: Hal March *(Larry);* Carol Haney *(Marion);* Jayne Mansfield *(Robin);* Georgann Johnson *(Francesca);* Julie Wilson *(Leslie);* Raymond Bramley *(Dunlap);* Harry Holcombe *(Wainwright);* Renzo Cesana *(The Count),* Peter Gennaro, Frank Derbas, The Ted Ralph Orchestra.

Musical comedy with March as a bachelor account executive with an advertising agency, who thinks he has the perfect set-up with three girlfriends (Mansfield, Johnson and Wilson). His loyal secretary Haney has the delicate job of seeing to it that the three girlfriends never learn of one another's existence. In the end he realizes it's Haney with whom he is truly in love. It was advertised as being the first TV musical comedy. Haney also choreographed the dances and the songs were written by popular TV host Steve Allen. They received solid reviews. Jayne, as the dumb blonde Robin, also sang one song.

SUNDAY SPECTACULAR: "ATLANTIC CITY HOLIDAY"
NBC — 90 minutes, Color and B&W
Original air date: August 12, 1956.

DIRECTOR: Ernest D. Gluckman. WRITERS: George Foster & Mort Green.

CAST: Jack Carter, Polly Bergen, Pat Boone, Jayne Mansfield, Rocky Graziano, Carol Morris, Jonathan Winters, Eddie Fisher, Debbie Reynolds, Bill Haley & His Comets.

Carter goes to the seaside resort of Atlantic City to visit his friend, nightclub songstress Bergen. Before they know it, Bergen and Carter have become the Earth guides for gorgeous visitor from the planet Venus,

Jayne Mansfield. Jayne is accompanied by her Venusian protector, Rocky Graziano. Jayne gets to meet a potpourri of entertainers and does an imitation of Marilyn Monroe; she's seen reading *The Brothers Karamazov* in a bubble bath and sings the Monroe number "Heat Wave". Portions of the show were filmed in color.

SHOWER OF STARS: "STAR TIME"
CBS — 60 minutes, Color.
Original air date: January 10, 1957.

DIRECTOR: Ralph Levy. WRITERS: Howard Snyder & Hugh Wedlock.

CAST: Jack Benny, Jayne Mansfield, Liberace, Vincent Price, Bob Crosby, George Liberace, Rod McKuen, Joan O'Brien, Jack Harmon, Russell Trent, Herb Vigran, Robert Williams, William Lundigan *(Host)*.

Originally filmed in color, the show highlights Jack Benny in a fifteen minute courtroom sketch with Liberace, Vincent Price and Jayne. Jayne playes Benny's defense lawyer in a murder trial. Liberace is the judge, Price the prosecutor and George Liberace is the bailiff. After Jayne's appearance on Shower of Stars, an Elvis Presley fan wrote to CBS: "If you can't show Elvis Presley from the waist down, don't show Jayne Mansfield from the waist up!"

THE RED SKELTON SHOW: "CLEM'S GENERAL STORE"
CBS — 30 minutes, B&W
Original air date: October 6, 1959.

DIRECTOR: Ed Hiller. TELEPLAY: Johnny Carson & Hal Hudson.

CAST: Red Skelton *(Clem Kadiddlehopper);* Jayne Mansfield *(Daisy June);* Jamie Farr *(Nose, Prison Escapee);* Jesse White *(Moose, Prison Escapee);* Art Gilmore *(Announcer);* David Rose and His Orchestra.

Dim witted Clem Kadiddlehopper takes a job at a General Store so he can earn the money to marry his sweetheart Daisy June. When two escaped convicts violently want to take shelter in the shop, Clem and Daisy June fight back. Daisy June points a gun to the crooks and tells Clem that she's got him all covered. To which Clem says: "And she's just

AYNE WITH RED SKELTON IN "CLEM'S GENERAL STORE" (1959).

the girl to do it!" In the end the bandits are caught, Daisy June and Clem get the reward which they spend on their honeymoon. This was the first time Jayne appeared with Red Skelton. She would appear with comedian Red Skelton in two other comedy shows in the following years.[6]

JAYNE WITH RICHARD ANDERSON, DIANA TRASK, AND JOHN ERICSON IN "THE HOUSE ON THE RUE RIVIERA" (1961).

KRAFT MYSTERY THEATER: "THE HOUSE ON THE RUE RIVIERA"
NBC — 60 minutes, B&W
Original air date: August 30, 1961.

DIRECTOR: Unknown. TELEPLAY: Douglas Heyes.

CAST: Richard Anderson, John Ericson, Jayne Mansfield, Diana Trask, Frank Gallop *(Host)*.

Originally titled *Monte Carlo* and intended as a pilot for a proposed NBC adventure series. It was filmed on the 20th Century Fox lot and had Anderson playing an American who is hired by the French national

6. On January 6, 1959 he had actress Edie Adams do and impersonation of Jayne Mansfield. The particular show was titled *San Fernando in Alaska*.

police to watch over American tourists and keep them from getting in trouble. The pilot show was aired as part of the Kraft Mystery Theater and had Anderson trying to clear his name after he becomes the prime suspect in a woman's murder. Jayne Mansfield: "Many have asked why my part was not bigger even though I got star billing. The truth is, that I did this short part only as a favor to my studio. This was to have been a pilot film and was never intended to be shown as a special show." In a publicity photo Jayne wears the white dress Marilyn Monroe had worn in *Let's Make Love* (1960).

THE RED SKELTON SHOW: "WILL SUCCESS SPOIL CLEM KADIDDLEHOPPER?"
CBS — 30 minutes, B&W
Original air date: September 26, 1961.

DIRECTOR: Seymour Berns. TELEPLAY: Johnny Carson & Hal Hudson.

CAST: Red Skelton *(Clem Kadiddlehopper)*; **Jayne Mansfield** *(Lorelei Lovely)*; Linda Loftis *(Miss Texas)*; Carolyn Lasater *(Miss Utah)*; Art Gilmore *(Announcer)*; David Rose and His Orchestra.

Clem wins a raffle, the first prize of which is a kiss from buxom movie queen Lorelei Lovely. But Clem is too shy to collect, so Jayne is forced to turn on the charm! Also appearing are several recent Miss USA contestants. The title is an obvious spoof on Jayne's own *Will Success Spoil Rock Hunter?* (1957). The name of Jayne's character is derived from Lorelei Lee, the famous dumb blonde of *Gentlemen Prefer Blondes*. It was the first episode of the 11th season of *The Red Skelton Show*.

FOLLOW THE SUN: "THE DUMBEST BLONDE"
ABC — 60 minutes, B&W
Original air date: February 4, 1962.

DIRECTOR: Robert Butler. TELEPLAY: Ellis Kadison.

CAST: Barry Coe *(Ben Gregory)*; Brett Halsey *(Paul Templin)*; Jay Lanin *(Lt. Frank Roper)*; Brian Keith *(Earl Patton)*; **Jayne Mansfield** *(Scottie)*; George Brenlin *(Mike Champion)*; Tom Palmer *(Al Brand)*; Gigi Perreau

(Kathy Richards, The Secretary); Rebecca Welles *(Beverly Willis);* Doris Edwards *(Betty);* Ray Kellogg *(Carter);* Paul Kent *(Kane).*

The show follows the adventures of two freelance writers (Coe and Halsey) in Hawaii. In this episode Gregory encounters Scottie, the 'dumb blonde' girlfriend of loudmouth Earl Patton. Gregory works on a story of a deal Patton is trying to cook up with a crooked financier. Because of Scottie's interference by talking to Gregory, the deal may fall apart. Gregory takes a liking to Scottie and introduces her to some of his friends and recommends

WITH BARRY COE IN "THE DUMBEST BLONDE" (1962).

WITH RED SKELTON IN "WILL SUCCESS SPOIL CLEM KADIDDLEHOPPER?" (1961).

some books to her. Scottie begins to feel alive again after the mental abuse and anguish she has suffered for years at the hands of her hoodlum boyfriend. The plot is very much like Judy Holiday's *Born Yesterday* (1950). *The Dumbest Blonde* was filmed for 20th Century Fox's Television division.

THE ALFRED HITCHCOCK HOUR: "HANGOVER"
CBS — 60 minutes, B&W
Original air date: December 6, 1962.

DIRECTOR: Bernard Girard. TELEPLAY: Lou Rambeau.

CAST: Tony Randall *(Hadley Purvis)*; Jayne Mansfield *(Marian)*; Robert P. Lieb *(Bill Hunter)*; Myron Healey *(Bob Blake)*; Tyler McVey *(D.A. Driscoll)*; James Maloney *(Cushman)*; June Levant *(The Saleswoman)*; William Phipps *(Bartender)*; Chris Roman *(Cliff)*; Richard Franchot *(Albert)*; Dody Heath *(Sandra Purvis)*; Alfred Hitchcock *(Host)*.

Hadley Purvis, an advertising man, finds himself facing a divorce if he doesn't stop his heavy drinking. This does little to slow him down as he continues to drink himself into an alcoholic stupor, and one morning, finds himself at home with a girl named Marian that he picked up the night before — and his wife is missing. Jayne plays an attractive and sympathetic girl Purvis meets in a bar. Jayne looks completely different with a short blonde hairdo; she was applauded because of her acting in *Hangover*. The hour play was adapted from two stories: *Hangover*, by John D. MacDonald, and *Marian*, by Charles Runyon. This was the second time Jayne worked with Tony Randall. Dody Heath, who played Randall's wife, would meet Jayne again on the set of *Dog Eat Dog*.

THE RED SKELTON SHOW: "ADVICE TO THE LOVEWORN"
CBS — 60 minutes, B&W
Original air date: February 19, 1963.

DIRECTOR: Seymour Berns. TELEPLAY: Johnny Carson & Hal Hudson.

CAST: Red Skelton *(George Appleby)*; Virginia Gregg *(Clara Appleby)*; Jayne Mansfield *(Dr. Joyce Sisters)*; Art Gilmore *(Announcer)*; David Rose and His Orchestra.

ITH TONY RANDALL IN "HANGOVER" (1962).

Henpecked George Appleby and his loudmouthed wife Clara seek help from marriage counselor Dr. Joyce Sisters. Her advice to George and Clara on how to spice up their marriage lands George in the hospital. During a session with Dr. Sisters, she asks Appleby where he got his less-than-impressive physique, he explains that he's rented his muscles from Mickey Hargitay. Jayne also sang a song called "Glory of Love".

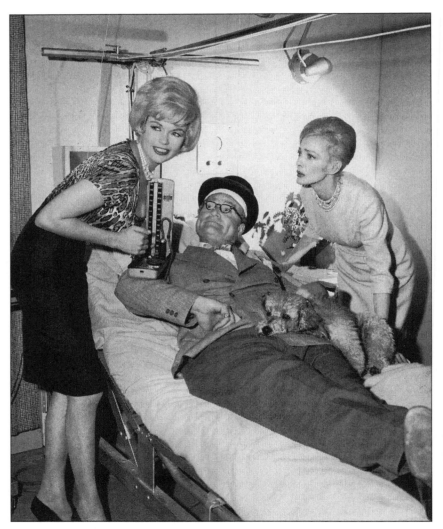

WITH RED SKELTON AND VIRGINIA GREGG IN "ADVICE TO THE LOVEWORN" (1963).

WITH JACK BENNY IN "JACK TAKES A BOAT FROM HAWAII" (1963).

THE JACK BENNY SHOW:
"JACK TAKES A BOAT FROM HAWAII"
CBS — 30 minutes, B&W
Original air date: November 26, 1963.

DIRECTOR: Frederick De Cordova. WRITERS: George Balzer, Hal Goldman, Al Gordon & Sam Perrin.

CAST: Jack Benny, Eddie 'Rochester' Anderson, Dennis Day, Don Randolph, Vince Williams, Ollie O'Toole, Dolores Domasin, Peggy Mondo, Don Wilson, Cliff Norton.

Jayne plays Benny's dream girl in a sketch aboard a cruise ship. Benny takes a little vacation to Hawaii. He falls asleep and dreams of meeting Jayne. When he wakes up from his daydream he finds fat lady Mondo instead of Jayne. It was almost the same sketch that Benny performed with Marilyn Monroe 10 years earlier. Jayne sings "You're Just Too Marvelous" to the love-struck Benny.

A piece of the dialogue: "I just can't control myself when I'm near you. I'm crazy about you," Jayne tells Jack. To which he replies: "Well, I'm crazy about you too, Jayne, but it's so ridiculous. I mean, look at the difference in our ages." Jayne: "There's not that much difference, Jack. I'm twenty-six, and you're thirty-nine." Jack answers: "I know, but I was thinking. Twenty-five years from now, when you'll be fifty-one, and I'll be thirty-nine." Of course Jayne wasn't twenty-six, but thirty years old, when the program was filmed.

BURKE'S LAW: "WHO KILLED MOLLY?"
ABC — 60 minutes, B&W
Original air date: March 27, 1964.

DIRECTOR: Don Weis. TELEPLAY: Albert Beich.

CAST: Gene Barry *(Capt. Amos Burke)*; Gary Conway *(Det. Tim Tilson)*; Regis Toomey *(Det. Les Hart)*; Leon Lontoc *(Henry, the Chauffeur)*; Nannette Fabray *(Mrs. Amanda Tribble)*; Joyce Nizzari *(Molly Baker)*; Jayne Mansfield *(Cleo Patrick)*; Jay C. Flippen *(Lt. Grogan)*; Hoagy Carmichael *(Carl Baker)*; Michael Fox *(Coroner George McLeod)*; Eileen O'Neill *(Sgt. Gloria Ames)*; Marianna Hill *(Dr. Goddard)*; Sharon Cintron *(First Stripper)*; Carol Anderson *(Second Stripper)*; Juli Reding *(Third Stripper)*; Irwin Charone *(Mr. Hoffmeyer)*; Larry Blake *(Robert Taggart)*; Allyson Ames *(Miss Halsey, First Landlady)*; Sandra Giles *(Mrs. Kurtz, Second Landlady)*; Sandra Wirth *(Miss Huntley, Third Landlady)*; Rachel Romen *(Georgia)*; Brenda Howard *(Waitress)*.

Capt. Burke is investigating the murder of housewife Molly Brown. The beautiful brunette is found dead in the shower, apparently the victim of a fall and drowning. But the autopsy shows that she was strangled and the discovery of blond wig hairs on four of her dresses is the first indication of her very busy secret life. The evidence leads Burke into the world of burlesque, where he meets a stripper called Cleo (Jayne). He questions her in her dressing room. The second scene Jayne was in was at Molly's funeral.

WITH GENE BARRY IN *BURKE'S LAW* (1964).

Magazine Cover Gallery

SHOW

A HILLMAN PUBLICATION

OCTOBER 15¢

U.S. THEATRE—
IS IT SEX
OR ART?

THAT
ROCK 'N' ROLL
RUMPUS!

BEST PIN-UPS
OF 1955

US MAGAZINE, OCTOBER, 1955.

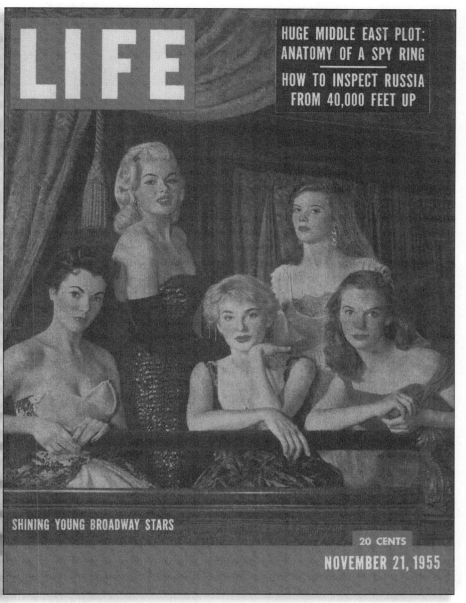

LIFE

HUGE MIDDLE EAST PLOT:
ANATOMY OF A SPY RING

HOW TO INSPECT RUSSIA
FROM 40,000 FEET UP

SHINING YOUNG BROADWAY STARS

20 CENTS

NOVEMBER 21, 1955

US MAGAZINE, NOVEMBER, 1955.

de Mascotte

VROLIJKE
MOPPENTROMMEL
PIN UP
PARADE

48 blz.
ELKE
MAAND

No 199   HUMORISTISCH MAGAZINE VOOR HEREN   10 Fr. (Ned. 90 cent)

BELGIAN MAGAZINE, JULY, 1956.

FRENCH MAGAZINE, DECEMBER, 1956.

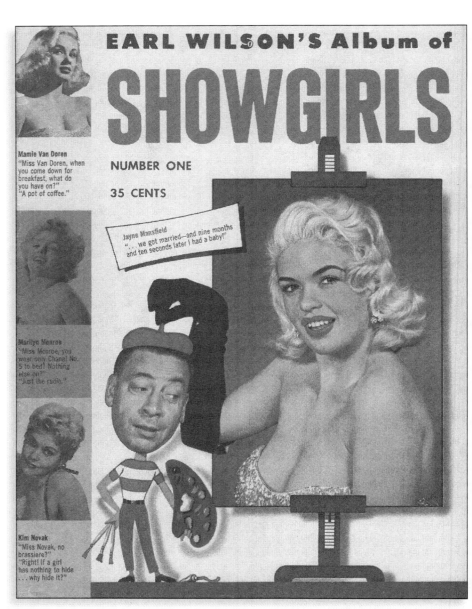

EARL WILSON'S Album of

SHOWGIRLS

Mamie Van Doren
"Miss Van Doren, when you come down for breakfast, what do you have on?"
"A pot of coffee."

NUMBER ONE

35 CENTS

Jayne Mansfield
"... we got married—and nine months and ten seconds later I had a baby!"

Marilyn Monroe
"Miss Monroe, you wear only Chanel No. 5 to bed? Nothing else on?"
"Just the radio."

Kim Novak
"Miss Novak, no brassiere?"
"Right! If a girl has nothing to hide ... why hide it?"

US MAGAZINE, 1956.

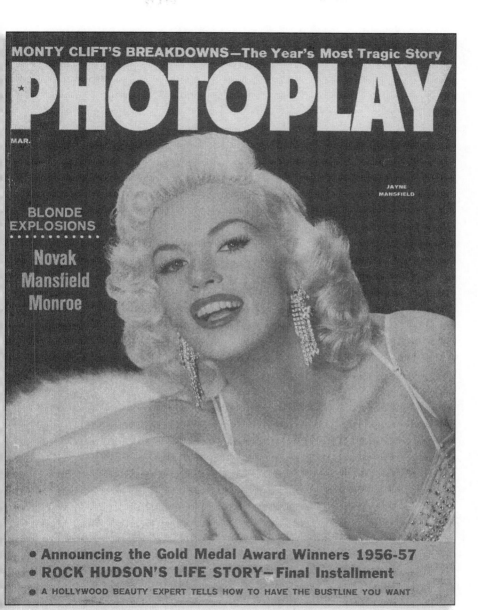

MONTY CLIFT'S BREAKDOWNS—The Year's Most Tragic Story

PHOTOPLAY

MAR.

JAYNE
MANSFIELD

BLONDE
EXPLOSIONS
• • • • • • • • • • •
Novak
Mansfield
Monroe

● Announcing the Gold Medal Award Winners 1956-57
● ROCK HUDSON'S LIFE STORY—Final Installment
● A HOLLYWOOD BEAUTY EXPERT TELLS HOW TO HAVE THE BUSTLINE YOU WANT

US MAGAZINE, MARCH, 1957.

AUSTRIAN MAGAZINE, MARCH, 1957.

JUNE—1957
1/6ᵈ

Hearts

Glamour & Fun

FILMS & T.V.

Records & Shows

FEATURE & FICTION

JAYNE MANSFIELD
20th Century-Fox

UK MAGAZINE, JUNE, 1957.

US MAGAZINE, JULY, 1957.

AUGUST 17th, 1957

6D

Blighty

JAYNE MANSFIELD

THE NATIONAL

HUMOROUS WEEKLY

UK MAGAZINE, AUGUST, 1957.

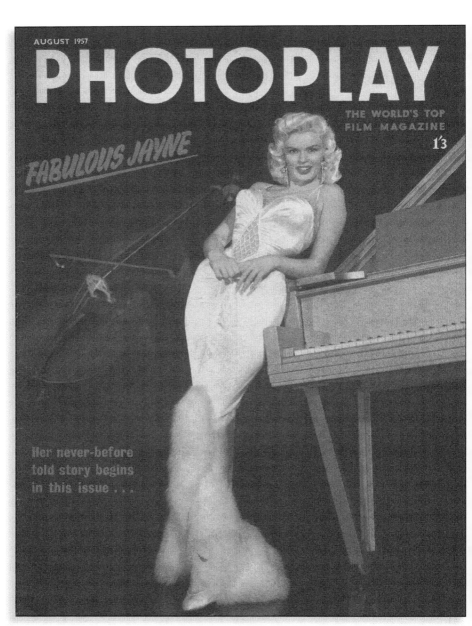

AUGUST 1957

PHOTOPLAY

THE WORLD'S TOP
FILM MAGAZINE

1'3

FABULOUS JAYNE

Her never-before
told story begins
in this issue . . .

UK MAGAZINE, AUGUST, 1957.

Nr 15 1957

Jayne Mansfield
Foto: FOX

SWEDISH MAGAZINE, AUGUST, 1957.

DUTCH MAGAZINE, SEPTEMBER, 1957.

VIJF DAGEN JAYNE MANSFIELD

DUTCH MAGAZINE, OCTOBER, 1957.

the magazine which is a souvenir book

66

PHOTOGRAPHS

OF

1/3

Jayne **MANSFIELD**
and Pin-up Stars

UK MAGAZINE, 1957.

SHOW

PAT BOONE —
The New Crosby?

What Next
Jayne Mansfield ?

23

BRITAIN'S BRIGHTEST
SHOW BUSINESS
MAGAZINE

1'6ᴰ

UK MAGAZINE, 1957.

PARIS

FROU FROU

LE 1ᵉʳ DE CHAQUE MOIS
Nᵒ 44   170ᶠ

JAYNE MANSFIELD

FRENCH MAGAZINE, 1957.

PARIS

FROU FROU

LE 1er DE CHAQUE MOIS
N° 48   170 F

JAYNE
MANSFIELD

FRENCH MAGAZINE, 1957.

GLANCE

DECEMBER . 35 CENTS

WHY
MEN GO
WILD IN
LAS
VEGAS

STRANGE
ALLIANCE
STRIPPER
AND THE
SNAKE

BEAUTIFUL
WOMEN WERE
HIS PREY
BEDROOM
BANDIT

VICE KING
TELLS ALL
I RUN
HONG
KONG

BRIGITTE BARDOT
EXCLUSIVE!

THE ACTUAL PHOTO
PAPA TRIED TO
SUPPRESS

A SALESMAN'S
FANTASTIC
EXPERIENCE WITH . . .
Farmer Ford's
3 Daughters

5
New Pin-up
Features

I'M GOING
BACK TO
PARADISE
ISLAND

JAYNE MANSFIELD

US MAGAZINE, DECEMBER, 1958.

M. R.
N.° 1454
$ 100
M/chilena

ecran

REVISTA DE CINE
INTERNACIONAL

Jayne Mansfield

ARGENTINIAN MAGAZINE, DECEMBER, 1958.

BRAZILIAN MAGAZINE, FEBRUARY, 1959.

Nr 17 1960

1:30
INKL. OMS.

Jayne Mansfield hälsar på i detta nummer

SWEDISH MAGAZINE, 1960.

das magazin
bolero

HEFT 4   2 DM   12 SCHILLING

MÄRZ 1961   H 8019 E

GERMAN MAGAZINE, MARCH. 1961.

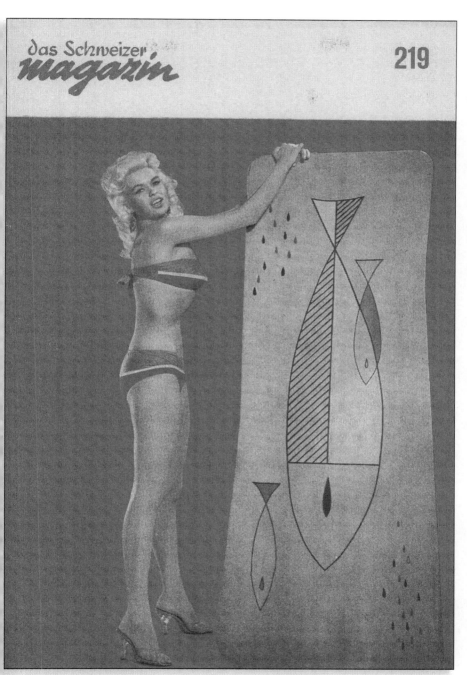

das Schweizer magazin

219

SWISS MAGAZINE, JULY, 1961.

FRENCH MAGAZINE, OCTOBER, 1961.

FRENCH MAGAZINE, MAY, 1964.

BIBLIOGRAPHY

Agan, Patrick. *The Decline and Fall of the Love Goddesses.* Los Angeles: Pinnacle Books, Inc., 1979.

Axelrod, George. *Will Success Spoil Rock Hunter?* New York: Bantam Books, Inc., 1957.

Bergsma, Auke & Selier, Herman. *De Terugkeer van Jayne Mansfield in Nederland.* Rotterdam, The Netherlands: 1997.

Betrock, Alan. *Battle of the Blondes — Jayne Mansfield vs Mamie Van Doren.* New York: Shake Books, 1993.

Betrock, Alan. *The I Was a Teenage Juvenile Delinquent Rock 'n' Roll Horror Beach Party Movie Book — A Complete Guide to the Teen Exploitation Film: 1954-1969.* London: Plexus Publishing Limited, 1986.

Bret, David. *Diana Dors — Hurricane in Mink.* London: JR Books, 2010.

Brode, Douglas. *Lost Films of the Fifties.* Secaucus, N.J.: Citadel Press, 1988.

Bubbeo, Daniel. *The Women of Warner Brothers — The Lives and Careers of 15 Leading Ladies.* Jefferson: McFarland & Company, Inc., Publishers, 2002.

Cameron, Ian & Elisabeth. *Dames.* New York: Frederick A. Praeger, Inc., Publishers, 1969.

Cocchi, John. *Second Features — The Best of the 'B' Films.* New York: Citadel Press, 1991.

Collins, Joan. *Past Imperfect — An Autobiography.* New York: Simon & Schuster, 1978.

Conrad III, Barnaby. *The Blonde — A Celebration of the Golden Era from Harlow to Monroe.* San Francisco: Chronicle Books, 1999.

Crivello, Kirk. *Fallen Angels — The lives and untimely deaths of 14 Hollywood Beauties.* Secaucus, NJ: Citadel Press, 1988.

Dauphin, Gerald. *Jan Cremer in New York & Jayne Mansfield.* Antwerp, Belgium: Celbeton, 1966.

Dempsey, Michael. *Movies of the Fifties.* London: Orbis Publishing Limited, 1982.

Diller, Phyllis. *Like a Lampshade in a Whorehouse — My Life in Comedy.* New York: J.P. Tarcher/Penguin, 2005.

Dors, Diana. *Dors by Diana — An Intimate Self-Portrait.* London: Macdonald Futura Publishers Ltd, 1983.

Dowdy, Andrew. *The Films of the Fifties — The American State of Mind*. New York: William Morrow & Co, 1975.

Eames, John Douglas. *The MGM Story — The Complete History of Fifty Roaring Years*. London: Octopus Books Limited, 1975.

Eaton, Shirley. *Golden Girl*. London: B.T. Batsford Ltd., 1999.

Ehrenstein, David and Reed, Bill. *Rock on Film*. New York: Delilah Communications Ltd., 1982.

Faris, Jocelyn. *Jayne Mansfield. A Bio-Bibliography*. Westport: Greenwood Press, 1994.

Feeney Callan, Michael. *Pink Goddess — The Jayne Mansfield Story*. London: W.H. Allen, 1986.

Ferruccio, Frank. *Diamonds to Dust, The Life and Death of Jayne Mansfield*. Denver: Outskirts Press, Inc., 2007.

Ferruccio, Frank & Santroni, Damien. *Did Success Spoil Jayne Mansfield?* Denver: Outskirts Press, Inc., 2010.

Finler, Joel. *Movies of the Fifties*. London: Orbis Publishing Limited, 1982.

Fusco, Joseph. *The Epitome of Cool: The Films of Ray Danton*. Albany, GA: BearManor Media, 2010.

Fusco, Joseph. *The Films of Mamie Van Doren*. Albany, GA: BearManor Media, 2010.

Garcia, Roger. *Frank Tashlin*. British Film Institute, 1994.

Gussow, Mel. *Don't Say Yes Until I Finish Talking — A Biography of Darryl Zanuck*. New York: Doubleday & Company, Inc., 1971.

Hirsch, Phil. *Hollywood Uncensored — The Stars-Their Secrets and their Scandals*. New York: Pyramid Books, 1965.

Hirschhorn, Clive. *The Warner Bros. Story*. London: Octopus Books Limited, 1979.

Hirschhorn, Clive. *The Columbia Story*. London: Pyramid Books, 1989.

Jackson, Jean-Pierre & Françoise. *Jayne Mansfield*. Paris, Edilig, 1984.

Jordan, Jessica Hope. *The Sex Goddess in American Film 1930-1965 — Jean Harlow, Mae West, Lana Turner, and Jayne Mansfield*. Amherst, New York: Cambria Press, 2009.

Kashner, Sam & Macnair, Jennifer. *The Bad and the Beautiful — A Chronicle of Hollywood in the Fifties*. London: Little, Brown, 2002.

Koper, Richard. *Fifties Blondes — Sexbombs, Sirens, Bad Girls and Teen Queens*. Albany, GA: BearManor Media, 2010.

Lowe, Barry. *Atomic Blonde — The Films of Mamie Van Doren*. Jefferson: McFarland & Company, Inc., Publishers, 2008.

Luijters, Guus & Timmer, Gerard. *Sexbomb. The Life and Death of Jayne Mansfield*. New York: Citadel Press, 1985.

Mann, May. *Jayne Mansfield: A Biography*. New York: Drake, 1973.

Mansfield, Jayne and Hargitay, Mickey. *Jayne Mansfield's Wild, Wild World*. Los Angeles: Holloway House Publishing Company, 1963.

Marshall, David. *The DD Group: An Online Investigation Into the Death of Marilyn Monroe.* Bloomington, IN: iUniverse, Inc, 2005.

Martin, Len D. *The Allied Artists Checklist — The Feature Films and Short Subjects, 1947-1978.* Jefferson: McFarland & Company, Inc., Publishers, 1993.

Mathias, Bob & Mendes, Bob. *A Twentieth Century Odyssey: The Bob Mathias Story.* Champaign, IL: Sports Publishing LLC, 2001.

McGee, Mark Thomas. *Faster and Furiouser — The revised and fattened fable of American International Pictures.* Jefferson: McFarland & Company, Inc., Publishers, 1996.

McGee, Mark Thomas. *The Rock and Roll Movie Encyclopedia of the 1950s.* Jefferson: McFarland & Company, Inc., Publishers, 1990

Nelson, Nancy. *Evenings with Cary Grant.* New York: Citadel Press, 2003.

O'Dowd, John. *Kiss Tomorrow Goodbye: The Barbara Payton Story.* Albany: BearManor Media, 2006.

Parish, James Robert. *The Fox Girls.* New York: Arlington House Publishers, Inc., 1972.

Pascall, Jeremy & Jeavons, Clyde. *A Pictorial History of Sex in the Movies.* London: The Hamlyn Publishing Group Limited, 1975.

Pendergast, Sara & Tom. *St. James Encyclopedia of Popular Culture.* London; St. James Press, 2000.

Pye, Michael. *Movies of the Fifties.* London: Orbis Publishing Limited, 1982.

Reid, John. *These Movies Won No Hollywood Awards.* Lulu.com, 2005.

Riese, Randall & Hitchens, Neal. *The Unabridged Marilyn — Her Life from A to Z.* New York: Congdon & Weed, Inc., 1987.

Ringgold, Gene & Bodeen, DeWitt. *Chevalier — The Films and Career of Maurice Chevalier.* Secaucus, N.J.: Citadel Press, 1973.

Romanski, Phillipe & Sy-Wonyu, Aïssatou. *Trompe(-)l'oeil: imitation & falsification.* Rouen, France: Publications Univ Rouen Havre, 2002.

Ross, Robert. *The Complete Terry-Thomas.* Richmond, GB: Reynolds & Hearn Ltd, 2002.

Saxton, Martha. *Jayne Mansfield and the American Fifties.* Boston: Houghton Miffin Company, 1975.

Seife, Ethan de. *Tashlinesque — The Hollywood Comedies of Frank Tashlin.* Middletown, CT: Wesleyan University Press, 2012.

Settel, Irving. *A Pictorial History of Television.* New York: Frederic Ungar Publishing Co., 1983.

Silver, Alain and Ward, Elizabeth. *Film Noir — an encyclopedic reference guide.* London: Bloomsbury Publishing Limited, 1988.

Silverman, Stephen M. *Dancing on the Ceiling — Stanley Donen and his movies.* New York: Alfred A. Knopf, Inc., 1996.

Solomon, Matthew. *Larger than Life — Movie Stars of the Fifties.* New Jersey: Rutgers University Press, 2010.

Strait, Raymond. *The Tragic Secret Life of Jayne Mansfield.* London: Robert Hale & Company, 1976.

Sullivan, Steve. *Va Va Voom — Bombshells, Pin-ups, Sexpots and Glamour Girls.* Los Angeles: General Publishing Group, 1995.

Sullivan, Steve. *Glamour Girls — The Illustrated Encyclopedia.* New York: St. Martin's Press, 1999.

Truffaut, François. *The Films in My Life.* New York: Simon & Schuster, 1978.

Thomas, Tony & Solomon, Aubrey. *The Films of 20th Century Fox.* Secaucus, N.J.: Citadel Press, 1985.

Van Doren, Mamie with Aveilhe, Art. *Playing the Field — My Story.* New York: G.P. Putnam's Sons, 1987.

Weldon, Michael. *The Psychotronic Encyclopedia of Film.* New York: Ballantine Books, 1983.

Yates, Paula. *Blondes — A History From Their Earliest Roots.* London: Michael Joseph Ltd, 1983.

Zec, Donald. *This Show Business.* London: Purnell and Sons Limited, 1959.

INDEX

Donen, Stanley 190, 191
Donlevy, Brian 290
Donovan, King 255
Dors, Diana 35, 65, 101, 102, 108, 199
Douglas, Paul 157
Drake, Betsy 167
Dru, Joanne 144, 343
Drusky, Roy 294
Duryea, Dan 147, 148, 149, 150, 151
Eaton, Shirley 103, 104
Edwards, Ralph 67, 340
Ekberg, Anita 35, 65, 101, 104, 105, 221, 223, 317
English, Mara 44
Ericson, John 346
Ewell, Tom 156, 157, 159, 162, 167
Faye, Alice 20
Feld, Fritz 256
Fonseca, Carolyn De 222
Fontaine, Eddie 157
Franchi, Franco 277-280
Francis, Connie 196
Frey, Nathaniel 189
Fuller, Lance 28
Funicello, Annette 277, 289
Furstenberg, Betty von 335
Gabel, Martin 320, 322
Gallagher, Robert 331
Gallo, Lew 318, 324
Gardner, Ava 223
Gavrib, Gustav 271
Gaynor, Janet 20,
Genn, Leo 204, 206
Giles, Sandra 99, 100
Gilling, John 214
Gorshin, Frank 235
Gowland, Peter 49,
Grable, Betty 21, 22, 23, 27, 113, 234, 235, 324
Grace, Carol 325
Grant, Cary 57, 184, 186-188, 190
Graziano, Rocky 344
Greene, Billy M. 300, 304
Gregg, Virginia 352
Gregg, Walter 299
Grey, Duane 133

Grimaldi, Hugo 298
Halliday, Hildegarde 331
Haney, Carol 342, 343
Hargitay, Mariska 77, 81, 94-96, 238
Hargitay, Mickey 28, 53, 55, 57, 59, 61-63, 66-69, 71, 73, 75, 77, 78, 85, 89, 93-95, 100, 118, 119, 125, 129, 197, 220-222, 247, 253, 255, 259-261, 277, 278, 315, 352
Hargitay, Miklos 63, 81, 86, 94, 95, 230, 264
Hargitay, Zoltan 66, 81, 86, 89, 93-95, 230, 264, 311
Harlow, Jean 19, 186
Harrison, Linda 310
Hartman, Elizabeth 328
Hathaway, Henry 179
Haupt, Ullrich 124
Haver, June 21, 22, 23
Hayworth, Rita 57
Heath, Dody 350
Hefner, Hugh 36, 75
Hoffa, Jimmy 91
Holliday, Judy 190
Holm, John Cecil 331
Holt, Joel 315
Hope, Bob 208, 290, 341
Hopper, Dennis 51, 339
Hopper, Hedda 124
Hudson, Rock 169, 229
Husky, Ferlin 294, 296, 297
Hyer, Martha 280
Ingrassia, Ciccio 277-281
James, Sonny 294
Jason, Rick 179
Johnson, Nunnally 157
Jones, T.C. 256
Kaiser, Burt 132, 133, 134
Keating, Larry 180
Keaton, Buster 280
Keim, Betty Lou 177
Kelly, Grace 186, 230
Knight, Arthur 315
Lansing, Joi 99, 100, 297
LaVey, Anton 87, 89
Le Maire, Charles 162
Lee, Belinda 101
Lee, Christopher 209

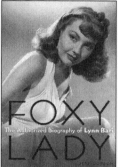

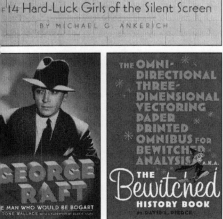
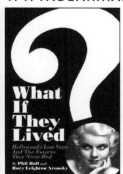

27620430R00224

Printed in Poland
by Amazon Fulfillment
Poland Sp. z o.o., Wrocław